THE
CHIMPS
OF FAUNA
SANCTUARY

THE
CHIMPS
OF FAUNA
SANCTUARY

ANDREW WESTOLL

HarperCollins Publishers Ltd

The Chimps of Fauna Sanctuary
Copyright © 2011 by Andrew Westoll
All rights reserved.

Published by HarperCollins Publishers Ltd

First Canadian edition

HarperCollins books may be purchased for educational, business,
or sales promotional use through our Special Markets Department.

HarperCollins Publishers Ltd
2 Bloor Street East, 20th Floor
Toronto, Ontario, Canada
M4W 1A8

www.harpercollins.ca

Library and Archives Canada Cataloguing in Publication
information is available upon request

ISBN 978-1-55468-649-0

Book design by Melissa Lotfy
Floor plan by Mapping Specialists, Ltd

Printed and bound in the United States
RRD 9 8 7 6 5 4 3 2 1

For Tom,
and all of us great apes

Resilience is more than resistance, it's also learning to live.

— BORIS CYRULNIK, *Un Merveilleux Malheur*

What kind of animals are we?

— FRANS DE WAAL, *The Age of Empathy*

CONTENTS

THE CHIMPHOUSE

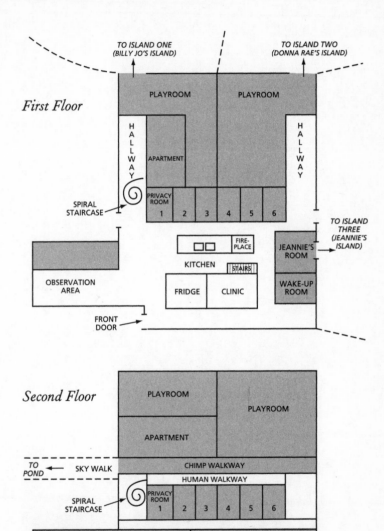

First Floor

TO ISLAND ONE
(BILLY JO'S ISLAND)

TO ISLAND TWO
(DONNA RAE'S ISLAND)

PLAYROOM

PLAYROOM

HALLWAY

APARTMENT

HALLWAY

SPIRAL
STAIRCASE

PRIVACY
ROOM

1 2 3 4 5 6

TO ISLAND
THREE
(JEANNIE'S
ISLAND)

FIRE-
PLACE

KITCHEN

STAIRS

JEANNIE'S
ROOM

OBSERVATION
AREA

FRIDGE

CLINIC

WAKE-UP
ROOM

FRONT
DOOR

Second Floor

PLAYROOM

PLAYROOM

APARTMENT

TO
POND

SKY WALK

CHIMP WALKWAY

HUMAN WALKWAY

SPIRAL
STAIRCASE

PRIVACY
ROOM

1 2 3 4 5 6

JEANNIE'S
ROOM

STAIRS

MEZZANINE

INDOOR CHIMP AREAS

THE
CHIMPS
OF FAUNA
SANCTUARY

Chapter 1

FULL-MOON WEEK

I am not interested in why man commits evil.
I want to know why he does good.
— VÁCLAV HAVEL

Chimp Art

"SMELL MY PHONE," says Gloria Grow as I climb into her Jeep at Montreal's Trudeau Airport. She guns the engine and hands me her cell phone. "Go on. Smell it."

These are Gloria's first words to me in person. We've already had two long phone conversations, between my home in Toronto and her farm in Quebec. By the end of those talks she'd invited me to move in with her family and write a book about them. But at no point did Gloria seem like the sort of person who would ask a virtual stranger to smell her phone.

There is nothing peculiar about the cell, a standard-issue flip phone. But upon closer inspection I notice a constellation of little divots—are they bite marks?—punched into the bright pink casing. I look at Gloria. She is frowning. A construction detour has sent us in circles.

"Go on," she says again. I raise the phone to my nose.

I smell a swamp. Rotten fruit. Fecal matter. The reek of a tropical jungle.

"I love it," I say.

"Me too. Richard got me pink. I hate pink. But now I can't bear to throw it out. Open it."

I flip the casing open, and the LCD comes to life. But instead of showing an orderly sequence of numbers and icons, the screen is a mess, a muddy squelch of black ink. The phone has been crushed, or chewed, beyond repair.

"These roads!" says Gloria, making her third consecutive left-hand turn. Then she reaches over and presses her thumb into the phone's screen. The inky cloud morphs into kaleidoscopic rainbows.

"Isn't that beautiful?" she says without looking over. "It's like chimp art."

I fiddle with the cell phone, making a few of my own psychedelic impressions on the screen. As we descend an exit ramp to nowhere, Gloria sighs. She reaches over and tears the phone from my hand. Closing her eyes, she presses the phone to her nose and inhales deeply.

"They only gave it back to me yesterday."

Cat Lady

THIS IS the story of a family of troubled animals who live on a farm in the French Canadian countryside. It is the story of how these animals came to be so troubled and how they are slowly becoming less so, in their own particular ways, through the actions of a small group of people led by Gloria Grow.

When I say these animals are a family, I don't mean they share a mother or father or brothers or sisters (although some of them surely do). They are a family in the sense that any group of beings who have lived together, suffered together, and triumphed together becomes a family. They are related in the way we are all related to one another, and here lies the source of their great misfortune.

I first contacted Gloria in 1998, when I was a college biology student. I wrote to inquire about volunteer opportunities at the Fauna Foundation, the sanctuary for rescued animals that Gloria had recently founded with her partner, a veterinarian named Richard Allan, on their 240-acre hobby farm near Chambly. The foundation had recently been all over the local, national, and international news because it had just become the permanent retirement home for a very special group of chimpanzees.

At the time I was one of thousands of young biology students who, inspired by the usual suspects (Jane Goodall, Dian Fossey, the breathless David Attenborough), would have done just about anything to get a job either working with or studying great apes—the orangutans, gorillas, bonobos, and chimpanzees most of us have seen only in a zoo or in the pages of *National Geographic*. So when I first heard of Fauna, I couldn't believe it. The place sounded like my own personal Shangri-la. Imagine: an opportunity to experience chimpanzee behavior in the flesh, just a short drive from Canada's most sophisticated and seductive city, thereby removing the need to fund a kamikaze trek to the remote Central African rainforest (something I, at a much younger age, had briefly considered until I did a little reading and learned what the "civil" in "civil war" actually meant).

I didn't know why the chimps had been shipped to Fauna from their home in New York State. I knew nothing of what they'd been subjected to there or of the struggles each one faced in adjusting to retirement in Canada. All I knew was I wanted to work with them. Looking back, I find it unsettling how selfish my curiosity really was.

Unfortunately, life got in the way, and the volunteering idea came to nothing. Soon after that I was offered a dream job of a different sort. After graduating, I spent a year in the jungles of Suriname, just north of the Amazon rainforest, studying wild troops of brown capuchin monkeys. Though they're no great apes, capuchins are known as the chimpanzees of the New World for their intelligence and primitive forms of tool use. I was employed by the University of Florida, funded by the National Science Foundation and the Leakey Foundation. My dreams fulfilled, my interests served, the chimpanzees of Fauna became a distant memory.

Fast-forward more than a decade, then, throw in a career shift from scientist to writer, and here I am with Gloria, searching for a way out of Montreal, struggling to correlate the embarrassing mental image I'd had of her with the real-life version sitting next to me.

The stereotype of the woman who dedicates her life to rescuing animals is a surprisingly powerful cultural image. Often referred to as the Crazy Cat Lady, but by no means limited to felines, she shuffles around in moldy slippers, the backs of her hands are raked with claw marks, and at any moment a minimum of four living creatures are buried somewhere in the folds of her robe. This woman is a walking menagerie of frumpy disillusionment, in desperate need of the unconditional love only an animal can provide. And although that image is a cruel exaggeration, I was half-expecting some variation on it when I climbed into the Jeep and finally met Gloria, more than ten years after my first attempt.

Gloria is nothing like that imaginary Cat Lady. Small but full-figured, with shoulder-length dark blond hair worn half up in a clip, she is disarmingly attractive, her face deeply tanned, her makeup tasteful, her smile full of intelligence. She is very fit, her shoulders and upper arms packed with the strength of a farmhand. She wears an elegant beige top, expensive-looking jeans, black sandals, and dark-framed glasses, a chic outfit that belies her age (mid-fifties), her roots (blue-collar Quebec), and her mode of transport (a dusty Jeep that smells vaguely of farm). As our quest for an escape route continues, Gloria speaks about the effects of captivity on animals, while my first impression of her changes to that of a woman caught between opposing worlds—something that could also be said of the Crazy Cat Lady.

"It's like *Shawshank Redemption*, right?" she says of the difficulties facing rescued animals. "The librarian finally gets out of prison, and what does he do? He kills himself." Gloria pulls a hard right, and we careen onto a packed highway. "Found it. The 20-East." She punches the gas. "We're free!"

Down on the Farm

IN FIFTEEN minutes we reach a major crossroad, a huge parcel of former pastureland now inhabited by a dizzying metropolis of big-box stores, movie cinemas, restaurants, and parking lots. Soon enough, we're driving along a pleasant country road, surrounded mostly by fields of corn and alfalfa, with occasional houses backing onto acres of open land. Another turn onto an even quieter road, a few more meanderings past farms and old barns, and we've completed our departure from the hurly-burly. We arrive at a stretch of white picket fencing that looks plucked from the western frontier circa 1890. Gloria slows, and I take in my first glimpse of her home—now my home, too, if only for a few months.

The large farmhouse where Gloria and Richard live is partly hidden behind a copse of trees, but I get a glimpse of its rural heritage—the gabled roof, the pillared veranda. To the left of the drive, in a narrow pasture, two cream-colored llamas are resting in the shade. A few billy goats nibble lazily at the grasses behind them.

We creep down the drive, the gravel crackling under our tires. At a gate, Gloria lowers her window, and I hear the wild barking of dogs, perhaps a whole pack of them. Then, from a small stable, two impressive horses emerge. One is black with a glint of gray, with white-booted back legs and a white stripe down his muzzle. The other, slightly taller, is a delicious chestnut brown with a gleaming black mane. As the horses get closer, I realize the black one must be fairly old, his gait hobbled in the rear.

"There's Jethro and McLeod, coming to say hello," says Gloria. "Eeyore's around here somewhere."

I spot an elderly gray donkey behind the stable. He stands perfectly still, his ears twitching, his gaze fixed intently on our passing Jeep, as if he's on surveillance, compiling data on our whereabouts and reporting back to some donkey strike force. I've never felt entirely comfortable around donkeys. I consider mentioning this to Gloria but decide it's probably best to keep it to myself for now.

"There he is," says Gloria, waving to Eeyore over her shoulder. "What a grumpy old man."

Continuing down the drive, we pass a small bungalow. This is the Fauna office, where I will be living for the next few months in the basement apartment. Gloria doesn't stop, though, and a beautiful country pond opens up on our left. Families of ducks and Canada geese cruise the surface, and two white swans sit preening on a promontory of rocks. A majestic fountain of water rises up in the center, and in the distance a gray heron high-steps through the shallows, hunting minnows and frogs.

On the far side of the pond are two barns with a tractor parked between them. A raging bonfire coughs a plume of black smoke into the air. Every now and then, an ATV with a payload of lumber zips past the blaze. A cacophony of sounds drifts across the water—the buzz of lawn mowers, the growl of a chain saw, the echoing thuds of a hammer. Fauna is much more than a mere hobby farm, I realize; it is a place of perpetual labor. Since we arrived, the walkie-talkie on Gloria's belt has been humming with the industrious voices of her French Canadian staff.

Between the pond and the driveway are immaculate gardens, with quaint pathways winding through them. A few rustic benches sit among the flowers, just a few weeks from full bloom. At a small clearing, Gloria slows.

A peculiar building comes into sight, three stories high, on maybe an acre of ground. The structure, surrounded by chainlink and electric fencing, resembles a medium-security prison. Above the entrance, a caged balcony looks tacked on, almost as an afterthought. But this is not what makes the building peculiar. The strange part is the chutelike appendage that protrudes from the second floor and stretches toward the pond we've just passed. Made of steel caging, it is supported by thick pillars reaching fifteen feet to the ground. It looks like some postapocalyptic contraption from the set of *Mad Max*.

Before I can ask Gloria about this, she directs my attention to our right, where an imposing steel cage sits in a thicket of native sumacs. The cage is about the size of a clothes closet, seven feet high and five feet wide. A small metal box with a hole in the top is affixed to the side. An old truck tire hangs from rusted chains inside the cage. The whole thing looks like something out of a medieval dungeon.

Gloria says nothing about the cage. We just creep past in silence. Then we rumble over a wooden bridge, and she parks in front of the chimphouse.

"Now remember," she says, climbing out of the Jeep, "today's crazy." She throws open a chainlink gate. "It's full-moon week, so everyone's a little off."

I'm a bit astonished. I hadn't expected Gloria to take me inside on my first day. By the time we reach the front door I've understood that by "everyone" she is not referring to her staff.

Full-Moon Week

THE FIRST thing I notice upon walking into the Fauna chimphouse is not, as I'd expected, the smell, a brooding stench of compost, urine, flatulence, and feces that apparently makes some visitors vomit. And it is not the sweltering humidity, an absurdity considering our northern locale.

No, the first thing I notice is the fear, which runs up my spine like a silverfish as Gloria leads me down a dark corridor. It is a familiar feeling, reminding me how I felt the first few times I walked alone in the jungles of Suriname, with only a machete to protect myself from the menagerie of rainforest predators. But this is not Suriname, and despite the smell and the heat, it is not a place where a bushmaster or a jaguar might roam. So I begin to wonder: is this *my* fear, or is it perhaps someone else's?

As we walk, an eerie sound rises, like something large and hollow being dragged across the floor.

Gloria turns to face me. "Rules," she says. "First: take your jacket off. The bigger you look, the more threatening you are. Second: you're tall, so I need you to crouch. Third: do not stand too close to me. They don't interpret it properly. They can't control it. It's threatening. Four: respect the red lines on the floor. They're there for a reason. Inside the red, believe me, they will try to get you."

"What's that sound?"

"The welcoming committee." Gloria smiles. "They already know you're here."

We walk on. The dragging grows louder. Then a terrible boom detonates up ahead. It echoes throughout the building, a crash of something extremely dense slamming into a wall of steel. I stop dead. The crash is followed by eerie silence; I hear birds chirping. But a few seconds later an identical blast goes off, followed by another and another, and I decide no, this fear may have started out as someone else's, but now it's entirely mine. The building fills with the booms. The cement walls seem to shake with the noise.

"Full-moon week," says Gloria between the blasts. "Everyone's in such a good mood."

I think of that machete and how good it would feel in my hand right now. I think of those nineteenth-century explorers who refused to enter the Congo without an arsenal of guns, for fear of attack by the murderous beasts known as *kivili-chimpenze* (Bantu for "mock-man"). One researcher actually built *himself* a cage in the jungle so that he could observe chimpanzees in safety. It wasn't until 1960, when the young Jane Goodall entered the Tanzanian rainforest accompanied by her mother, that Western culture slowly began to lose its irrational fear of the chimpanzee.

Easier said than done, I think, as a different sound now emerges above the fray—the chimpanzee pant-hoot. It begins almost imperceptibly, a series of low-pitched *hoo*ing sounds, as if someone were panting in and out through their mouth. It builds slowly, the *hoo*ing getting faster, louder, the in-breaths growing shorter and the outs longer, *uh-hoo, uh-hooo, uh-hoooo,* until finally they climax in a sequence of hysterical, near-human shrieks. The silverfish scuttles up my neck. My ears ring. Then silence. The birds. Scraping. Pounding. More howls. I turn a corner and come across a woman.

Her back turned to us, she is folding linens from a towering pile of laundry. When the woman sees me out of the corner of her eye, her body quakes, and she lets loose a terrified scream. For an instant her voice extinguishes the crashes and shrieks, and a flurry of bed sheets parachutes to the floor. A moment later, realizing what species I am, the woman grasps her chest with her hands, rolls her head back, and in a spasm of hysterical French thanks God for sparing her life.

"I thought a chimp was out," she says breathlessly. "I thought you were a chimpanzee."

And that's when I see him. Over the laundry lady's shoulder, past Gloria. A massive black body behind a wall of steel caging, thundering back and forth.

"Come and meet Binky," says Gloria, waving me over. "It's OK. Really. Come and meet the Bub."

Of all the dramatic arrivals and new beginnings that have occurred in the Fauna chimphouse over the years, few can compare with one that happened on a cool September day back in 1997, when the first members of Gloria's new family arrived at sanctuary.

Late that morning, a black pickup truck towing an ordinary horse trailer pulled into the Fauna Foundation's driveway after a long journey. It had begun before dawn in the Ramapo Mountains, about an hour's drive north of New York City. But for the animals inside that horse trailer, arrival at Fauna marked the end of a much longer and more difficult journey, one that had lasted their entire lives.

Inside that trailer were seven young chimpanzees. Until that morning they had been the property of New York University and had lived at a biomedical research facility called the Laboratory for Experimental Medicine and Surgery in Primates, or LEMSIP. As research subjects, these animals had endured years of pain and deprivation as living test tubes for the study of human diseases. They'd been torn from their mothers just days after birth. They'd been imprisoned in cages, sometimes in solitary confinement. They'd undergone blood draws, invasive surgeries, and viral experiments. Some had been knocked unconscious with dart guns almost every week.

And when the trailer turned in to the Fauna driveway that morning, these animals were met by a distinctly human welcoming committee and became the sole responsibility of Gloria Grow.

Over the next few months, those seven were joined by eight more chimps from LEMSIP, many of them much older and more troubled, some having been singled out for infection with multiple strains of the human immunodeficiency virus, or HIV, in studies aimed at developing a vaccine for AIDS. Upon arriving at Fauna, these animals became the first HIV-positive research chimps on the planet to be retired to a sanctuary.

As the years passed, these apes were joined by four more from nearby zoos. Six members of this assorted family have since died. The day I arrive, the Fauna Foundation is home to thirteen chimpanzees, all of whom bear the psychological and, in some cases, physical wounds of having spent much of their lives either in biomedical research or simply behind the bars of a cage. This is their retirement. This is their Shangri-la. And with Gloria's help, they've slowly begun to heal.

The Bub

BINKY, OTHERWISE known as the Bub, reminds me of a boxer crossed with a gymnast. Beneath his luxurious black hair he is a brawny middleweight, stocky and barrel-chested, his shoulders rounded into thick tussocks beneath his ears, his arms wrapped with power, his thighs like industrial pistons, his wrists and ankles thicker than my neck. But the artistic ease with which he swings his bulk down to the platform where he sits, halfway up the wall of his room, gives Binky the air of an elegant floor tumbler, the perfect mixture of strength and grace. As I approach, my jacket wrapped around my waist, making sure to keep outside the red lines on the floor, and lowering myself into an awkward crouch, it occurs to me that few animals have ever been so inappropriately named as the magnificent being before me.

Binky stares at me, and I stare back. I am immediately, hopelessly entranced. The monkeys in Suriname never looked at me this way (I barely registered in their world), and the only chimps I've seen have been in zoos, where they do everything they can to ignore their human visitors. But Binky holds my gaze. What's more, he returns it. With most primates, looking an individual in the eye is seen as a threat. Not so with the chimpanzee. It is a good thing I am no longer a primatologist in training, a blessing that this moment has not been mediated through the lens of a scientific agenda. We are simply two great apes considering each other, sizing each other up, perhaps wondering what the other is thinking, much like two prospective roommates.

I am surprised by Binky's beauty, his lack of any visible signs of distress. I mention this to Gloria.

"Binky is the luckiest one in here," she says. "He had three whole months with his mother before he was taken." Gloria reaches up and gently strokes his enormous fingers. Binky keeps his eyes on me. "He's only recently started pulling his hair out."

The room in which Binky sits is six feet wide and six feet deep, with a loftlike second story. I count three sliding doors, two in the rear and one in the ceiling, all of which are open. On our side of the caging sits a trolley overflowing with a vegetarian feast — apples, pears, lettuce, cucumbers, red and yellow peppers, tomatoes, leeks, potatoes, onions — and countless bottles of water. Just above the trolley is a space in the caging wide enough for a chimp to reach his arm through. This, Gloria tells me, is called the porthole. Below the porthole a red line is painted on the floor. Gloria stands well inside this line; I keep a few feet outside.

Gloria retrieves a small container from the counter behind us, and Binky immediately starts vocalizing—*Aow! Aow! Aow!*—the happy food grunts of an excited chimpanzee. He pushes his mouth up against the cage and extends his lower lip through the bars as if unrolling a miniature carpet.

"His mother died in a lab in New Mexico," says Gloria as she pops gummy-bear vitamins onto Binky's lip one by one. "She was Minky, and his half sister was Inky. His brother lives in Florida. Guess what his name is."

"Dinky? Stinky?"

"Pumpkin," says Gloria. "His brother's name is Pumpkin."

As I listen to Binky chew, his food grunts muffled but still delightful, I realize my fear is gone, replaced by something quite different. I'm not sure how to describe the feeling. Disappointment isn't quite right. Neither is sadness. I guess I'd always imagined that the first time I saw a chimp outside of a zoo we would be lost together in a vast African rainforest, in the Congo, maybe, or Ivory Coast. But instead we're in the Canadian countryside, just a ten-minute drive from a Tommy Hilfiger and an Urban Planet.

Another great shriek echoes through the chimphouse. The sound breaks Binky's spell on me, and I sense movement all around. "Tommie!" yells Gloria. "Where are you, big boy? Come and say hello!" I look up and see hulking black bodies everywhere—huddled in the caged walkways above, slinking past the caged walls to my left and right, peeking through the caged windows. The chimphouse resembles an Escher drawing come suddenly to life, a surreal playground complete with impossible staircases, walled-in balconies, sideways doorways, and ropes leading to nowhere. Upon first glance, one might think evolution had been twisted by some mysterious force here, that a family of animals *resembling* chimpanzees had taken up residence in a place *resembling* a humid rainforest of half-ladders and hiding places. It is only the ubiquitous crosshatching of steel that gives this place its final, terrifying logic.

I can feel their eyes on me, the intruder.

Gloria pours a half-dozen gummy vitamins into Binky's out-stretched hand. His grunts become hysterical squeaks of pleasure as he stuffs the treats in his mouth. Jumping down from the platform, he rushes out of the room on all fours, squeezing his massive frame through a doorway, squeaking the whole way.

"I'm amazed he stayed," says Gloria. "He normally hates strangers."

Full-moon week.

Over the next three hours, we wander the chimphouse, and the residents slowly reveal themselves: Regis, the diabetic who refuses to take insulin; Jethro, the alpha male who runs around mediating everyone's disputes; Sue Ellen, a senior citizen whose teeth were knocked out with a hammer and chisel when she was young; Pepper, Sue Ellen's best friend and protector, who is extremely intelligent and terribly claustrophobic; Chance, who spent the first five years of her life completely alone; Petra, the resident escape artist; Yoko, the smallest chimp here but apparently a warrior; Toby, Spock, and Maya, the zoo chimps, who are trying hard to fit in with the LEMSIP crew; and Tom, the wise old man, Gloria's savior, Fauna's most famous chimpanzee.

The afternoon passes in a whirlwind of crashes, screams, and sudden silences. By the time Gloria lowers the lights, around five P.M., I am exhausted. I've spent the entire day on display, trying to make a good first impression. I have no idea if I have succeeded. My eyes fixed on the red lines on the floor, I inch my way back through the murk toward the laundry room.

And then the caging to my left erupts with a violent crash. I leap back in terror as, not three feet away, a distraught chimpanzee hangs on the caging and slams her feet repeatedly into the steel. *BANG! BANG! BANG! BANG! BANG!* It looks as if she might come clean through. Having gotten my attention, she lets go of the caging, drops to all fours, runs across the room, and pounds her fist into a steel door. *BANG!* She is pilo-erect, her hair standing on end. She looks enormous and not the least bit sleepy. After striking the door, her display abruptly ends. She sits down with her back to me as if nothing had happened. At her feet sit a pair of ragged stuffed animals—gorillas, maybe. The only remaining sign of her outburst is the violent shaking of her head.

"Oh, Rachel, honey," says Gloria softly. "Rachel, sweetheart, honey."

I slip out the way I came in.

Chapter 2

ZIHUATANEJO, QUEBEC

Not for him the soft colors of the forest,
the dim greens and browns entwined.

— JANE GOODALL, *Visions of Caliban*

The Safety Briefing

THE NEXT MORNING, life with the chimps begins with a safety briefing. Cyndi, the office manager, takes me through the Fauna Code of Conduct, the Roles and Responsibilities. Then she gives me a cell phone, a walkie-talkie, and a list of emergency phone numbers.

"If you hear 'Code Red' over the walkie-talkie, it means one of two things," she says. "Either a chimp has escaped the safety perimeter or a human has been attacked. The odds of these things happening are very, very small. But we need you to be prepared." Once a Code Red has been confirmed, a senior staff member activates the emergency siren, the equivalent of an air-raid warning that blasts from speakers atop the chimphouse and the welcome center. The alarm is deafening, audible for miles. When it goes off, emergency calls are automatically placed to 911, fire, police, Richard's veterinary clinic, and Gloria's sisters' houses in nearby Chambly.

"When the siren sounds," says Cyndi, "you have only one responsibility: get off the property as quickly as you can."

I picture myself hightailing it through the woods that surround the farm—a distant siren wailing, branches whipping my face, a knuckle-running phantom hot on my heels—and emerging in a quiet cul-de-sac in the subdivision that backs onto the Fauna property. I imagine trying to explain my panic to the kids playing street hockey, the dads soaping their sedans. *Ch-ch-ch-chimp*, I would stammer. *Ch-ch-ch-chimp!*

"What if I can't get away?"

"You hide."

"Where?"

"If you're here in the office, get into the garage. If you're outside, get into the water. If you're in the chimphouse . . ." Cyndi laughs.

"Why are you laughing?"

"Well, there's really nowhere in the chimphouse to hide."

The nearby public school has been briefed on the remote possibility of a chimp escape. In the early years, the teachers ran a simulation "chimp drill" every few months to keep the students and staff on their toes. Picture a tornado drill in rural Oklahoma, but instead of kids hiding under their desks, imagine children huddled in the arts-and-crafts closet or locked in the gymnasium, a lone custodian, mop in hand, standing guard.

Cyndi slides a piece of paper across the table toward me. Her timing needs some work: it's a health indemnity waiver. And just as I am freeing Gloria and the Fauna Foundation from all legal responsibility for whatever might happen to me here, a faint scream drifts into the office.

"That's nothing," says Cyndi, seeing my face. "Wait till you hear that in the middle of the night."

The Crazy House

GLORIA PEELS into the driveway on a golf cart, her ride of choice on the farm. She has a cell phone in one ear, has a walkie-talkie in the other, and is carrying on a third conversation with a man in his mid-sixties dressed in baby blue medical scrubs, who stands in front of an idling pickup truck. He is Richard Allan, Gloria's partner and the owner of one of the area's most successful vet clinics. Before he goes to work each morning, he visits the chimps and then checks in at the office.

As I approach, Richard gives me a blank stare, as if he'd heard of me but didn't believe I really existed. "So," he says. "How long do you think you're going to be here?"

"Richard . . .," Gloria groans.

"I'm joking," says Richard. He shakes my hand and smiles warmly. "Seriously. Welcome to the farm. I just want to get a sense of what the electric bill's gonna look like."

"Richard, please . . ."

"It was a joke," says Richard, giving me a wink. "It's summer. The electric's gonna be nothing."

With that, he climbs into his truck and leaves for a long day at the clinic. Suddenly a great racket—an enthusiastic chorus of honking—rises up from behind the office. It sounds like a regiment of circus clowns. Then a pair of enormous white swans come barreling around the corner. They run straight for me, wings splayed, beaks wide open in warning. And just as I think they might launch a full-on attack, they stop, lower their wings, and sit down in the grass.

"There you have Jekyll and Hyde," says Gloria. "They can be really protective of their space, especially around the office, so you gotta watch it. OK, hop on. You're already late for work." I climb onto her golf cart, and she floors it.

When we enter the chimphouse, a pleasant new aroma cuts through the stench. It is a comforting smell, one that reminds me of my childhood.

A bizarre morning ritual is in full swing. I can't see any chimpanzees, but I can hear the same dragging and pounding sounds they welcomed me with yesterday. The door to one of their rooms is flung wide open, and inside stands a woman. She is about forty-five years old and wears a faded T-shirt, a denim skirt, yellow dish-washing gloves, and black rubber boots. In her hands is an industrial-strength pressure washer, at her feet sits a coil of thick hose. She is spraying the resting bench that Binky sat on yesterday. The woman looks like a half-mad firefighter battling an imaginary blaze. A soapy brown sludge streams down the wall and creeps toward a distant drain.

Through this disgusting flood wades another woman, perhaps thirty-six, wearing athletic shorts, a sweat-stained tank top, and heavy-duty rubber shoes. She is pushing three trolleys, each strewn with half-eaten fruits, smashed vegetables, torn paper bags, mangled paper cups, and toppled water bottles. After a brief struggle (two of the trolleys have wonky wheels), she delivers her cargo to a queue of similarly ransacked trolleys and then splashes off down a distant hallway. Then another trolley—this one on its own and moving at high speed—zips down the hallway after her as if propelled by an invisible hand. I hear the woman yelp, then a watery crash. A lone tomato rolls into view. "Maya!" yells the trolley woman. "They're almost ready!" I glimpse a long, hairy arm withdrawing from a half-hidden porthole.

In the kitchen stands a third woman, older than the others, who leans against the marble countertop as she whips up something in a large steel bowl. Every now and then, she glances at a bulky old television, where a soap opera plays, the volume muted. She is oblivious to the commotion around her, as if she were alone in a quiet country kitchen, just watching her stories. On the stovetop next to her, I spot the source of the soothing aroma: four pans of freshly baked muffins—by my guess, apple cinnamon.

For a place with only eight full-time employees, forty-eight muffins seems like a lot. And more are in the oven. Is it someone's birthday? Is Fauna holding a bake sale?

"Petra would eat the whole tray if she could," yells Gloria.

Petra is a chimpanzee.

Gloria lights a stick of Nag Champa incense, transporting me from my childhood straight to an ashram in India. "I know it sounds pretty rich—a bunch of great apes eating muffins fresh from the oven. But think about this: the only thing *less* natural is where they came from."

Gloria leaves the incense burning on top of the old wood stove, which, along with the island countertop, divides the human area from the chimp area. On the other side are the caging, the portholes, the beginning of the chimpanzee world, mapped out in precise detail by the red lines on the floor and the crosshatched steel bars that rise to the ceiling.

Gloria introduces me to her staff. The woman operating the pressure washer is her younger sister, Linda. The woman who has now returned with the ghost trolley is Kim, the full-time manager of the chimphouse. And the baker is Kim's mother, who drives in every Wednesday from her home in the Eastern Townships to make a week's worth of stews, pastas, and assorted baked goods for the chimps.

"Feel like a muffin?" Kim's mom asks me.

"Feel like making lunch?" asks Kim.

Linda slams the door to the room she's just cleaned and snaps the padlock into place. She yanks on it three times just to be sure. Then she drops the pressure washer, peels off her gloves, and reaches out a hand.

"Welcome to the crazy house," she says.

Every chimpanzee in here is struggling to overcome some level of psychological disturbance. To refer to their sanctuary as the "crazy house" might seem unkind. But for the last few years, Linda has spent the better part of every morning spraying down and stripping bare the intimate world of another species. She has dragged countless sleeping blankets and shoveled innumerable children's toys out of this world. She has chipped hardened shit off the walls and mopped piles of diarrhea from the floors. She is, for all intents and purposes, a fully ordained citizen of this world—hell, she's arguably the head janitor. Right now, every inch of Linda save what's covered by gloves or clothing is coated with a fine mist of liquid ape feces. Not far from the surface of her "crazy house" comment is a subtle self-admonishment, I think, a sneaking suspicion that *she* might be the crazy one for being here. The chimps, of course, had no choice in the matter.

The Tragedy of Travis

I SPEND the next hour in and out of the walk-in refrigerator. This was Gloria's idea. "Chimpanzees are like men," she told me. "The way to their heart is through the kitchen." If I am going to have a relationship with these apes, they need to see me preparing their food.

"Making lunch" means lugging countless armloads of fruits and vegetables from the fridge and restocking the trolleys, which Linda has emptied of last night's leftovers and sprayed clean. Compared to the warm humidity of the chimphouse, the fridge might as well be a freezer. Every time I go in I shiver uncontrollably; every time I return to the kitchen my glasses fog up. Kim tells me the fridge is usually packed floor to ceiling with a huge variety of fresh produce. Today, though, supplies are running low; it's delivery day. Even so, I am able to piece together a modest smorgasbord of apples, oranges, grapefruit, lettuce, tomatoes, potatoes, carrots, and leeks for the chimps.

The chimpanzees, still out of sight, have quieted down. Linda relaxes in the kitchen, munching on a muffin, her shift finally over. As I walk back and forth, she gives me her own version of the safety briefing.

"They will try to grab you," she says.

"Linda," says Gloria. "You don't need to scare him."

"It's true. When you least expect it, you will step over one of those red lines and they will try for you. They're just testing you, usually. But I'm telling you, it's like being trapped in a vice."

Gloria rolls her eyes, disappears down a side hallway. "I'm outta here," she says. "I've got a million things to do."

Linda continues her pep talk. "Doesn't matter who you are, either," she says, polishing off the muffin and snapping into a red Delicious. "Gloria's been grabbed. So have I."

I'm beginning to feel that Linda and Cyndi got their wires crossed this morning. Clearly, they had planned to play a modified version of Good Cop, Bad Cop with me on my first day of work, but somehow they've gotten their roles mixed up. Both seem hellbent on scaring the living daylights out of me.

Their tactics don't surprise me. After all, it's only been a few months since the horrifying news broke about Travis.

When most of us think of a chimpanzee, our minds conjure the image of an adorable, rambunctious, and profoundly childlike animal who wears clothes, enjoys human foods, rides a bike or plays sports, makes rude gestures, and acts the loyal sidekick in countless television commercials and movies. But the truth is, this image is of a prepubescent chimp in captivity. Most of us have no mental concept of what these apes eventually become as they grow up, and what usually happens to them.

Travis was a pet chimpanzee who lived in Connecticut with his owner, Sandra Herold. In February 2009, Travis viciously attacked one of Herold's closest friends, Charla Nash. By the time Travis was fatally shot by police, Nash had suffered unfathomable injuries. She had lost her hands, her jaw, her lips, her nose, and her eyelids; she will be blind for the rest of her life.

An adult male chimpanzee can weigh well over two hundred pounds and be approximately five to seven times stronger than a human male of similar size. To put this in some perspective, not long ago at an exhibit at the Natural History Museum in Ottawa, I had my grip strength tested and compared to that of other primates. When I squeezed as hard as I could, the needle barely flickered up from its resting place. A chimpanzee's grip would have swung the needle 180 degrees. Turns out I had the grip strength of a tarsier, an adorable, bug-eyed primate of Southeast Asia that is no more imposing than a kitten.

Every human-raised chimpanzee, no matter how well adjusted she is or how loving her bond is with her owner, has the potential to become dangerous. In fact, Travis's profound bond with Herold may have contributed to the ferocity of his attack on Charla Nash. One theory holds that Nash had recently had her hair cut in a different style, and the increasingly territorial and anxious Travis didn't recognize her when she came to the door. The attack followed the same script that wild chimps follow when engaging with a foreign intruder.

Unlike dogs and cats, the chimpanzee has never been bred for domestication. Every chimp in America is no more than two or three generations away from their wild ancestors in Africa. So where does a person who adopted a cute baby chimp go to get rid of an uncontrollable adult? An entire industry in the United States exists that is all too willing to take these unwanted apes off the owners' hands. Oftentimes the strung-out owners will simply walk the chimpanzee they've raised since birth, the being they once thought of as their child, straight into a cage in a biomedical laboratory, where the pet will undoubtedly be appreciated as a virgin test subject. Once he is no longer cute and cuddly, a home-raised chimpanzee in America faces a rather predictable fate.

When the story of Travis broke, it became the latest in a long list of cautionary tales about the dangers and ethical quandaries of raising chimpanzees in human homes. But for some reason this tragedy seemed to hit people more deeply than usual. Perhaps it was the catastrophic nature of Nash's wounds: the hospital where she underwent seven hours of surgery had to provide counseling to staff members who initially treated her. Or perhaps it was the recording of Herold's horrifying 911 call during the attack, which serves as a testament to the spectacular range of a terrified human's vocal chords, which, thanks to YouTube, anyone with an Internet connection can now hear. Regardless, for captive adult chimpanzees, the world after Travis will never be the same. Many sanctuaries across the United States went into lockdown mode, revisiting their safety procedures and intensifying emergency preparedness, knowing that their best practices would soon be thrust into the media spotlight. Cyndi and Linda have clearly taken the reaction of their American brethren to heart.

The Lay of the Land

As I apply the finishing touches to the trolleys—paper bags filled with monkey chow, paper cups of freshly brewed tea, plastic bowls of cold spaghetti—a new sound makes me jump. It's easily the strangest sound yet.

Pwbbt!

I look up. Binky is staring at me from a nearby room. No one else is around. He wears a sort of "What, me?" look on his face. I drop my gaze to the trolleys. Sure enough, the noise again. *Pwbbt!* It sounds like a rude child making farting noises with his armpit. I look up. Still just Binky. But this time he nods his head a few times and stretches an upraised hand through the porthole. I look back to the trolleys, fiddle with a lettuce. Then I look up quickly. Binky jumps, nods excitedly, shakes his waiting hand. Then he purses his lips together and emits a series of enthusiastic raspberries, or zerberts.

Pwbbt! Pwbbt! Pwbbt!

"The Bronx cheer," says Gloria, coming around the corner. "It means he wants something." Gloria rolls the nearest trolley over to Binky. "He'll do it for hours until you give in."

The Bronx cheer is a silly, childish sound. But there is much more to it than meets the ears. Wild chimpanzees do not make this vocalization; only captive chimps do. According to scientists, when Binky makes these zerbert sounds he is creating a "novel communicative signal," engaging in a form of tool use.

Binky lifts the bowl of spaghetti from his trolley, squeezes it through the porthole, and tips the contents into his mouth. He grunts happily, just as he did yesterday, and at the sound of his excitement, the chimphouse erupts in a chorus of pant-hoots. Then Linda emerges from the walk-in fridge.

"Has Gloria shown you where not to walk?" asks Linda.

The red. Stay outside the red.

Linda throws her head back and laughs. "Come with me."

The chimpanzee enclosures at Fauna form a labyrinth of private and communal living spaces, a complex of rooms and playgrounds connected by crossover walkways and sliding pulley doors; the building is one part Alcatraz and one part Rube Goldberg. In another context, the Fauna chimphouse might be lauded as an accomplished piece of postmodern industrial sculpture—a comment on human vulnerability, perhaps, or on our tragic tendency to imprison those we love. In reality, however, the chimphouse is not a work of art so much as a stage upon which the intimate dramas of thirteen remarkable lives play out every day.

Natural light pours into the building through reinforced windows and skylights. The six individual rooms that front on the kitchen area (where Binky was just doing his Bronx cheers) are called the privacy rooms. These rooms are the most popular with the chimps for relaxing alone, eating, and interacting with staff. From these rooms, exit doors lead either straight up to a crossover walkway or back into the rest of the building.

Behind the privacy rooms are two playrooms, separated by a three-story wall of caging. The playrooms are furnished with wooden climbing structures, wood and plaster shelters, raised walkways, rope systems, and huge tractor tires. They provide the chimps with a range of nooks, crannies, and wide-open spaces in which to gather, run, leap, or hide.

In one of the playrooms, I spot three chimpanzees, each sitting alone in a corner. "The big guy up there is Jethro," says Linda.

"He's sort of our alpha male. Down there is Toby, who is having some issues these days. And over there is Rachel, whom you've met already, I think. Rachel is such a sweetheart. But she's pretty messed up."

The playrooms cannot be seen from the kitchen area. To view them, an observer must walk down one of two hallways or climb a spiral staircase to the upper walkway, which runs above the privacy rooms and allows Gloria and her staff an invaluable lookout, as well as access to many of the pulley doors. From here I can see into the other playroom, where two chimps are grooming each other.

"The big girl lying on her back is Petra," says Linda. "She doesn't like to move much these days because of a sore knee. Her little sidekick is Yoko, and he's a bit of a bully."

The walkway is also where the strange appendage I noticed yesterday, the Sky Walk, begins. This 250-foot-long elevated walkway stretches from the chimphouse all the way to a lookout spot near the pond. The caging of the Sky Walk is spaced wide enough to allow the chimpanzees unobstructed views of the driveway, the farm, and the surrounding countryside. From up there the apes can also see the islands.

Chimpanzees are terrible swimmers. Place a robust, two-hundred-pound male chimpanzee in just enough water to cover his nose and watch him turn into a panicking, two-hundred-pound sack of cement. Sanctuary directors have long known that the best way to confine a chimpanzee is to dig a ditch around him and fill it with water. So a few years ago, Gloria had more than two acres of farmland just west of the chimphouse transformed into three connected islands. Each is surrounded by a shallow moat as well as wooden, steel, and 9,000-volt electric fencing. These outdoor playgrounds can be accessed through pulley doors in the chimphouse walls. Each island has a tall bandstand, some excellent hiding places, a boardwalk, a few trees, and a lawn of fresh green grass. In the summer months, some of the chimpanzees sleep on the islands. Pepper is a huge fan of overnight campouts. And a few of the more courageous apes have been known to venture outside during the harsh Quebec winters to play with the snow.

Linda takes me back through the kitchen to the other side of the building. She wants to show me the one area I'm not allowed to walk through, affectionately known as Grab Central. This is an especially tight space to the right of the kitchen, a place that wasn't in the original building plan. In Grab Central, the floor is almost entirely enclosed by red lines. On one side is a privacy room; on the other is Jeannie's Room.

Before she passed away in 2007, Jeannie was probably the most troubled ape ever to live at Fauna. To help her cope, Gloria turned a large area next to the kitchen into a private, two-story enclosure that Jeannie had exclusive access to. Today Jeannie's Room is where Fauna's most troubled individuals still choose to live. Here they can feel especially safe and secure, with frequent contact with humans, access to the outside, a good view of the television, and proximity to the fireplace — it's the best seat in the house. These days, says Linda, the place might as well be called Rachel's Room.

The chimphouse was constructed from scratch in 1997. To reach its current grand proportions, though, the place has undergone many expensive renovations. The Fauna sanctuary now provides its residents with more than 5,500 square feet of heated indoor floor space and over 100,000 square feet of outdoor recreation area. And as Gloria told me yesterday, the architects of the entire operation are the chimpanzees themselves.

"We didn't design it. The folks who live here did. Every change we have made came from watching them closely, and everything we've added came from something they showed us they needed." In this way the chimphouse and the islands are expressions of chimpanzee creativity as much as of human smarts.

Day to day, though, it is human ingenuity that allows this place to succeed. Gloria uses the maze of rooms, islands, crossover walkways, and pulley doors to create as many as five entirely separate living quarters for the chimps. Gloria and her senior staff decide who lives where and with whom, but these decisions are made after many hours, if not days, of careful observation and consideration. Only then are pulley doors either locked or unlocked accordingly.

These decisions are informed by a deep understanding of each chimpanzee's background, each one's likes and dislikes, abilities and shortcomings, personalities and moods, friends and foes, even individual tolerance for stress — in other words, a deep understanding of each chimp's intimate life. This knowledge, which Gloria wields via the thick bundle of keys wrapped around her wrist, is the glue that holds the Fauna family together.

But no matter how much "glue" she applies, Gloria's family sometimes comes unstuck. Although she hopes that one day her charges will be able to live "as one big family," Gloria realizes that some of the chimps are simply far too disturbed to engage in the normal, healthy chimpanzee social arrangement, in which each individual lives with one group for a while and then abruptly shifts allegiance to another. Occasionally, the more anxious chimps can't adjust to these changes and must be separated from the others in order to preserve the peace.

For many months now the chimpanzees have been living in three social groups, nearly without incident. I don't realize it yet, but the tranquility of this arrangement is beginning to unravel.

Signore Tom

AFTER THE tour, Linda and Kim roll the lunch trolleys around the chimphouse. The building comes alive with excited screams and bodily crashes as the chimpanzees heave themselves down to the portholes. The commotion soon attracts a crowd to the privacy rooms facing the kitchen, where Tom appears, looking for lunch.

Tom is the only chimp currently at Fauna who was born where he should have been, somewhere in the lush rainforests of Central Africa. His friends Pepper and Sue Ellen might have been wild-caught as well, but Gloria can't be sure because records for them don't exist. Tom was about three years old when he was caught in 1967 or so, after his family was slaughtered by hunters employed by the local bushmeat trade, the exotic animal market, or the American biomedical industry. Regardless of the hunters' affiliations, Tom, as was often the case with orphaned primates back then, was quickly sold into the booming biomedical research industry in the United States.

In his early lab years, Tom was a model test subject, a totally trusting ape who would actually present his arm for injections. As a result, he went on to a distinguished "career" as a living testing ground for human diseases. Before being sent to LEMSIP, where he lived for fifteen years, Tom spent sixteen years in the Alamogordo Primate Facility in New Mexico and some time at the Buckshire Corporation, a Pennsylvania lab that leases animals for cosmetic and scientific testing. For more than thirty years, he was repeatedly infected with increasingly virulent strains of HIV, went through numerous hepatitis-B studies, and survived at least sixty-three liver, bone marrow, and lymph-node biopsies. Tom has gone through more surgeries than anyone else at Fauna—by Gloria's estimate, he was knocked unconscious at least 369 times, but this number is based on incomplete medical records and is certainly an underestimate. Only Tom knows how many surgeries he's been through.

As a veteran of the biomedical industry, Tom's body is in horrendous shape. He begins each day by gagging uncontrollably, the legacy of decades having feeding tubes and respirators shoved down his throat. Who knows what destruction has gone on inside his body? But somehow Tom's demeanor is that of a suave elderly gentleman, and he is something of a grandfather figure to the other chimps.

Tom finds it incredibly difficult to trust humans. Unless he has had a long-term relationship with you, he will rarely look you in the eye. I am a complete stranger, so his full attention is now on the lettuce and apples on his trolley.

I have known about Tom for a long time, and I have known about his special bond with a man named Pat Ring for a long time, too. Pat is the rancher who used to own this land. When he sold the farm to Richard and Gloria, he agreed to stay on for a few years and help them manage it. When he accompanied Gloria on a few of her visits to LEMSIP, he met Tom the chimpanzee, and that changed his life forever. Pat doesn't work at Fauna anymore, but he still stops by on his Harley-Davidson every month or so to hang out with his old buddy.

Like many people who come to Fauna, I had high hopes of striking up an immediate friendship with Tom the way Pat did, a relationship for the ages, a heartwarming example of human-chimpanzee communion that flies in the face of accepted wisdom. But if Tom and I are going to bond, it's clearly not going to happen today. Although I'm crouching right in front of him, he refuses to acknowledge my presence.

Tom is one of Fauna's most distinctive chimps, his face fringed with gray hair, his protruding jaw marbled black and white, his eyes soft and glassy. His is perhaps the most famous chimpanzee mug in America today, for Tom is the face of Project R&R: Release and Restitution for Chimpanzees in U.S. Laboratories, a nationwide campaign to end invasive research on chimps and to release all federally owned laboratory apes in the United States to sanctuaries like Fauna. Project R&R is spearheaded by the New England Anti-Vivisection Society (NEAVS) in Boston. The project's centerpiece is the Great Ape Protection Act (GAPA), a landmark piece of legislation that was introduced to the U.S. Congress in 2009, in collaboration with the Humane Society of the United States (HSUS). Gloria is one of the lead campaigners for GAPA, and so is old man Tom. His wise, dignified face is used in many campaign documents, pamphlets, brochures, posters, Web pages, and videos.

At Fauna, Tom can often be found slumped against a wall, one hand clinging to the caging above or resting on a windowsill. In this position he looks like he's slumped on a sofa in a seniors' home midway through slipping his arm around his sweetheart. When Tom walks on all fours, when he claps his hands to get Gloria's attention, or simply when he's lunching, the calmness of his movements suggests he knows all about time — how it works, how it can ravage you, how best to reconcile yourself to these facts. Something about Tom puts the lie to that old cliché *time heals all*. As one of his Project R&R posters points out, time doesn't heal all. Of course it doesn't. Tom knows this better than most.

Zihuatanejo, Quebec

I WATCH Tom chow down on his favorite food in the world: Washington State apples. He crunches into one, strips off a piece of flesh with his teeth, sucks the juice out, then spits the flesh to the ground. The process takes about three seconds. Tom can "eat" a whole apple in about thirty seconds flat. He is similarly discerning when it comes to lettuce. He grabs one of the huge heads of romaine from the trolley, holds it by the lush green leaves, bites straight into the white heart, chews this part for a few moments, and then spits it out, dropping the leaves as well. If Tom disappeared, he would be the easiest ape to track. You'd know where he'd been by the huge pile of lettuce leaves and apple shavings left behind.

Tom still won't look at me. I creep right up to the red lines outside his room, say his name a few times, but he pays me no attention. In fact, he looks the other way, purposefully ignoring me. At one point he stops eating and cranes his neck around to face the back of his room. Chastened, I back off a little. Tom is going to be a tough sell.

Then something wet and extremely hot lands on my forearm. I yelp and rub the offending substance off. Mystified, I look up to find a massive female chimp looking straight at me from her bench in the next room over. Her cheeks are puffed up a bit. She holds a paper cup in her hand.

"Did you just—"

The chimp spits another stream of hot tea at me. This time it hits me in the neck. It burns for a split second and then cools. My assailant refills her cheeks from her cup.

"What did I do to—"

Another searing mouthful of tea arcs in my direction. I duck, and it lands with a splat on the kitchen counter. Gloria laughs from the far hallway. "That's my big girl, Petra," she says. "She's teasing you. Petra loves to spit. So does Regis. Watch out, because here he comes."

A skinny black figure approaches in the walkway above Petra. I look back at Tom. He's been watching me, and I detect a subtle amusement on his face before he remembers to turn away. Then something hard slams into my shoulder and crashes to the floor.

"Ha!" yells Gloria. "Binky got you good!"

At my feet sits a thick carrot. In the room next to Petra, playful Binky sits with his hand through the porthole. Having gotten my attention, he nods vigorously. *Pwbbt! Pwbbt! Pwbbt!* Then, as a threat, he grabs a tomato from his trolley.

I walk a few steps toward Binky's room. I have no idea what to get for him, and Gloria isn't offering any suggestions. Just as I imagine the feeling of a tomato smashing into my chest, big Petra goes at it again. Splat! Hot tea right between my eyes. This time it really burns.

Pwbbt! Pwbbt! Pwbbt! Binky is really excited now, enjoying the show. I remove my glasses and wipe them on my mucky T-shirt. Then I hear something behind me. I turn just in time to see Maya's arm disappearing through her porthole, and the ghost trolley zooming toward me. I try to leap out of the way, but its wonky wheel catches. A feast of fruits, vegetables, water bottles, cups of tea, and bowls of pasta smashes to the floor at my feet.

I take a deep breath, replace my glasses, and gaze up at the caging in frustration. And there I see skinny Regis staring down at me. At first he does nothing, just gives me a sympathetic look, as if he's sorry for the trouble his friends are causing. Then he purses his lips, makes a soft squirting sound, and a ball of chimpanzee spit explodes on my forehead.

Finally, Gloria comes to the rescue.

"You wanna quit?" she asks.

"No."

"I warned you on the phone, didn't I?"

"Yeah, you warned me."

"What did I say?"

I recite the litany: "It's like a mental institution, a maximum security prison, a Zen sanctuary, an old folks' home, a daycare center, and a New York deli during lunchtime rush."

"Good."

Gloria goes looking for the mop. I begin gathering up the remains of Maya's lunch. And then, without the slightest warning, the chimphouse explodes in a tremendous riot of hoots and screams. All thirteen chimpanzees clamber and crash to the south end of the building. Some heave themselves out onto the Sky Walk, while those in the adjacent enclosures leap at the windows like raging two-hundred-pound frogs, pounding their fists on the glass. I run outside and sprint the length of the Sky Walk to see what the problem is.

Out near the pond, the potbellied Jethro is going berserk. His hair on end, he looks twice as big as usual. He throws his enormous body at the caging, slamming it with his fists and feet, letting loose a series of high-pitched alarm barks, his mouth wide open in a fear grimace. He does this again and again—I wonder if he's injuring himself, such is the ferocity of his display—and only now do I realize just how huge Jethro is, what a powerful frame lies beneath the ample flesh of his retirement. Back along the Sky Walk, three other chimps are alarm-barking and displaying, but their efforts are nothing compared to the might of Jethro's performance. This terrifying, terrified alpha male is very angry about something. There is danger in the air. Danger to himself, certainly, but danger to his family, too.

And then I see the source of his anger. Or, more accurately, I hear it. A large produce truck, with its weekly delivery of groceries, is slowly backing down the driveway toward the chimphouse. Its engine rumbles, its tires crackle, and the wooden bridge creaks beneath the vehicle's weight. But these aren't the sounds causing turmoil in the chimphouse. No, it's the high-pitched beeping of the reversing truck that has sent the apes into a frenzy. It's the constant *beep-beep-beep* that has inspired Jethro's ferocious displays. As Gloria will later explain, it is the same sound the forklifts at LEM-SIP used to make, the forklifts that delivered the cages to the cage-washing machine once a month. Before the cages could be washed, of course, the chimps had to be moved into temporary quarters, and for many this meant being shot with a dart gun.

Although I'm covered in tea and spit, and I might get a bruise on my arm from that carrot, and Tom may never look me in the eye, and I'm going to spend the next half-hour cleaning up after moody Maya, and the produce delivery guy looks like he might have peed his pants, somehow my mind flips back to the day before, to what Gloria said in her Jeep. Something about animals in captivity. Something about *The Shawshank Redemption*.

For Gloria, one of the most telling moments in the movie is when Brooks, the old prison librarian, commits suicide after finally being freed. The idea that a lifelong convict would kill himself when presented with the vast possibilities of freedom rings true for Gloria. She sees a tragic connection between Brooks and the chimpanzees of Fauna. After all, what good is freedom when you've given up hoping for it? And what good is Shangri-la when you arrive there in the twilight of your life?

But surely Gloria understands the real message of that movie as well. Yes, these chimpanzees were cheated out of the best years of their lives. Yes, they lived in tiny cages and underwent invasive procedures that left them deeply wounded. And yes, if they were able to choose, perhaps a few of these apes *would* choose to end their suffering (what an eerie question to ask about another species). But there is another way of looking at Fauna, another perspective on Gloria's work here that is far more uplifting. Because the most telling moment of *Shawshank* is not when the prison librarian kills himself but when, at the end of the film, the narrator, Red, is released after spending forty years in the clink.

Red is so overwhelmed by his freedom that he, too, considers committing suicide. But he doesn't. Instead, he keeps a promise he made to his best friend, Andy, who'd escaped a year earlier. Red travels to that hayfield in Buxton, Maine, finds the beautiful old oak tree, digs up the metal box, and reads the letter Andy left for him.

And then what does Red do?

He heads for retirement, with the only person on Earth who understands the horrors he's been through, in Zihuatanejo, Mexico.

As the lights go down after my first day on the job, I search the chimphouse for Tom. I can't find him anywhere, so I ask Kim, who points to a mountain of blankets in a walkway up near the roof. Somewhere in that disorderly muddle lies Tom, munching away on his evening wedge of raisin bread, oblivious to his symbolic importance as the chimpanzee ambassador of the Great Ape Protection Act. Way up there near the roof, all alone in the quiet, Tom is simply one of the lucky few — an unfortunate, fortunate soul who finally made it to sanctuary.

Chapter 3

OUR DISQUIETING DOUBLES

One chimpanzee is no chimpanzee.

— ROBERT M. YERKES, quoted in *On Aggression*, by Konrad Lorenz

The Fauna Two-for-One

SUE ELLEN HAS a weakness for large, bearded men. This could be a remnant of her childhood in the circus. Gloria suspects that at some point in Sue Ellen's difficult life, she enjoyed a deep and loving friendship with a broad-shouldered man who preferred not to shave, and that's why she has warmed up to me faster than any of the other chimps have. Apparently, I'm just Sue Ellen's type.

For the first week, my job in the chimphouse consists of two simple tasks: stocking the dinner trolleys and washing dishes. And for the entire week, every time I look up from my work, Sue Ellen is sitting on a resting bench in one of the privacy rooms, adorned in whatever fashion statement she's been able to rustle up. Sue Ellen, otherwise known as Susie or Susie Goose, loves to drape herself in clothing whenever she can, another legacy of having been reared by humans.

When I approach her to say hello, which I do approximately twenty times a day, Sue Ellen presses her face against the caging between us and literally shakes with excitement. She purses her lips and squeezes them between the bars, offering a kiss. It doesn't take long for her to figure out that I am not allowed to return the gesture, but she is not one to be deterred. She usually just leaves her lips, thin and pink and mottled with black, out there for a while, and I can hear her stuttered breathing as she attempts to control her pleasure at my presence.

Today is Wednesday, the day the chimphouse is cleaned top to bottom. Although I don't know it yet, on Wednesdays "washing dishes" takes on a whole new meaning. I will spend the next six hours standing at the sink, my hands submerged in putrid wash water, while Gloria, Kim, and Linda deliver an endless mountain of poop-stained and urine-soaked enrichment items that they've rescued from the chimp enclosures.

The word "enrichment" is used to describe anything that improves a captive animal's quality of life. A new climbing structure is enrichment, as are new toys, new windows, new activities, or simply a new kind of food. The best sanctuary directors, lab technicians, and zookeepers are constantly in search of novel forms of enrichment for their animals. But Gloria has always had a problem with the term "enrichment." It has always felt like a sham to her, something dreamed up by a public relations firm to help zoos and research labs gussy up their image. Add a short length of rope to a tiny unkempt cage, and you can claim to be *enriching* the lives of your animals. Add an old tractor tire to an enclosure overflowing with animals, and you can claim they are *richer* for the experience. To Gloria, the cheerful term "enrichment" glosses over a very simple truth she wants everyone to understand — that the quality of life for the average animal in captivity is exceedingly dismal and that enrichment objects only serve to lessen, by a small margin, the profound impoverishment of the animal's life. It occurs to me, as I stand here wrist-deep in muck, that Gloria might be right — that the more appropriate term might be something closer to "compensation."

It is a disturbing experience to spend fifteen minutes chipping week-old feces off the jingles of a plastic tambourine (it helps, by the way, to let it soak first). But it is altogether more disquieting when you can feel two pairs of chimpanzee eyes boring a hole right through you while you do it. Sue Ellen's best friend is an intense little chimp named Pepper. They go everywhere together, and Pepper seems to share Sue Ellen's fascination with me. "Pep and Susie are like two words in the same sentence," Gloria tells me. "They're like the Fauna two-for-one deal."

As I struggle to liberate an especially foul tennis ball from the folds of a rank beach towel, I look up to see Pepper peacefully grooming Sue Ellen's shoulders. Sue Ellen is wearing a long string of plastic pearls and has managed to get herself stuck inside a particularly tight-fitting tube top. The bright red number is stretched up and over her head and one of her shoulders, but she hasn't been able to squeeze her other arm through. As Pepper tries to calm her, Sue Ellen sits staring in my general direction, a look of supreme annoyance on her face.

Washing dishes provides ample time to think. As the revolting pile by my side continues to grow, I can't help but wonder at the absurdity of this situation. Sue Ellen is a full-blooded chimpanzee of the species *Pan troglodytes*, endemic to the rainforests of equatorial Africa. But she is also a connoisseur of inexpensive fabrics and plastic jewels, and at one time she carried the human immunodeficiency virus in her veins. How did we come to this place, we humans and chimpanzees? How did all this begin?

Chim & Panzee

It is strange to imagine a time when the Western world knew nothing of the great apes. But only a few centuries ago the idea of supernaturally strong humanlike creatures roaming the wilds of far-off lands was consigned to the realms of superstition, mythology, and fairy tale. It wasn't until 1607, when an English sailor named Andrew Battell returned home after two decades in West Africa, that superstition turned into fervent speculation. In the published account of his experiences, Battell provided Europe with its first written descriptions of gorillas and chimpanzees.

Battell writes of "two kinds of monsters, which are common . . . and very dangerous." One of them "hath a man's face, hollow eyed, with long haire upon his browes." These creatures, known to the locals as *pongo* and *engeco,* "sleepe in the trees, and build shelters for the raine. They feed upon Fruit that they find in the Woods, and upon Nuts . . . They cannot speake, and have no understanding more than a beast."

With the publication of these words in 1625, Western culture's fraught relationship with the chimpanzee began. And fifteen years later, the first live ape arrived on European shores. The creature, which had likely been captured in Angola, was a gift for the prince of Orange, who kept his new prize in a menagerie in Amsterdam. This ape was immortalized by a Dutchman named Nicolaes Tulp, who made a now-famous engraving of it slumped against a boulder in an eerily thoughtful pose. Tulp included the engraving in his work *Observationes Medicae,* known to the wider public as his "book of monsters." In the accompanying essay, according to the philosopher Raymond Corbey, "Tulp confirmed what others before him had already suggested: the hairy, impudent Dionysian satyrs, described by ancient authors such as Pliny the Elder and familiar from literature and art, really existed."

Almost sixty years later, another chimpanzee arrived in Europe, this time in London, only to die soon after from a jaw infection. The English anatomist Edward Tyson dissected its body and published his findings in 1699, emphasizing the surprising similarities between this strange new creature and humankind. Now speculation about these animals became an insatiable curiosity. Not only did these powerful creatures of legend actually exist, their resemblance to humans went far deeper than anyone had dared to suppose.

To explain the profound impact these early observations on chimpanzees had on the philosophy, literature, religious thought, and almost every other aspect of the Western psyche at the time would require a book all its own. Many writers have dealt with this topic, most notably Raymond Corbey in his classic *The Metaphysics of Apes*. But for the purposes of this story, it is sufficient to say that by the end of the seventeenth century, thanks to men like Tulp and Tyson, invasive research on chimpanzees had begun. It would take another 250 years for modern laboratory research on captive chimps to establish a scientific foothold. The pioneer in this field was Robert M. Yerkes.

Already a towering figure in American psychology, Yerkes became fascinated with chimpanzee behavior after living for some time during the 1920s in Cuba, where he spent months observing a captive colony owned by a woman named Madame Abreu. Upon his return to Florida, Yerkes vowed to begin raising his own chimpanzees for study, and in 1923 he bought two young chimpanzees, Chim and Panzee, and began raising them in his home. Yerkes' most popular book, *Almost Human*, is an engaging account of the summer he spent with this pair of apes, especially his relationship with the one he called Prince Chim, whom experts now believe was a bonobo (a distinction that had yet to be made in Yerkes' time).

Although Chim and Panzee both died within the year, Yerkes' professional involvement with chimpanzees had only begun. In 1924 he was hired by Yale University to become the first professor of psychobiology, and by 1925 he had bought four new chimpanzees: Bill, Dwina, Pan, and Wendy. These four were the original members of what would eventually become one of the world's most storied chimpanzee research colonies. In 1930 Yerkes founded the Yale Laboratories of Primate Biology in Orange Park, Florida, which Yale renamed the Yerkes Laboratory of Primate Biology in 1941, on the occasion of Yerkes' retirement. When he died in 1956, the laboratory was taken over by Emory University and moved to Atlanta, Georgia, where it remains to this day. The facility, known informally as Yerkes, is easily the most famous primate research lab in America.

What is most notable about Robert Yerkes' work on chimpanzees (and, it should be said, the work of his contemporary Wolfgang Köhler) is that the professor was entirely comfortable attributing reason, insight, and humanlike emotions to his ape subjects, concepts that were many decades ahead of their time. "Many, if not all, the chief categories of human emotional expression are represented in chimpanzee behavior," wrote Yerkes in 1943. He also had an innate understanding of the importance of social life to a chimpanzee's emotional well-being. "One chimpanzee is no chimpanzee," he famously wrote, referring to the chimp's biological need to live surrounded by others.

These statements seem innocuous by today's standards, but back then they were severely at odds with the behaviorist school of thought, which was dominant at the time. The behaviorists held that nonhuman animals were little more than furry bundles of muscle, bone, and rudimentary brain matter and that only humans expressed emotions. The concept of an "animal mind" was worthy only of extreme ridicule. Perhaps the best way to illustrate that prevailing wisdom is to compare Yerkes' work with that of his colleague at Orange Park, Henry Nissen.

While Yerkes was beginning to elucidate the vast emotional range of his captive chimpanzees, Nissen was conducting a very different sort of research on apes. To determine whether certain arm movements (such as reaching or scratching) were innate or learned behaviors, Nissen encased the arms of an infant chimpanzee in plaster cylinders and left him this way for two years. When the baby chimp was finally freed, after twenty-four months with his arms immobilized, Nissen poked the poor ape to test his reaction. When he failed to defend himself with his arms, Nissen was left with two plausible conclusions: either the infant chimp had failed to learn the proper motor responses (as Nissen would argue) or the muscles in his arms had atrophied to the extent that, try as he might, he just couldn't move them. The study produced an entirely useless data set, while one unfortunate chimpanzee was put through unimaginable misery. This ugly pattern would be repeated countless times in laboratories around the world over the next sixty years.

Even though it meant bucking the conventional wisdom, Robert Yerkes refused to ignore the emotional intelligence he saw in his apes. And in doing so, he (along with Köhler) opened a line of scientific inquiry that two decades later would be blown wide open by a certain young Englishwoman in the jungles of Tanzania. "Chimpanzee emotional expression is fascinating and at the same time baffling in its complexity and variability," wrote Yerkes in 1943. "It is important as material for the investigator."

With this statement, we reach the extent of Robert Yerkes' enlightenment. Because no matter how progressive he may have been about the emotional capacity and intelligence of apes, Yerkes was nonetheless in agreement with the mainstream in one very important way: a captive chimpanzee was, above all else, "material for the investigator." He believed chimpanzees should be used "as a means of approaching the solution of various human problems for which we may not freely and effectively use ourselves as materials of observation and experimentation." It is this attitude, pervasive throughout Western science in the 1950s, that would soon launch our increasingly complicated relationship with the chimpanzee straight into outer space.

Our Disquieting Doubles

BY LUNCHTIME I can hardly stand being at the sink anymore. The stench is overwhelming, the drain is almost clogged with dead cockroaches, and no matter how many times I empty and refill the sink, the water turns instantly brown. The skin on my hands is the texture of wet prunes, and when I casually point this out to Linda she is horrified, but not for the reason I expect.

"Trolley Boy!" she yells. "Why didn't you use the gloves?" (Trolley Boy is now my official nickname in the chimphouse.)

"What gloves?" I ask.

"The ones below the sink."

I look under the sink and find a pair of yellow dishwashing gloves.

"These would have been useful."

"You've had your shots, right?" Linda asks, only half-joking.

As I squeeze my hands into the gloves, Linda is for some reason reminded of the time Tom got out of his enclosure one winter. Perhaps to take my mind off the germs that are surely circulating through my body, she tells me the whole story.

Every padlock in the chimphouse comes with a built-in safety mechanism. The only way to lock one is by inserting the proper key, which will not release until the lock is firmly shut. The chimps at Fauna are continually listening for that telltale *click* and are always double- and triple-checking the padlocks on the off chance that one might have malfunctioned. One January day, as Gloria closed up, this is exactly what happened. The padlock on Tom's enclosure released the key, but it wasn't locked. Once Gloria left for the night, it probably didn't take Tom very long to free himself.

The next morning, Linda was the first one on the scene. "I got to work, opened the chimphouse door, and there's Tom, at the far end of the hallway, sitting in the laundry room." Every instinct in Linda's body urged her to run, but she didn't. "I just said, 'Oh, hi, Tommie.'" And then, as calmly as she could, she walked back out and called Gloria at the house.

Linda said only two words to her sister on the phone — "Tom's out" — but Gloria instantly understood the scope of the problem. Tom wasn't living alone that winter; he was in a group with fragile Rachel, skinny Regis, enormous Jethro, and the two best friends, Sue Ellen and Pepper. If Tom was out, that meant the others were out, too. Gloria told Linda to go up to the office building, call their other sister, Dawna (who lives in nearby Chambly), and wait there. Then Gloria walked down to the chimphouse.

It was a bitter January morning, with a foot of snow already on the ground and a vicious south wind blasting across the fields. Gloria circled the building, peering into the side doors and windows, trying to figure out where everyone was. Gloria could see the faulty padlock on Tom's door, and she briefly considered sneaking in a side door to see if she could rectify the situation. Unfortunately, Regis was sitting at this door, and he looked pretty nervous about the situation.

So instead of trying to get inside right away, Gloria sat and talked with Regis for a while to calm him down. Jethro, meanwhile, took one look at Gloria through the door and went running back into his enclosure, as if he'd been caught stealing cookies by his mother and already knew he was grounded. And it didn't take long for Gloria to surmise that Sue Ellen and Pepper had never left their enclosure, even though the door was wide open. They were huddled together up on the second floor, watching the drama unfold below and wanting no part of it.

Just then it started to snow. Mario, the Fauna project manager, brought his truck down to the chimphouse so Gloria could warm up inside. And for the next four hours, Gloria interacted with the chimps through the windows and caged doors, trying to keep them calm and reassured. Slowly the chimps began to relax. At one point Rachel disappeared for a while, and Gloria began to fear for her. But soon enough, she heard a strange scraping noise from up on the roof. When she looked up, she was astonished to see a long, hairy arm reaching out of the second-floor window, holding a plastic snow shovel. Rachel was trying to shovel snow from the roof, just as she'd seen her human friends do countless times before.

Thankfully, by midafternoon, Regis had grown bored with his little adventure and had rejoined Jethro, Sue Ellen, and Pepper in their enclosure. Now Gloria just had Tom and Rachel to think about. She felt comfortable being in the chimphouse with those two loose, so after sneaking in to replace the faulty padlock, she stayed inside and started cleaning up the incredible mess the chimps had made. Tom, of course, had spent the day eating his fill from the walk-in fridge, and he had already made himself a sleeping nest on top of the walkway in which he usually slept. When Gloria entered the ransacked kitchen for the first time and opened the fridge door to survey the damage, Tom actually clapped three times, as he always does when he wants a treat. Meanwhile, Gloria eventually found Rachel fast asleep in the observation room, curled up on top of the television set.

Within an hour, Gloria had led a sleepy Rachel and a sated Tom back into their proper enclosure while making a mental note to have every door in the chimphouse outfitted with two padlocks instead of one and to add a set of sliding steel bars to each door mechanism for triple protection against escapes. Crisis averted, Linda and Dawna joined her inside to begin the long cleanup. And it was while they were surveying the damage that the women realized an unsettling truth about the chimps of Fauna Sanctuary.

The bathroom and medical clinic had been trashed, and the walk-in fridge was a little emptier, to say the least. But the floor of the laundry room was coated with a thick layer of liquid detergent, and two brooms from the storage closet lay across the slick surface. The kitchen sink was filled with soapy water; the oven door was flung open, its walls smeared with oven cleaner, and sponges were scattered around the interior. Apparently, Rachel's attempt to clear the snow from the roof had been more than just an adorable anomaly—the chimps had also tried to clean the floors, wash the dishes, and scrub the oven. Peter Singer calls chimpanzees "our disquieting doubles," and what was most disquieting to the Grow sisters that January day was that when presented with the closest thing to freedom they'd ever known, Tom, Rachel, Regis, and Jethro had done everything they could to act like human beings.

Chimps in America

BY THE 1940s, scientists at Yerkes had begun conducting the first large-scale invasive research studies on chimpanzees. Many of the studies were focused on human infectious diseases, mainly poliomyelitis, which chimpanzees can carry in their blood without developing symptoms of the disease. Around the same time, an increasing number of experimental neurologists and psychologists began working with live chimpanzees, cutting open their skulls and performing partial lobotomies, implanting electrodes in their gray matter, or simply crushing their skulls to test the effects of blunt-force trauma on the brain.

These experiments are surely disturbing, and the list goes on and on, but for sheer absurdity and shock value, nothing comes close to what the Soviet scientist Ilya Ivanov had attempted back in the 1920s. According to recently discovered documents, Ivanov was recruited by Stalin himself to create "a new invincible human being" by artificially inseminating female chimpanzees with human sperm. Stalin wanted Ivanov to put an army of these creatures at his disposal, both for military purposes and as an inexhaustible labor force. The project ended in utter failure, but it is probably the closest humanity has ever come to creating the chimpanzee-human hybrid, or humanzee, of legend and lore.

A new area of chimp research began stealing headlines in the 1950s. In an effort to get a leg up in the burgeoning space race, the U.S. Air Force founded a breeding colony of sixty-five chimpanzees at Holloman Air Force Base in Alamogordo, New Mexico. These chimps would be used to test the effects on the primate mind and body of high-speed and high-altitude travel, g-force pressures, and space flight itself.

All of the Holloman chimps were wild-caught in Africa, a practice that was enormously destructive to existing ape populations. By one estimate, for every infant chimp sold into research in America before 1975 (when the United States stopped participating), ten other chimpanzees may have been killed during its capture. The full impact of this practice is impossible to measure, but it could be argued that it made a significant early contribution to the modern decline of wild chimpanzee populations across West and Central Africa.

The Holloman Air Force chimps were essentially used as living crash-test dummies. They were strapped into spinning capsules, tied down in decompression chambers, and ejected from aircraft while traveling faster than the speed of sound. In one particularly grisly experiment known as "the sled," chimpanzees were strapped into a metal seat outdoors in the dry desert heat. The sled was catapulted at very high speed down a long track, and then the brakes were applied rapidly, bringing the sled to an immediate stop. The fastest sleds could reach a speed of Mach 1.7, or nearly 1,300 miles per hour. Chimpanzees regularly emerged from these sled rides either brain-damaged, seriously burned by the supersonic air, or with a broken neck caused by the inevitable whiplash. Some of them died after just one ride.

Meanwhile, a few of the Holloman chimps were being trained for space missions. By means of straitjackets, neck rings, and limb restraints (and electric shocks when they did something wrong), these apes were forced to master a series of simple tasks, such as pushing the correct lever whenever they saw a light flash on their screen. Once they'd mastered these tasks on Earth, the apes could theoretically be launched into space and asked to perform the same tasks in orbit. This would provide researchers with conclusive data on the effects of space travel on primate motor response.

In January 1961, just seven months after Jane Goodall launched her own groundbreaking research on wild chimps in Tanzania, a three-year-old chimpanzee named Ham became the first hominid to be launched into space. His voyage was considered a great success, even though he experienced g-forces 30 percent greater than expected and went 122 miles farther than planned, and his capsule lost partial pressure on its return to Earth, landing 60 miles off course in the Atlantic Ocean. None of this mattered to the scientists, because aside from a broken nose and a dose of profound terror, Ham was alive, and he had performed very well on the lever tests. A few months later, a chimp named Enos did equally well when he was launched into orbit, even though the electric shocking mechanism in his capsule malfunctioned and began administering zaps even when Enos pulled the right lever.

These results suggested to the air force that space might indeed be a safe and productive place for humanity. In many ways the chimpanzees of Holloman Air Force Base helped pave the way for Neil Armstrong's first steps on the moon. But their relevance to this story begins long after Ham and Enos returned from orbit. By the late 1960s, the air force had ended its aeronautical research with chimpanzees and needed to find another use for the colony. At that time, biomedical research on apes was beginning to boom in America. Hundreds of chimps were being captured in Africa and shipped across the ocean to take part in human disease research and toxicology tests for products like insecticides and industrial solvents. Also, the National Institutes of Health (NIH), having created eight National Primate Research Centers in 1960, was pouring hundreds of millions of tax dollars into invasive research on chimpanzees and monkeys. Rather than retiring their chimps to sanctuary as a reward for military service, the air force decided to lease them and the facility to Frederick Coulston, a toxicologist who eventually set up the Coulston Foundation on the site, which became one of the most notorious animal research facilities in American history.

In addition to their use in infectious disease research, by the late 1960s chimpanzees were being exposed to amphetamines, LSD, marijuana, nicotine, and alcohol in behavioral labs; their teeth were being knocked out so that dental students could practice reconstructive surgery on them; and their livers, kidneys, and hearts were being harvested for human transplantation (none of these transplants were ultimately successful, and the practice ended in the mid-1970s). By this time the famed ape-language experiments had begun, in which chimpanzees such as Washoe and Lucy were taught to communicate with their human caregivers using American Sign Language. In 1969 the journal *Science* published a groundbreaking paper entitled "Teaching Sign Language to Chimpanzees." In addition to the remarkable discoveries emerging from Goodall's research at Gombe, the world was being offered provocative glimpses into the mind, intelligence, and emotional expressiveness of the chimpanzee.

But for many observers, the most significant result to emerge from a chimpanzee behavioral lab in the early 1970s was reported by a young psychologist named Gordon Gallup. Working at Tulane University, Gallup devised a deceptively simple research tool called the mirror test. To conduct the test, Gallup applied little dots of odorless red dye to the foreheads of sleeping chimpanzees. Then he watched what happened when these chimps awoke and looked in a mirror. Every chimp responded by immediately trying to rub the offending red dot off his forehead, proving that the chimpanzees understood they were looking at themselves in the mirror. Their self-recognition led Gallup to an unavoidable and profoundly meaningful conclusion: chimpanzees must possess a sense of self.

Gallup first reported his findings in *Science* in 1970, and since then many other species have been put through his mirror self-recognition test. So far, bonobos, gorillas, orangutans, elephants, bottlenosed dolphins, orcas, and even European magpies have joined the chimpanzee in passing the test. All are therefore considered to have some sense of self-identity. And as Gallup has written, the results of the mirror test often call into question many of our traditional beliefs about animals: "Perhaps someday, in order to be logically consistent, man may have to seriously consider the applicability of his political, ethical, and moral philosophy to chimpanzees."

Little Red Dots

As my first Cleaning Day draws to a close, Gloria and I sit outside near one of the islands. The sun slips behind the farmhouse in the distance, and a few of the chimps emerge from their freshly washed home to spend some time in the grass. Binky shuffles to the bandstand, walks halfway up the staircase, and then stops for a moment to think, perhaps taking in the evening breeze. Then Yoko joins Binky on the lawn below, and the two engage in a mock-wrestling match. Binky pulls Yoko around by his feet, and the diminutive bully huffs with laughter. Meanwhile, old man Tom, on the next island over, is busy chasing a gaggle of white geese back into the moat where they belong.

The scene playing out before me could be considered absurd: retired chimpanzees surrounded by electric fencing and a moat, frolicking on a farm that is covered in a foot of snow four months of the year. But it is far less absurd than the place these apes came from.

Soon Sue Ellen and Pepper appear and sit down right in front of us. Susie, having managed to extricate herself from her ridiculous outfit, seems much more relaxed. Gloria disappears for a moment and returns with a handful of grapes, and when the girls see the bright green fruit, they utter excited food grunts and squeeze their hands beneath the caged wall. Gloria shares the bounty, handing them over one by one or popping them into the chimps' open mouths. When the grapes are gone, Gloria sits with her legs pressed to the fencing, and Pepper and Susie Goose proceed to groom her kneecaps through the bars.

I wonder what it was like for Gordon Gallup to see the first of his sleepy chimpanzees recognize himself in a mirror. I wonder if it was a genuine eureka moment for him, or if the little red dots just confirmed something he'd always known to be true. Watching Susie watch me, and watching Pepper watch Susie, and watching Gloria speak to both of them as if they were her oldest friends, I can't help thinking how disquieting it is that Western culture demands irrefutable proof for so many things that our sensing bodies already know. The chimps of Fauna are animated by their own self-identities; that much is obvious to me, and I've been here only a week. The unbelievable part, the story I want to focus on, is that these particular selves are still in existence at all. Because back in the units at LEM-SIP, a radically different set of red dots held sway and threatened to destroy them. These were the colored stickers that the lab technicians would apply to selected cages at night. If they marked your cage, it meant that you were one of the unlucky chimps destined for the surgery room come morning.

Chapter 4

BLUEPRINTS OF A DREAM

By the time I turned fifty, I knew I wanted to be
judged not by what I wrote in scientific journals
about chimpanzees but by what I *did* for them.

— ROGER FOUTS, *Next of Kin*

Mr. Puppy

ALTHOUGH THE CHIMPANZEES are Fauna's most famous residents, the heart and soul of the farm is not an ape at all. The truth is, while the chimps have been the subjects of countless radio spots, television shows, and documentary films over the years, the sanctuary's founding mascot flies, or barks, far below the celebrity radar. This brave leader of the rescued and rehabilitated goes by the simple yet dignified name of Mr. Puppy. He is a mutt, a mongrel, a mix — or, as I prefer to say, "a dog of a thousand fathers." And I have had to learn two important lessons about him right off the bat.

First, never ask anyone why Mr. Puppy doesn't have a real name. This is the most reliable way to make people at Fauna furious with you. "He *does* have a real name," they will say through clenched teeth, with a look of utter insult. "His real name is *Mister Puppy*." The second lesson to learn is that Mr. Puppy basically runs the show here. So for someone like me — a stranger living in the studio apartment directly below the Fauna office, smack-dab in the middle of Mr. Puppy's home turf — this means His Highness will be spending every night, whether I like it or not, chasing dream-rabbits and snoring like a chain saw at the foot of my bed.

Mr. Puppy dates to the beginning of the farm in 1990, when Gloria and Richard bought this parcel of rural pastureland near Chambly, Quebec. The purchase was a dream come true for both of them, and it marked the beginning of a period of great transition in Gloria's life. A paralyzing case of carpal tunnel syndrome had recently forced her to hand over Salon Gloria, the dog-grooming business she had started sixteen years earlier, to one of her assistants. Now, with business at Richard's vet clinic flourishing, Gloria could focus all of her energies on turning the new farm into . . . something. All she and Richard knew was that it would involve animals, a lot of animals, and that most of them would be rescues.

Back then great apes were the furthest thing from Gloria's mind. She was more concerned with cats and dogs, specifically those trapped in Quebec's notorious kitten and puppy mills. Even today the province battles its reputation as the puppy-mill capital of North America. Although Quebec tightened its regulations on animal breeders in 2005, the problem continues, with ever-more-gruesome cases coming to light nearly every year.

During those early years on the farm, Richard would often get phone calls from the local police asking him to accompany officers on raids of suspect properties. The cops needed an expert on animal welfare, someone who could pronounce with authority on the horrific conditions they inevitably found on-site. But the cops also needed someone who could offer temporary shelter to any despairing animals they might find. Gloria, the fiery, animal-loving partner of one of the busiest and most respected veterinarians on Montreal's South Shore, often filled in for Richard on these gruesome outings. And it was during one such raid, not long after they'd bought the land near Chambly, that Gloria stumbled upon Mr. Puppy.

The property in question was a typical junkyard, littered with the rusted hulks of abandoned cars and farm equipment, the melancholic debris of an increasingly depressed farming region. A ramshackle manor house tilted on its foundation, and a column of black smoke rose from a distant tire fire. When Gloria arrived on the scene, the authorities had just gotten there, along with a whole team of veterinarians, who were already getting down to business.

Gloria described the scene: "The vets just fanned out through the junkyard and started pulling these terribly malnourished and sickly dogs from beneath the cars. They were everywhere. There must have been more than three hundred dogs in that place. And each time they dragged one out, the vets would jab it with a needle, inject Euthanyl, and move on to the next one. They weren't even considering the fact that some of them might have been saved. Some of them didn't look all that badly off. But the vets just went around killing everything they could find."

The cops had asked Gloria along on the raid so she could rescue the farm animals at the junkyard: two pigs, a horse, and a cow. But Gloria was horrified by what was happening to the dogs. And she wasn't the only one who didn't like it. Soon gunshots rang out from the old manor house. Everyone took cover, and the cops moved in on the residence. This is when Gloria, fearing for her own life as the bullets flew, sprang into action.

"I couldn't just sit there and watch all those dogs be killed. So I started driving around, plucking dogs from where they were lying, and throwing them into the van." Gloria managed to save only three dogs from the needles before the cops saw what she was doing and ordered her to stop. By then the insurrection at the house had been brought under control, and the occupants, members of a proud but dirt-poor family, were being frog-marched to the police cruisers. They were dressed in rags, and some had no shoes. Apparently, the house was even worse than the junkyard: the stench of garbage was overpowering, and the floor was a mat of hardened dog feces. One of the cops wouldn't let the young daughter into his cruiser because, he said, she "stunk like a pig."

"I felt terribly for that family," says Gloria. "It's not like they were living the high life and abusing those animals. They thought they were rescuing them, giving them a place to live. The problem was, they couldn't provide for the animals because they couldn't even provide for themselves. And that's not right. But can you imagine watching people come onto your property and start murdering your dogs?"

That night, Gloria brought her precious cargo back to the farm: two pigs, a Belgian workhorse, a Holstein cow, and three little dogs—a male with a touch of collie in him and two females. All three dogs had scabies and mange and were obviously deeply traumatized. One had lost all its fur. Gloria set them up in the barn to convalesce for the next month.

Gloria decided to name her new charges in ways that would pay homage to the anonymity of the dogs she was powerless to rescue that day at the junkyard. She named the female with no fur Pinky because her bare, infected skin was the color of a bright blush. She named the second female simply the Girl. And she named the male Puppy, because that's what he was, no more and no less.

Once they'd recovered, the Girl was sent to live at Gloria's mother's house. But Pinky and Puppy stayed at Fauna. Pinky became a loving but somewhat introverted little dog, while, in the hands of his new caregivers, Puppy's natural charisma soon began to shine through. Consequently, he became known by the more sophisticated Mr. Puppy.

That was sixteen years ago. Today, Pinky and Mr. Puppy are still the best of friends. And along with an old calèche horse from Montreal, they've been here as long as Fauna has been. But both are now showing signs of significant aging. Pinky, whose fur eventually grew back into a luxurious white coat, is now stone deaf, very thin, and a little unstable on her feet. With her frail body and slinking gait, she resembles a nervous ghost. Mr. Puppy is losing his sight and is increasingly incontinent, and the muscles in his hips are deteriorating. Most worrying of all, Pup-Pup has begun showing signs of dementia, suffering occasional seizures and panic attacks and barking at the moon. Gloria has begun weighing the options should Mr. Puppy's health continue to decline. Although she hates to think about it, she and Richard would never deny Mr. Puppy a peaceful, painless end if it became necessary.

But even with all that is wrong with him, nothing can keep this dog from his single most important duty on the farm. "Mr. Puppy has been here since the beginning," says Gloria. "He has greeted every volunteer and every worker who has ever come through our gate."

I quickly learned just how seriously he takes his job. At 6:00 A.M. sharp every weekday morning, having felled a forest of snore-trees and vanquished his kingdom of dream-rabbits, Mr. Puppy wrenches himself up from his spot at the foot of my bed, shimmies his sack of bones to my apartment door, and starts whining piteously. I open the door, he drags himself upstairs, and I go back to bed. And the next thing I know I am awakened by the sound of His Highness barking to high heaven. The door to the office opens upstairs, Mr. Puppy taps a happy claw-dance on the roof above my head, and Cyndi banishes any hope of my returning to sleep with her distinctive, piercing greeting.

"Monsieur Pup*pee!*" she yells. "Mon a*mour!*"

For sixteen years now, that's how every workday at Fauna has begun.

Running on Instinct

IN THOSE early years, the young sanctuary grew and grew. Gloria and Richard received animals from just about everywhere. As word spread, more and more people showed up at the door of their farmhouse with sick or unwanted dogs and cats, guinea pigs, pot-bellied pigs, roosters, geese, swans, goats, even ostriches and llamas. Whatever the animal, they took it in, and not all were of the cute and cuddly variety.

"You buy a farm," says Richard, "and suddenly everyone starts giving you farm animals." Soon the back paddocks were being grazed by a ragtag family of retired dairy cows and Highland cattle. Gloria even received a group of pigs who'd been destined for slaughter. After a few months of relative freedom, these pigs—who'd been pumped full of growth hormones and were dangerously overweight—had dropped significant poundage and were beginning to look almost svelte.

When a deer was hit by a car or otherwise injured in the area, someone would call the cops to report the incident, and the police would immediately call Dr. Allan. If the animal was beyond assistance, as was often the case, Richard would dispatch it with a humane injection or, when time was of the essence, a shotgun. But occasionally, a wounded animal ended up at the farm. One, a young buck who had slipped on a patch of ice and broken his leg, lived in the barn at Fauna for a year and made a full recovery. Unfortunately, when Richard moved this buck, named Buddy, into a brand-new outdoor enclosure so he could finally see the sun and breathe some fresh air, a grisly scene unfolded. Driven by instinct to flee the moment he was outside, Buddy ran repeatedly into the heavy-duty fencing, crashing into it with his head until he collapsed, unconscious. Richard pumped him full of anti-inflammatories and pain medication, but in the end he couldn't save Buddy. Richard and Gloria still rue their decision to erect that fencing instead of just letting him run free.

The pair continued going on police raids and returning with vanloads of rescues. On one particularly ghastly evening they returned with crates and crates of ailing rabbits, which they'd found stacked one on top of the other in the basement of a wealthy restaurateur's house, their food molded into inedible heaps, their coats matted with feces and urine.

Gloria and Richard's participation in these raids was perfectly legal, and most of the animals they rescued were never reclaimed. But on rare occasions, the animals had to be returned to their original owners. Sometime after the junkyard raid, the Montreal police arrived at Fauna with a warrant and a large truck. Incredibly, a local judge had concluded that the animals had been unlawfully seized and must be returned. Luckily, the Belgian workhorse had already been fostered to another farm, and the dogs had become so healthy and had regrown so much of their fur that the cops couldn't identify them. But they took away the two pigs and the Holstein. According to Gloria, as the truck was backing out of the driveway, the bailiff admitted to her that he was ashamed of what he was doing. He likened his actions to ejecting the animals from a five-star hotel.

A Purposeful Escape

ALTHOUGH THE early years of Fauna may sound idyllic, full of rural happiness and sweet liberation, for Gloria that time was unexpectedly hard. As her sanctuary began to thrive, she found herself falling into a debilitating funk. The more animals she took in, the more she sensed that something was missing. She was desperate to fix Quebec's puppy-mill problem but felt powerless to do so; she was a member of the only two animal rights groups in the province, but both were relatively toothless and soon went defunct. Gloria wanted to do something big and audacious in the name of animal welfare, but she didn't know where to start. She began to feel disillusioned, inadequate, and helpless. She was about to turn forty, and none of her larger plans for Fauna had panned out. She'd wanted to start a doggie spa or an elite boarding kennel on the farm, but Richard eventually put his foot down. He spent his days spaying, neutering, and treating household pets, and the last thing he wanted was to be greeted by hundreds of them when he arrived home at night.

Predictably, as Gloria struggled, their relationship began to suffer. Richard buried himself in his work, and Gloria in her malaise. She considered going back to school or starting a nonprofit to promote vegetarianism to the elderly. She felt she'd been put on Earth for a reason, but she couldn't figure out what it was. In other words, she was nearing a full-blown midlife crisis. Soon her feelings of inadequacy, coupled with a growing emotional distance from Richard, transformed into an overwhelming sense of guilt. Just two years after starting her sanctuary, Gloria knew she needed to make a drastic change or risk being unhappy for the rest of her life.

"You come up with a lot of ideas when you're trying to get out of your real life," she tells me. "At first I was going to run away to Africa. I was like, 'I'm getting the hell out of here. I'm going to hang out with Jane Goodall.' I've always been the type of person who wants to run away from home."

This romantic notion—that she could circumvent the complications of real life by disappearing into the wilds of East Africa and bunking with Jane Goodall—would surely be echoed by innumerable kindred spirits the world over, myself included. Because although it was her scientific discoveries that made Goodall famous, it was also her sense of adventure, the sheer panache with which she escaped the predicted drudgery of her life as a young woman in 1960s England, that captivated the world and that made her a household name. How many of us, scientists and nonscientists alike, have fantasized about going off into the jungles as she did, to live an unorthodox and thrilling life as an honorary member of a society of great apes? How many of us, even while reading this sentence, are experiencing an existential tug on our psyches, a yearning to just get up and leave our lives, in all their muddy confusion, for the glorious riot of the rainforest? Here is one of Jane Goodall's less acknowledged legacies: half a century later, she is still a powerful icon for one of Western society's most common fantasies, that of *the purposeful escape*.

The truth—which I feel obliged to point out, having been lucky enough to follow through on exactly this fantasy at the age of twenty-three, when I spent a year studying monkeys in the jungles of Suriname—is that the act of disappearing, no matter how exotic the destination or how lofty the enterprise, is more a delay tactic than an actual solution to spiritual malaise. Imagine my dismay when I arrived at Monkey Camp on the remote shores of Suriname's Coppename River in the fall of 2000 and found that the very voices I was so desperate to run away from had tagged along for the ride inside my head.

For Gloria, the attraction of Africa was not the chimpanzees or even spending time with Jane Goodall. It was the profound sense of purpose she hoped such a trip would give her life. "I hadn't found my vision or my dream yet," Gloria says now. "I was aimless and casting about." She didn't end up going to Africa. Instead, her turning point arrived in a much more innocuous way. It came from a friend in the form of a catalogue from the Earthwatch Institute, a nonprofit organization that matches volunteers with scientific research projects around the world.

"I went nuts when I saw that thing," says Gloria. "One of my biggest fears about Africa was the vaccinations I'd have to get. But some of the Earthwatch programs didn't even require needles!" At first, Gloria focused on a program rehabilitating injured sea turtles in Central America. But then she saw one called Caring for Chimpanzees, a two-week course at the Chimpanzee and Human Communication Institute (CHCI) in Ellensburg, Washington, and she was sold. Richard, thrilled to see Gloria excited after watching her spirits decline for so long, bought the Earthwatch package for her as a birthday gift. She would spend two weeks in Ellensburg that coming February.

"I just thought it was going to be an experience, something different to do," says Gloria. Little did she or Richard know what lay in store for them in the mountains of central Washington.

The Blueprints

ONE MIGHT think the decision to transform a small animal sanctuary into a retirement home for traumatized chimpanzees must have required years of careful consideration and forethought. But Gloria made her decision in a heartbeat, almost without realizing it. In fact, she didn't think about it at all.

CHCI is run by a well-known husband-and-wife team of primate researchers, Roger and Deborah Fouts. Roger is renowned for his role in teaching a chimpanzee named Washoe to communicate using American Sign Language (ASL). Washoe was the first nonhuman primate to learn and correctly use ASL, and the discoveries made possible by this breakthrough revolutionized the way we think about the interior lives of other animals. To me, one of Roger's most incredible findings was that chimpanzees, like humans, often talk to themselves when no one else is around. Roger would sometimes catch Washoe signing to herself while she played with one of her dolls. When Washoe realized she wasn't alone, she would stop mid-sign, but the moment she thought Roger had gone away, she'd resume her internal conversation.

CHCI is first and foremost a sanctuary for the three remaining chimpanzees from the ASL studies. But its secondary goal is to encourage respect and compassion toward all great apes through education, public advocacy, and humane primate research. The Earthwatch courses are part of these activities.

For the first few days at CHCI, Gloria and her fellow participants were put through a demanding series of lectures. They were taught the basics of ASL, of chimpanzee behavior, and of chimpanzee society. During this rapid-fire education, they never met Roger or Deborah, nor did they lay eyes on a live chimp. Instead, they learned to identify individual apes from photographs and video footage.

At night the participants bunked together in university dorm rooms. This arrangement was not to Gloria's liking. "There were differences of opinion," she says, putting it mildly. "I was animal rights, and a few of them weren't. What was I supposed to do? Some of them even ate meat." Gloria had to switch roommates a couple of times.

On the third day, the group watched a series of videos recounting our thorny relationship with chimpanzees, from the wild chimps studied by Goodall to famous bonobos like Kanzi and Panbanisha, to chimps subjected to neurological, toxicological, and pharmaceutical testing in military and biomedical labs. "You're pretty much a blubbering idiot by the end of the videos," says Gloria. "It's the day you realize how horrible we've been to chimps. It's the day you just want to die."

On the fourth day, having survived their initiation, the group finally got to meet Roger and Debbie Fouts. The couple sat at the front of the room and asked each participant a single question: Why are you here? As each one answered in turn, the Foutses heard the usual catalogue of earnest responses — "to experience a great ape in the flesh," "to carry on a conversation across the species divide," "to explore our primal connection to the animal kingdom." But when they got to Gloria, they heard something entirely new.

I want to start a sanctuary.

Gloria was as surprised as anyone. "I just blurted out the first thing that came into my mind." At the end of the session, Gloria received a summons. "A woman came up to me afterward in the hall. She said Roger and Debbie would like to meet with me tomorrow. I thought, Oh, great. I'm getting booted out. Someone has said something behind my back, and now they're going to send me home." Gloria assumed the Foutses had heard about her "differences of opinion" with her ex-roommates. She fully expected to be kicked out for not playing nice.

Nothing could have been further from the truth. The woman who had delivered Gloria's summons was Mary Lee Jensvold, the assistant director of CHCI.

"So I went in there the next day, and Roger just asked me point-blank: Are you serious? It took me a minute to figure out what he was talking about. The sanctuary. And so I said, Well, yeah. Sure, I'm serious. I mean, I said it, so I guess I'm serious. I am a believer in myself. I believe I can do anything I want to do. So I thought, Yeah, sure, of course. And before I knew it, we were having a really confusing conversation about zoning bylaws."

Roger and Debbie told Gloria that they would help her with absolutely anything she needed to start a sanctuary for chimpanzees: plans, designs, funding contacts, guidance through the legal labyrinth, training, anything. They took her into an adjoining room and pulled out a set of blueprints. "I was looking at the plans for their building," she says. "The actual blueprints. I gotta say, that was one hell of an Earthwatch visit."

As soon as Gloria was alone, she ran to the phone to call Richard at the clinic in Quebec. She told him she wanted to start a chimpanzee sanctuary and wanted to know what he thought of the idea. Gloria and Richard now agree that their future together may have been hanging in the balance that day. As it turned out, Richard's response may well have rescued them both.

"Tell me what you need me to do."

Two hours later, Richard called Gloria back, and she relayed his encouraging news to Roger. Richard had managed to speak with a vet in Ottawa, as well as officials with the federal and provincial governments, and apparently no one could see a problem with the idea. When Richard called an official at city hall, the person who answered the phone was also amenable. "A barn for monkeys?" he said, perhaps not realizing that Richard was serious. "A monkey barn sounds fine."

"I told Gloria nothing is impossible," says Richard now. And that was exactly what she needed to hear. Every time Gloria talks about those ecstatic days at CHCI, the memories come pouring out in an emotional jumble. Looking back, she seems dumbfounded by the luck and happenstance of it all, but also extremely thankful for the sense of conviction she found there, the strength and certainty of purpose she'd long been searching for. The messages from those two weeks in central Washington will never cease to evolve and circle back upon one another in her heart and in her mind. When she speaks of her gratitude to Roger Fouts for the help he gave her, she is also speaking about her gratitude to Richard for sticking by her during a very difficult period.

"He believed in me," says Gloria. "And if someone believes in you, you can do just about anything. You have to have people who have faith in you, and then you'll be fine. Even if your dream is the wonkiest dream in the world."

With the CHCI blueprints in hand, Gloria returned to Montreal revitalized. But when she and Richard began pricing out the construction of a building similar to the Foutses' on their property, they hit a significant snag. Richard had pledged his entire life's savings to the project—$250,000—but the first quotes they received from builders were well north of $2 million. After interviewing countless contractors and modifying the CHCI plans as much as possible, the lowest bids were still more than $1 million. Richard couldn't afford that, and over the next six months, Gloria slowly began to lose faith in her dream. How could it be that only the rich could afford to rescue chimpanzees? she wondered. How could an idea that felt so right be stymied by something so pedestrian as a lack of funds?

Gloria's passion for animal rights was blossoming in new and exciting ways. She joined an alphabet soup of influential animal rights organizations—from AAVS to NAVS to NEAVS to PETA to HSUS—and when their promotional materials arrived in the mail, she devoured them cover to cover. This was around the mid-1990s, when some of the first eyewitness accounts were emerging from inside primate laboratories. These tales of animal suffering helped keep Gloria's faith and commitment going, as she and Richard struggled to find a feasible way to construct their chimphouse.

One summer, Gloria made the long drive to Washington, D.C., to participate in a historic march for animal rights. There she met Roger and Debbie Fouts again, and they introduced her to some of the biggest names in the movement. She met Jane Goodall for the first time and heard Peter Singer, the father of animal liberation, speak. As she listened to Theodora Capaldo from the New England Anti-Vivisection Society, Neil Barnard from the Physicians Committee for Responsible Medicine, the eminent scientist Carl Sagan, the author and animal rights activist Cleveland Amory, and Alex

Pacheco and Ingrid Newkirk of People for the Ethical Treatment of Animals (PETA),Gloria was finally able to see beyond her frustrating local problems in rural Quebec. She discovered an international community of passionate, like-minded people who were actually getting things done. It didn't hurt that she was welcomed with open arms. Roger Fouts always made sure to introduce Gloria as an important new member of the clan who was starting a much-needed chimpanzee sanctuary in Canada. At that time she was secretly considering rescuing elephants instead (elephants, after all, could live mostly outdoors and wouldn't require an expensive, sophisticated building), but as the old wisdom goes, the more you tell people you're going to do something, the more likely you are to do it. It didn't cost Roger a cent to introduce Gloria that way, but his words gave her invaluable encouragement.

And then, finally, a breakthrough. Richard found a contractor willing to build a greatly scaled-down version of the CHCI chimphouse for around $250,000. Suddenly presented with the very real possibility of pumping his entire retirement savings into an extremely risky enterprise, Richard added one important stipulation: before breaking ground, he needed assurances that there would be chimps available to retire to the sanctuary. He wanted to be sure that if they built it, the chimpanzees would come.

The final word came from Roger Fouts. Six months after the march on Washington, and just a week after Gloria had taken Richard to CHCI so he could see the place for himself, Fouts called the Fauna sanctuary and left the couple a rather cryptic message.

"Here's the number for Dr. James Mahoney," he said. "Give him a call as soon as you can." Apparently, Mahoney was planning to smuggle some chimpanzees out of a biomedical research lab somewhere in New York State and was quietly looking for takers.

Two weeks later, Gloria, Richard, and their friend Pat Ring were driving south from Montreal through a raging snowstorm in the dead of night. Their destination was the small town of Tuxedo in New York's Ramapo Mountains.

Chapter 5

THE CAGE HOSPITAL

> Ask the experimenters why they experiment on
> animals, and the answer is: "Because the animals are
> like us." Ask the experimenters why it is morally
> OK to experiment on animals, and the answer
> is: "Because the animals are not like us." Animal
> experimentation rests on a logical contradiction.
>
> — CHARLES R. MAGEL

Racing the Bub

BINKY IS DOING his best to keep me in shape. When I'm not
stocking trolleys or washing dishes or whispering sweet nothings to
Sue Ellen and Pepper, the Bub will often challenge me to a footrace.
He'll lie on the floor of his privacy room and try to get my attention with a few Bronx cheers. When I approach, instead of reaching
his arm through the porthole and asking for a piece of fruit, Binky
will suddenly lurch to his feet, squeeze himself up into the walkway
above, and sprint to the Sky Walk door. There, with both hands
gripping the door frame, he will turn back to look at me, frozen in
place.

Now the ball is in my court. As soon as I take a step toward
him, the Bub will hurl himself out of the chimphouse onto the Sky
Walk, where he will run as fast as he can to the roundabout overlooking the pond. It doesn't matter how well I disguise that first
step; Binky always gets a head start, and with his long, powerful
strides there is no way I could catch him. And that's not his only

advantage. Aside from the fact that the Bub gets to use his knuckles as well as his feet as he runs, he also has a pretty straight shot to the pond, while I have to open a heavy sliding door, negotiate two finicky gates, and leap a small ditch—all the while keeping my eye out for passing golf carts. No matter how deftly I exit the chimphouse, by the time I reach the pond the Bub is already sitting quietly on his haunches, not one glossy hair out of place, a look of smug satisfaction on his face. The moment I stop to catch my breath or nurse my bruises, he's off, knuckle-running back to where we started.

The Bub and I run together like this every day. We usually make five or six trips to the pond before he loses interest or my lungs give out. Often, once the race is over, we'll sit out there together and stare across the water to the monkey house. The chimps are not the only primates at Fauna. Gloria has rescued a number of monkeys and a gorgeous olive baboon named Theo. They live together in a scaled-down version of the chimphouse on the far side of the property.

When Gloria says Binky is the luckiest chimp here, she is not referring just to the few months he spent with his mother as an infant; an ape with Binky's marvelous physique and relatively clean bill of health would be worth a fortune to a biomedical lab. Most of the chimps of Fauna were ready for retirement; they were either too old or too disturbed or had been infected with too many different viruses to be of much experimental value anymore. But not Binky. Whenever we run together, I can't help but marvel that such a strong and vigorous ape managed to escape the lab, where strength and vigor are so highly prized. So how did Binky get so lucky?

The Bub's story proves that with chimpanzees, as with humans, survival is all about whom you know. Binky's escape from LEMSIP is a testament to the power of friendship. It was because he had such wonderful friends that his life was finally spared.

Mahoney

GLORIA, RICHARD, and Pat arrived in Tuxedo, New York, at nine o'clock in the morning. On edge after driving all night through a snowstorm, they eventually found their way to a nondescript driveway. Stopping at the main gate of LEMSIP, they were greeted by James Mahoney.

The more I learn about Mahoney, the more he seems like the phantom antihero of this story, an enormously conflicted figure who could have come straight from the pages of a graphic novel by Peter Singer. So far, no one has been willing or able to supply me with a phone number at which I might reach him, and the only e-mail address I have for him has swallowed my increasingly insistent messages, pleading to let me speak to him. Because of his critical role in the creation story of Fauna, part of me quakes at the idea of writing about him without talking with him first. But sometimes a character's absence speaks volumes.

James Mahoney—or Jim, as both friends and critics refer to him—was the chief veterinarian at LEMSIP for over twenty years. He was the gynecologist, obstetrician, pediatrician, general physician, and occasional surgeon to hundreds of captive chimpanzees, monkeys, and baboons in a private biomedical lab during a period in America defined by an increasingly influential animal rights movement. Not surprisingly, Mahoney was called many things throughout his career, both good and bad: a doctor, a scientist, a philosopher, a ghoul, a traitor, a user of helpless creatures, a man of two minds. Jane Goodall once wrote that "Jim is one of the most gentle and compassionate people I know." His most memorable nickname was the Kissing Vet, a moniker he came by honestly, for Mahoney was deeply affectionate with his apes. But perhaps no description comes closer to the truth than that put forth by Roger A. Caras, who wrote that Mahoney is "a man trapped in the middle of a storm."

Mahoney's memoir, *Saving Molly*, was published the year after LEMSIP shut down. The book details Mahoney's strange journey from enthusiastic large-animal vet in rural Ireland to a morally conflicted researcher in one of the world's largest nonhuman primate research laboratories. By the time he was hired at LEMSIP in the mid-seventies, Mahoney had been working with primates for years, researching the reproductive physiology of macaque monkeys, "the wondrous, hopeful beginnings of life." But after his first visit to LEMSIP, Mahoney fell prey to the allure of working with the intelligent, humanlike chimpanzees. For the next eighteen months, he lobbied LEMSIP's founding director, a man named Jan Moor-Jankowski, who got his start in primate research at Yerkes, to hire him. When Moor-Jankowski finally did, Mahoney was thrilled. He thought he'd been given his dream job. "Working with chimps," he imagined, "must be the ultimate experience."

Little did he know what he'd signed on for. By taking the job at LEMSIP, Mahoney had entered a sort of waking nightmare. He was a passionate animal lover, but he was also a firm believer in the importance of animal-based research in saving human lives. His new job would require him to facilitate scientific procedures on animals that would leave many of them psychologically traumatized for the rest of their lives. As Mahoney writes in *Saving Molly*, by taking that job at LEMSIP, "without realizing it, I was setting myself up for years of heartache and doubt."

A Blessing and a Curse

FOR THE first few years, Mahoney's work revolved around LEMSIP's breeding program. But soon enough, he was pulled into what he calls "hard-core" research, the real bread and butter of a privately funded biomedical laboratory in the 1970s: viral hepatitis studies in chimpanzees.

Chimpanzees infected with hepatitis virus do not develop the debilitating liver inflammation that humans do. They do, however, act as excellent incubators for the virus, allowing it to proliferate in their bloodstream with few adverse effects. In theory, this makes the chimpanzee an attractive model for developing and testing hepatitis vaccines. Here is the great misfortune I spoke of at the beginning of this story, the paradox that underlies our fraught relationship with chimpanzees. It is their overwhelming similarity to humans, coupled with very specific differences, that have condemned so many of them to lifetimes of torment in laboratories around the world. As Deborah Blum writes in *The Monkey Wars*, the genetic differences between humans and chimpanzees are "next to nothing" and yet "next to everything." Perhaps Dale Peterson puts it best in *Visions of Caliban*, his remarkable book written with Jane Goodall: "The chimpanzee is blessed and cursed by the honored shape." Although chimpanzees and humans are in the same taxonomic family — Hominidae — chimps are not quite members of the *human* family. And when it comes to the moral standing of that particular club, almost is not close enough.

Hepatitis vaccine studies usually involve infecting the apes with live virus and then inoculating them with a potential vaccine. Blood samples are taken every two weeks or so. These samples are measured for viral load, antibody response, and serum chemistry; in other words, the proliferation of the virus is tracked over time. The vaccinated apes may also be challenged with reinfection to test the vaccine's robustness, and uninfected apes may be used in safety tests for potential vaccines.

An infected chimp will usually undergo a series of punch biopsies of the liver under general anesthetic; a long needle is pushed through the abdomen wall and "punched" into the organ, retrieving a small piece of fresh liver for analysis of the viral load. In rare instances, an infected chimp might undergo an open liver biopsy, a full-scale surgery in which the abdomen is opened and a larger, wedge-shaped piece of liver is removed. Open biopsies are the most invasive of all hepatitis protocols.

"By and large," Mahoney writes, "the research procedures themselves weren't hard on the animals." He justifies this remark by pointing out that chimps don't suffer the symptoms of hepatitis, and the protocols do not require the apes to be killed. And while it's true that Mahoney's boss, Moor-Jankowski, was well respected for resisting research contracts that called for terminal studies (those that require the animal subjects to die) or the most invasive sorts of surgeries, Mahoney's comment does gloss over one brutal reality of the science protocols. Even a routine blood draw may require the ape to be "knocked down," which is lab lingo for being knocked unconscious. The most popular knockdown method in biomedical laboratories is with a dart gun.

I've seen videos of technicians wielding these guns. The target chimpanzee goes berserk with terror inside his cage as the technician lines him up in the sights. If the chimp is lucky, his cage might have an old car tire suspended in the middle that he can hide behind, but even so, he doesn't stand a chance. As he spins and crashes his body against the steel bars, the other chimps in the unit—his friends, perhaps his family—begin screaming and howling and banging with all their might. Every time a chimpanzee is shot with a dart gun, those in nearby cages watch him grow groggy and lethargic and then crash to the floor in a matter of minutes, sometimes from high up on a resting bench. As far as these innocent bystanders know, a dart gun equals something close to death. When they see a chimp about to be shot, they react as if their friend's life is about to be taken.

Their reaction makes sense when you consider that when the knocked-down chimp is removed from the unit for surgery or a new study, his friends may never see him again. The last image they'll have of their friend is an unconscious heap on the floor. This explains the extreme level of fear, punctuated by a riot of screaming and involuntary urination and defecation, exhibited by a chimpanzee caught in the crosshairs of a dart gun. Even if the knockdown is only for a blood draw or cage transfer, to the casual observer it looks and sounds and smells as if the ape believes it is about to be murdered.

According to the partial LEMSIP medical records that Gloria managed to acquire for some of her chimps, most of the Fauna chimpanzees were subjected to tens, if not hundreds, of dart-gun knockdowns. In the first nine years of her life, Petra was knocked down at least 185 times, and 79 of those were by dart. Regis was knocked down at least 177 times, with 92 by dart. Binky was knocked down at least 136 times, with 74 by dart. Since the medical files are incomplete, these numbers are likely underestimates. Of the surviving Fauna chimps, it seems that only Jethro and Pepper managed to avoid a lot of dartings.

A brief perusal of the incomplete files reveals LEMSIP chimps being darted by accident, taking ill-aimed darts in the lips, forehead, chest, and, in one particularly horrifying case, the very sensitive skin of the vagina. Mario, the Fauna project manager, once tested the strength of a standard laboratory dart gun by shooting it at an inch-thick wooden board. From a considerable distance away, many times farther than a technician would be from a caged chimpanzee, the dart exploded from the gun with such force that it splintered the wood with a loud *crack!*

But it wasn't the physicality of the protocols per se that eventually led Mahoney to question the LEMSIP enterprise. Instead, it was his gradual understanding of the psychological impact on his chimps of the hepatitis studies—and the toll of captivity itself—that began to shift the ground beneath his feet.

Junior Africa

AT LEMSIP a chimpanzee usually began her research "career" around the age of two. In the wild, chimps are not weaned until they are four or five, and they remain tightly bonded to their mothers, emotionally and physically, until they're about eight. For all intents and purposes, then, most of the LEMSIP chimps entered the world of scientific research as babies.

This seemed especially harsh to Mahoney, and he repeatedly lobbied for the chimps to be given at least a four-year childhood before entering protocols. But he did not own these young chimpanzees; they were leased by the pharmaceutical companies that LEMSIP did business with. These companies essentially paid Mahoney's salary, so there was little he could do—the chimps had to earn their keep. So Mahoney and his staff focused their efforts on improving the housing arrangements and enrichment programs for the apes. In collaboration with Jane Goodall, he set up a nursery where infants who had been taken from their mothers after birth could be weaned by human surrogates while surrounded by other baby chimpanzees.

One night in my apartment beneath the Fauna office, I watch a series of home videos shot in that nursery. It looks like a very happy place. Youngsters dressed in OshKosh overalls and diapers chase each other through a child's paradise. Toys are scattered everywhere, there's a kiddie pool in the center of the room, classical music on the stereo, the chimps' human mothers laughing and playing with them, watching out for their adopted children with great care and affection. Infants wearing human onesies, being bottle-fed by caregivers in rocking chairs. "Have fun," says one surrogate as she delivers an infant into a bustling playpen in the adjoining room. "Finished product," says another, without a hint of irony, as she finishes swaddling an infant and holds him up for the camera.

With the volume muted, these videos are surreal, a bunch of happy women caring for a bunch of cute, cuddly, costumed baby apes. But when you turn the volume up, the clips are more disturbing. Because this idyllic little corner of LEMSIP was actually within earshot of the regular units, and every once in a while, paradise was riven by the voices of frightened chimpanzees. Each baby chimp could hear the panicked screams of the older apes, the constant cage-rattling of the juvenile and subadult chimps, for whom the nursery was now just an unreliable memory. No one can say if the youngsters understood what they were hearing, if at some point in their development they put two and two together and realized that nursery life wouldn't last forever. "It's hard to picture him as a big, two-hundred-pound adult, rattling his cage and shrieking," says one female caregiver, speaking about one of her favorite charges on her last day of work in the nursery. "I've made so many new friends," she says wistfully, "[but at least] I've got lots of pictures and lots of wonderful memories."

Mahoney was admired for his commitment to providing his apes with something approaching a happy childhood. Staff members threw occasional parties in the nursery and in the adult units, with music and toys and balloons, and they would paint their white smocks all the colors of the rainbow. One staff member even started a kindergarten program in the nursery, in which the youngsters could play together while solving puzzles. In addition to the nursery, Mahoney created something he called Junior Africa, a way station for chimpanzees who had graduated from the nursery but who were still, in his opinion, too young for the stresses of life in the adult units.

Junior Africa was the first of its kind in an American biomedical lab, a place where young chimps were housed in pairs, allowing them crucial companionship as they developed and adjusted to life without a mother, to a life inside a cage, and to lab technicians occasionally drawing their blood or knocking them unconscious. This is where Binky, Jethro, and Regis grew up together after leaving the nursery, either in the same cage or housed side by side. Junior Africa is where their friendship solidified into the powerful support system that would eventually save Binky's life.

Suffering and Solace

EARLY ON, when research at LEMSIP was focused mainly on hepatitis-B research for Merck Sharp and Dohme, Mahoney made sure that young chimps entered studies with the friends they'd grown up with. Although they had to be housed singly in cages during the protocols, they were usually surrounded by cages containing their closest companions. But as the science at LEMSIP became more complicated, these social provisions became more difficult to meet. With the discovery of non-A, non-B hepatitis (now known as hepatitis C), and an increasing number of different vaccine studies going on at the same time, biocontainment became the priority. Researchers didn't know if the hepatitis virus could be spread through the air, so to guard against cross-infection and protect the rigor of the study findings, chimps on different virus studies had to be singly caged in separate rooms. Apes who had grown up together soon had to be separated, often for several years. The rambunctious social groups the chimps had enjoyed as youngsters were now torn asunder, and the effects were terrible.

According to Mahoney, prolonged separation from their closest companions transformed even the most independent, brash young chimps into "whimpering masses of loneliness." He watched as more and more of them began falling victim to depression, anorexia, and self-mutilation as the studies ramped up. Even Mahoney's most trusted lab technicians, those passionate young women who had helped wean the chimps from their mothers in the nursery, were now unable to provide solace. Back then the conventional wisdom about hepatitis was that to hug an infected chimpanzee was to risk becoming infected yourself. Of course, it wasn't just the young who suffered enormous emotional trauma. "For all their piss and vinegar," writes Mahoney about his subadult males, "they can be psychologically demolished in a moment."

Meanwhile, Mahoney began to chafe at his colleagues' habit of referring to the chimpanzees as either "clean" or "dirty," depending on which studies they'd been involved in. Some of the lead scientists—many of whom rarely (if ever) laid eyes on their study subjects, so distanced were they from the realities of their research—used the term "old dogs" to refer to exposed individuals. By contrast, Mahoney was beginning to see each chimp as an individual, animated by her own spirit, with her own personality, moods, sense of humor, and special gifts. This gradual awakening would spell trouble for any committed animal researcher, but it was especially torturous for Mahoney because he was also tasked with selecting the chimpanzees to be used for each study. He had become, to paraphrase the psychologist Gay Bradshaw, an "agent of suffering and solace." By his own admission, he viewed this part of his job as "giving the kiss of death."

Mahoney considered quitting LEMSIP at least once a week for nearly twenty years, but he never went through with it. Like most lab workers who end up falling in love with their animals, Mahoney couldn't bear to think of leaving his friends behind.

In late-1970s America, biomedical research on chimpanzees was all the rage. The NIH's 1978 National Primate Plan claimed the chimp was an "irreplaceable model" for studying human diseases. It anticipated that an additional 180 chimps would have to be added to the federal colonies every year to keep up with scientific demand. The challenge was that the United States had recently signed the Convention on International Trade in Endangered Species (CITES), which outlawed the wild capture and importation of chimpanzees. LEMSIP had been the last lab in America to legally import chimpanzees from Africa, in 1976. So breeding facilities across the country soon received massive amounts of public money to ramp up their programs.

But by the early 1980s, many of the pharmaceutical companies that had commissioned hepatitis research on chimps were moving on to human trials of their products. By 1981 the first hepatitis-B vaccine was approved by the FDA for human use (this product was replaced in 1986 by the vaccine still in use today). Almost overnight, laboratories found themselves with colonies of infected chimpanzees that few researchers needed anymore. Considering the high cost of housing a captive chimp, let alone more than 1,500 of them, this quickly became a big financial and political problem.

So the NIH formed a committee to discuss how best to deal with the apes. According to Mahoney, mass euthanasia topped the list of possible solutions.

As it turned out, the lives of most of these "surplus" chimps were eventually spared. But it wasn't because of the outrage of people like James Mahoney or Roger Fouts or Jane Goodall, all of whom battled against the euthanasia policy. And it wasn't because of a moral decision by the NIH brass. The reason most of those chimps were spared was that in the early 1980s the world awoke to a new epidemic, a disease much more destructive and politically charged than hepatitis or malaria or polio.

"AIDS saved the chimp," says Mahoney with an ironic smile, in a documentary on the subject that aired in the late 1990s. With the appearance of HIV-AIDS, biomedical research on chimpanzees received a new lease on life.

Use Him and Lose Him

FOR CHIMPANZEES in America, LEMSIP was a crossroads of sorts, a place where many were destined to live at one point or another. Air force chimps from Holloman, sign-language chimps from Oklahoma and Washington, entertainment chimps who'd outgrown the circus and the movies, even chimps who'd grown up in people's homes—animals from all walks of life passed through LEMSIP's doors, and Mahoney was a common experience for them all. By his count, he met some six hundred to seven hundred chimpanzees during his career, including those he met on sojourns in Africa as a traveling veterinarian. One could argue that Mahoney has directly touched more chimpanzee lives than just about anyone else on Earth.

By all accounts, LEMSIP was unique among American biomedical laboratories. Moor-Jankowski and Mahoney encouraged an open-door policy with scientists and activists, believing that the public deserved to know what sort of research New York University was involved in. This attitude garnered much respect and goodwill, even among die-hard animals rights advocates. As Alex Pacheco, cofounder of PETA, once said, "Why can't they [primate research directors] all be like Moor-Jankowski?" But no matter how hard Mahoney and his staff worked to improve the lives of their apes, and no matter how much goodwill they fostered, they still had to face the reality of what they were doing every day. For Mahoney, the pain of their situation came to a head when an elderly chimp named Calvin, who had been retired from invasive research, was assigned to an AIDS-related study in spite of Mahoney's strenuous protest. Calvin suffered a massive heart attack the moment the anesthesia was started.

Calvin was mourned by everyone at LEMSIP, but in very different ways. The researchers mourned the loss of a useful study subject, while Mahoney and his technician colleagues mourned the loss of a "unique and very special soul." And with Calvin's death, Mahoney began to mourn something else, too.

"I was beginning to find it increasingly difficult to use the animals without considering the costs to them, as individuals, in spite of the benefits to man," he writes. "I was becoming a moral fence sitter, ready to hop off on either side whenever the occasion suited me."

The Cage Hospital

YEARS PASSED, and Mahoney continued living a conflicted existence. And then, in 1995, NYU announced it was getting out of the chimpanzee research business. The school had decided to shutter LEMSIP at the end of 1997 and to sell its chimpanzees and monkeys to the Coulston Foundation (TCF) in Alamogordo, New Mexico. Finally, James Mahoney had the opportunity to come down on the other side of that moral fence, to repay a small portion of the debt he owed his chimps.

TCF, the most infamous biomedical laboratory in America, was at one point home to the world's largest colony of captive chimpanzees—nearly eight hundred by one estimate. Many of them were refugees from the air force space program of the 1960s or their direct descendants, leased to TCF by the U.S. government or subsequently bred there. In those days, for an animal to end up there was a cruel fate indeed. Not only did TCF do toxicology studies involving cosmetics and insecticides in addition to the usual infectious disease research, it was repeatedly cited by numerous federal agencies for violations of animal welfare regulations. Stories surfaced of "unintended deaths" at TCF, of primates dying from prolonged exposure to extreme heat, dehydration, and experimental procedures. One poor chimpanzee named Donna apparently died from complications from carrying a dead fetus in her womb for several months. Estimates suggest that at least thirty-five chimps died at TCF as a result of substandard care between 1993 and 2001.

According to Jane Goodall and Roger Fouts, TCF had "the worst animal care record of any primate research facility in the history of the Animal Welfare Act." So when Mahoney heard that TCF had been awarded the LEMSIP chimps and that his friends would soon be shipped to Alamogordo, he devised a stunning plan. In the dead of night and in collaboration with only his most trusted lab techs, Mahoney began smuggling chimpanzees and monkeys out of the lab in the Ramapo Mountains and into sanctuaries across the country.

In a series of undercover operations—immortalized by National Geographic in the television special *Chimp Rescue*—Mahoney risked his reputation and career to save as many animals as he could from certain doom. It was a race against time. He had to get as many out as he could before Fred Coulston got them. "I have been two-faced for many, many years," Mahoney tells the camera as we watch unconscious chimps being loaded into cages and then wheeled through the dark into the back of a trailer. "They have served," he says, "and I think they damn well deserve a break."

Fred Coulston would occasionally show up at LEMSIP to check

on the animals he expected to receive. He always made a head count, and Mahoney knew that if Coulston found a discrepancy between these head counts and the numbers that eventually arrived in New Mexico, there would be trouble. So he did the only thing he could do: whenever a head count was ordered, he would gather up a group of chimps or monkeys and hide them somewhere on the LEMSIP property. What ensued was a campus-wide game of musical primates. According to Gloria, the best hiding spot was the abandoned building where damaged cages were taken to be repaired, known as the cage hospital.

No one knows how many monkeys and apes saw the inside of the LEMSIP cage hospital. But by the time Mahoney's covert operations finally ended, he had sent more than 200 primates to sanctuary, including 109 chimpanzees.

One morning in early 1997, not long before Mahoney began moving animals out of his lab, the vet welcomed Gloria, Richard, and Pat Ring to LEMSIP for their first visit. After donning the eerie garb of lab technicians — white Tyvek suits, protective booties, masks covering eyes and mouth — the three visitors were taken through the nursery and then into Junior Africa.

"Jim was smart," Gloria says. "He introduced us to the little guys first." In Junior Africa, they met Jethro, Regis, and Binky. The youngsters hadn't been involved in protocols for a few months, and Mahoney had recently connected their cages so they could play and socialize together. "My first image of Binky was of him tumbling through the cages, doing somersaults. Regis was chasing him, and Jethro was sitting there like Jethro always does, just kinda shaking his head at their antics. They were seven and eight years old. Those were my cute little sweet little darling little boys."

What Gloria didn't know at the time was that one of those darling little boys wasn't supposed to go to sanctuary at all. Binky was by far the healthiest and best adjusted of the three, and along with his mother, Minky, and his half brother, Pumpkin, the Bub was among those headed to TCF. But as Mahoney began formulating his rescue plans, he realized that the youngsters presented a problem. In Junior Africa, whenever Binky had been removed from the unit, Regis and Jethro immediately sank into deep depression. Regis stopped eating; Jethro whimpered and hugged himself. The two stopped playing together entirely. It was as if Regis and Jethro couldn't survive without their best buddy.

Perhaps Regis and Jethro felt disconsolate because they were worried about what Binky was going through. Or perhaps they just missed the Bub's playful presence. No matter what the reason, Mahoney knew that if he didn't send Binky to retire with his pals, Regis and Jethro might never adjust to life outside the lab. Without friends, Mahoney realized, sanctuary meant nothing, so Mahoney added Binky to the group bound for Fauna. Now he and I race each other to the pond every day on my lunch break.

Minky and Pumpkin, however, weren't so lucky. Without a coalition of close companions to advocate on their behalf, the rest of Binky's family ended up being sent to Coulston. Minky eventually died there. Pumpkin endured five more years of research until the facility finally went out of business.

Gloria visited LEMSIP eight times over the next few months. Sometimes she went alone, and sometimes Richard, Pat, or Dawna went with her. On each visit, she spent every moment in the units with the chimps destined for her farm, learning as much as she could about their individual personalities, laying the groundwork for the relationships she would need to build with them. After each visit, Gloria would hop back into her Jeep and drive north to Quebec for six hours, sobbing the whole way. With each return journey, Gloria became more and more committed to rescuing the chimpanzees.

What Gloria witnessed at LEMSIP during those preliminary visits utterly changed her life and the lives of many chimpanzees. But nothing could have prepared her for the three days in the fall and

winter of 1997 when she became the legal guardian of fifteen traumatized chimpanzees. The chimps arrived at Fauna looking skinny
and sickly and missing swaths of hair, in the same cages they had
lived in for years. Those cages were their sole inheritance from a
life spent in the lab, so Gloria decided to repurpose the steel and in-
corporate it into the chimphouse design. And as a tribute to the resilience of her new charges, Gloria left one of the cages intact and
on permanent public display. Today it sits nestled among the native
sumacs next to the wooden bridge. No one can visit the chimphouse
and meet its inhabitants without passing this monument.

Chapter 6

TOBY AND THE HOODLUMS

To say [peace] is beyond our nature is to know
too little about primates, including ourselves.

— ROBERT SAPOLSKY, "A Natural History of Peace"

Chimpanzee Dreams

EARLY ONE MORNING during my third week at Fauna, I am awakened by a knock at my door. As I struggle to kick away the bed sheets, the knocking grows more impatient. Soon the door is shaking on its hinges—*BANG! BANG! BANG!*—but my legs are hopelessly entangled. The more I struggle, the more tightly the sheets wrap around me, so I call out. Come in! Just come in! Then the knocking stops. The door is thrown open, and in walks Tom the chimpanzee.

Tom looks at me, sitting up in bed like a half-risen mummy. He bobs his head, huffs that glorious chimpanzee laugh—some human, he seems to be thinking. I feel like I'm in the presence of the Godfather. Then he takes a step toward me. I smell his wild, vegetable breath. He takes another step closer. I can't tell if he's menacing me or being friendly. Another step. This can't be happening. I should drop to the floor, but I'm stuck. What the hell is Tom doing in my room? Where's my walkie-talkie? And where the hell is Mr. Puppy? Alarm bells begin to sound.

When a person spends long periods of time in the presence of chimpanzees, something very strange happens. The best way to describe this phenomenon is to say that boundaries that once seemed inviolable begin to blur. This blurring occurs not only in the conscious realm but in the unconscious as well. Everyone who works with chimps has dreams about them.

The primatologist Frans de Waal, in his groundbreaking book *Chimpanzee Politics: Power and Sex Among Apes,* acknowledges this phenomenon on the first page of chapter one. He describes his first dream about chimps:

> In it my preoccupation with the distance between them and me was apparent. During this dream the large door to their quarters was opened for me from the inside. The apes were pushing each other aside in order to get a good look at me. Yeroen, the oldest male, stepped forward and shook my hand. Rather impatiently he listened to my request to come in. He refused point blank. That was out of the question, he said, and besides, their society would not suit me: it was much too harsh for a human being.

Doors. Boundaries. Seeking permission to cross from one side to the other. These are the themes of my chimp dreams, and Tom is always their star.

If chimpanzees also have dreams—and there is little reason to assume they don't—then Toby surely dreams about Maya. For the last week or so, Toby has followed her everywhere she goes in the chimphouse. Although they are currently living in different social groups—Toby with Rachel and Jethro, Maya with her old friend Spock—Maya can never really hide, and Toby always knows exactly where she is. No wonder Maya is so moody these days.

The male chimps at Fauna have all had vasectomies, and Gloria has never seen any of them successfully follow through on their sexual desires. "They wouldn't know what to do," she says. That might seem hard to fathom, but consider the perverse sterility of the average LEMSIP chimp's childhood and adolescence: taken from his mother soon after birth, raised in a quasi-nursery by women, then housed in a small cage suspended like a birdcage a few feet above the floor until his body is required for science. Perhaps Gloria is right: how would these chimps ever learn about the birds and the bees? Maya isn't even on her sexual swell these days, so Toby's fascination with her is perplexing. Perhaps his obsessive attraction to females has nothing to do with sex. Or perhaps, as Gloria suspects, Toby just likes the grumpy girl's company.

Whatever his motivation, Toby spends his days following Maya and banging incessantly on every obstacle that stands between them. He is desperate to join her, while Maya and Spock want nothing to do with him. Theirs is a strange sort of love triangle. And as with all such arrangements, the longer it goes on, the more likely it is that someone will get hurt.

Thirteen Humanzees

TOBY IS a terrified ape. Unlike many terrified animals, though, he rarely looks terrified. If Toby believes anything, and I would wager he does, it is this: go through life looking scared all the time, and something scary is sure to happen.

At times Toby seems utterly at peace, like when he's lying motionless on his back, grasping his feet with his hands in that sublime chimpanzee yoga pose. Or when he's crouched beside Rachel, his best friend, carefully grooming her shoulders (Rachel is also a terrified ape, but in a very different way: she is terrified of herself).

But no matter what lies his body is telling, Toby's face tells the real story. His anxiety is apparent in the rapid head bobs, the slack-jawed mouth, the way he quickly scans my body for a suitable place to groom, then pokes his massive fingers through the caging, probing for friendly skin. Toby is desperate to please, the way only a victim can become. He reminds me of the children I used to work with at summer camps, the quiet kids whom no one liked and everyone picked on and who sometimes arrived in the morning with mysterious bumps and bruises on their arms. They would look up at me as Toby does now, expecting that whatever occurs, it will be beyond their control.

Toby has reason to be terrified. Three years ago, the Hoodlums nearly killed him.

Nobody knows where Toby was born. Some say he was wild-caught in Africa, others say he was born in a small-town zoo in Quebec. Either way, Toby spent much of his first twenty-four years at the Saint-Félicien Zoo, on Lac Saint-Jean, Quebec. The zoo bought him to be a companion to their young male, Benji, who had recently been rejected by his own mother, Samba. Luckily, Toby and Benji hit it off, and soon they were as close as brothers.

When they were young, the chimpanzees were often taken home on weekends by one of the zookeepers. On these excursions they learned to wear children's clothes, use utensils, eat potato chips, drink soda pop, and color in coloring books. Partially raised by humans, Toby still enjoys donning a cool pair of sunglasses every now and then or wrapping his wrist in bracelets.

Although the psychological consequences of being from one world (the jungles of Africa), living in another (a low-budget zoo in central Quebec), and occasionally visiting a third (a home in a small town) must have been immense, by all accounts Toby was relatively well adjusted. And when the keepers arrived one morning to find that he and Benji had broken into Samba's enclosure and that the three were living peacefully together, as if Samba had never abandoned Benji, the zoo allowed them to live together as a family. In no time, Samba was treating Toby as her own.

In 2000 the zoo officials decided to get out of the chimp business, so they called Gloria to see if she'd be willing to make room for three more chimps. Gloria was very willing, though a bit anxious about mixing zoo chimps with lab chimps. The problem was, she couldn't do so without breaking the law. The Agriculture Commission, in an attempt to calm tensions caused by the arrival of the HIV-positive chimps a few years earlier, had changed their land-use laws, and now it was illegal to house exotic animals on farmland in Quebec. Here is another small irony of Gloria's situation: because chimpanzees have already been allowed at Fauna, she is prohibited by law from accepting any more.

Gloria had to say no. Soon after, Samba died of pneumonia, leaving the boys motherless once again. Gloria received another phone call, another plea from Saint-Félicien, but her situation had not changed. She was powerless to help.

The following summer, tragedy struck once more. With their regular caregiver away on vacation, Toby and Benji were locked in an outside area during a terrible heat wave with no water. The next morning, the keepers arrived to find a distraught Toby clutching the body of his adoptive brother. Benji had died of severe dehydration.

Toby spent the next three days screaming and tending to the corpse of his best friend. Gloria received another phone call, and this time she couldn't say no. She had to get Toby out of the zoo, so she mobilized a few of her most influential friends. Jane Goodall wrote a letter to government officials appealing them to force the Quebec Agriculture Commission to make an exception to their exotics law. Roger Fouts did the same. Against such high-profile firepower, the government relented and granted Gloria a transfer permit for Toby. Soon he was unconscious in a cage in the back of a truck, headed for sanctuary.

It is hard to underestimate the trauma Toby was suffering upon his arrival at Fauna. Having lost everything that had meaning in his life, he sank into a deep depression. As he hugged himself, rocking from side to side and displaying a permanent fear face—lips pulled back to expose his teeth and gums—he screamed almost nonstop for the first four days. Housed alone in Jeannie's Room, he could see his new housemates lurking all around, but now he was a complete outsider. Considering how a community of chimps usually deals with foreign interlopers—that is, with extreme violence—Toby was probably petrified by his new status. Having never lived in a community of apes, having never learned the intricate set of interpersonal and social skills so fundamental to group living, Toby was totally out of his element. He'd been partly raised as a human, and the dimensions of his life were defined entirely by human-made constructions. A primatologist would say Toby is a "highly enculturated" ape. His identity lies somewhere between chimpanzee and human. Toby is a member of a strange new tribe of beings we have forged from the formal shape of the wild chimpanzee, a new hybrid fashioned in human laboratories, circuses, movie sets, and living rooms over the past one hundred or so years. Toby is, for all intents and purposes, the confused and conflicted humanzee of lore, without the Soviet experiments. And although he may not have known it when he arrived, so were his new housemates.

Toby's regular caregiver from Saint-Félicien visited a few times, but he was so distraught at Toby's situation that he couldn't stop crying, which only made Toby sink deeper into despair. Gloria had to make a decision. Toby was refusing to eat. If she left him there all alone, she was sure he would die, if not of hunger or thirst then surely of a broken heart. So she did what she usually does when faced with a difficult choice—she went with her gut.

"I opened a door and let him go in with Sue Ellen and Donna Rae."

Considering how important social contact is to a chimpanzee, this may not seem like a tough decision. But Toby was a fully intact male. He hadn't had a vasectomy yet, and Gloria had put him in with her two oldest girls. What's more, the animal behavior literature is full of examples of chimpanzees, especially young males, displacing their powerful emotions onto innocent bystanders, often with horrifying results. Allowing Toby access to Sue Ellen and Donna Rae at a time of such heightened emotion could have been disastrous.

But it wasn't.

"I've never seen a hug like that between chimps," says Gloria. "My two girls have never been treated so well by any male they've ever known. Toby just embraced them both, and they had a group hug for probably three hours. Sue Ellen was like, 'I don't know what to do about this, but I'll let him hug me because he seems so happy.' That moment saved his life."

Under the watchful eyes and compassionate touches of Susie and Donna Rae, Toby's depression eventually lifted. He started to eat and drink. He even started to groom the girls, a very reassuring sign. But for some reason, Toby was never able to fully integrate himself into the Fauna family of apes. And five years later, during a time of great upheaval in the chimphouse, Toby would learn the terrible reality of his outsider status.

Impossible Days

BEFORE WE can understand what Toby was in for at Fauna, we must go back to the late 1990s, just after the LEMSIP chimps had arrived. For Gloria and her sisters, those first years were a whirlwind of frantic days and sleepless nights. In her more unguarded moments, Gloria refers to that time simply as hell, mostly because of the Hoodlums.

Gloria called the youngsters who had grown up together at LEMSIP—Jethro, Regis, Binky, Petra, Rachel, and Chance—the Hoodlums. But she didn't use this term to suggest that they were innately violent or ill tempered. Being the youngest and least troubled chimps, the Hoodlums had been the first to arrive at Fauna, and Mahoney had assured Gloria that they would be easier to care for than the older, stronger, more emotionally compromised apes, many of them HIV-positive, who were to arrive a few months later. But Mahoney was wrong about the youngsters being easier. From the very beginning, they were more troublesome by a long shot than the older ones, so Gloria started calling them the Hoodlums, in memory of their lost childhoods. "They raised themselves," she explains. "They had no time with their mothers, so they had to figure it all out by themselves." In many ways, Jethro, Regis, Binky, Petra, Rachel, and Chance were like a powerful gang of street kids.

• • •

In the beginning, the chimphouse was a simple two-room building, with the caged area on one side facing a quaint wood-paneled kitchen. The chimp enclosure was divided down the middle, with the youngsters on one side and the older apes on the other. There was no medical clinic yet, no Sky Walk or islands, and only one refrigerator to store enough food for fifteen ravenous apes.

The noise level in the chimphouse was almost unbearable. The apes, especially the Hoodlums, were always fighting, displaying, or screaming at the top of their lungs, and no one could do anything to calm them. With no dedicated medical clinic, a chimp injured during a skirmish had to be knocked unconscious, which sometimes took hours, and Richard had to treat the chimp's wounds right there on a stretcher in the kitchen. Gloria would throw blankets up and over the caging so the other chimps couldn't see what was going on, but often this just made their anxiety worse.

Added to this was the near-constant presence of reporters. Linda estimates that in the first two years, Fauna hosted at least twenty-six television crews and magazine writers, and the chimps were the subjects of more than one hundred news items. One begins to wonder how the sisters managed at all. "We went into animal care to get *away* from people," Linda jokes, "but we had more people around than ever."

And then there was local opposition to deal with. When the citizens of Chambly heard that a bunch of HIV-positive apes had moved in nearby, a public furor ensued. Fueled by a fear of AIDS and an understandable ignorance of chimpanzee behavior, a few locals began complaining to the press, painting nightmare scenarios of rampaging, disease-ridden, escaped chimpanzees wreaking vengeance on unsuspecting schoolchildren. Ultimately, a motion to shut down the sanctuary was put before the Chambly town council. If it passed, Gloria and Richard would have to close Fauna and send the chimps away, likely to another American laboratory. Fortunately, after a few raucous public hearings, the motion was narrowly defeated. The chimps were allowed to stay.

Meanwhile, the sisters' attempts at building trust with the chimps met nothing but cold glares or uninhibited displays of strength—if they were lucky. Many of the older chimps, like Tom, Pepper, and Donna Rae, simply ignored their new wardens for months. In the world they had just left, every human wanted something from them. They had been let down and deceived countless times by the lab technicians, who held treats in one hand, with needles hidden in the other.

"A part of me thought that the chimps would come here, they'd see they were finally safe, and they'd just relax and become friendly," says Linda now. "God, how wrong I was."

At one moment early on, Gloria and her sisters did realize the extent of what they'd gotten themselves into. The incident involved Petra, a beautiful young female chimp who, in addition to physical and psychological torment, had endured serious verbal abuse in the laboratory. Petra, who is very strong-willed, was notoriously uncooperative and occasionally malicious with the lab techs, grabbing them and slamming them into the bars of her cage whenever she could. She was also the resident escape artist, an expert at identifying malfunctioning padlocks. Along with Chance, who had different yet equally valid reasons for being difficult, Petra was known among frustrated employees at LEMSIP as "the bitch" or "the asshole."

Linda remembers the incident as if it were yesterday.

"Me and Dawna were standing there at the sink, washing vegetables the local grocery store had donated. Workers from the power company were here, and the animals were totally stressed out about having strangers in the building. Gloria was walking between the counter and the cages, popping monkey chow into the feed boxes. And as she went down the line, every single chimp reached out and tried to grab her." Today the only way a chimp can reach out from a privacy room is through a porthole. But back then, the privacy-room walls were nothing more than repurposed LEMSIP caging, and the spacing between the bars was much wider. Also, the chimps were a lot skinnier then.

"We saw a line of hands come shooting out," says Linda. "And they all missed. Until Gloria got to the end. That's where Petra got her." Unbeknownst to Gloria, Petra was displaying at the workers, who were in the closet directly across from her privacy room. When Gloria walked between Petra and the cause of her upset, Petra quickly pulled on her arm and wrenched her against the caging. "Gloria slipped on the wet floor and crashed into the bars," says Linda. "She pulled and pulled, trying to get away, but it's like your arm is in a vice when they grab you. It's like cement. And then, after a few seconds, Petra just let her go. Gloria fell backward onto the floor. She looked up at us, half scared out of her mind and half amazed to be free. I remember yelling, as loud as I could, 'Gloria, what have you done? What the hell have you done?'"

For years Gloria worked well into the night just about every day of the week. And no matter how many times she was grabbed, or threatened, or tested, she always made sure the chimps understood that nothing bad would happen to them as a consequence. "That's called unconditional love," Gloria says now. The sacrifices she and her sisters made to build a better life for these apes would boggle the mind of the average animal lover. But Linda and Dawna are quick to point out that their sacrifices were nothing compared to Gloria's. At least they could leave the farm at night and relax with their families. Gloria couldn't leave—she was already home. Richard and the chimps were her only immediate family, and for the first three years, she didn't leave the farm at all. "I was always the one late to Christmas," Gloria would later tell me. "I barely saw my nieces and nephews, and now they're all moving away. I don't regret the chimps one bit. But I definitely miss what I missed."

When I ask Linda how Gloria made it through those impossible days, Linda just shakes her head. "She just lets yesterday be yesterday, and tomorrow be tomorrow. She went back in there every single day, no matter what had happened the day before. It's like she has no fear. At least, not in the moment. Somehow, she can turn it off in the moment."

A Similar Resilience

MONTH AFTER painstaking month, the women continued to hope, against all odds, that these damaged souls would be receptive to some measure of rehabilitation. It was at this point that Gloria received some sage advice from Jane Goodall herself, when the primatologist and activist visited the Fauna sanctuary for the first of many visits.

Gloria couldn't believe that she had once planned to visit Jane in Africa, and now Jane was visiting her farm. She was very excited to meet her heroine, but she was also terribly anxious. "I was so embarrassed," she says now. "I had to show Dr. Goodall where the chimps were living. What would she think of all the caging, all the padlocks? She'd seen them at LEMSIP already. In many ways, this place is still a prison."

But Goodall was delighted with Fauna. She spent the day interacting with the chimpanzees and speaking to Gloria and her staff. Her visit was a priceless source of inspiration during a very difficult time. "She told me we were doing the right thing," says Gloria now, tearing up as she remembers the relief that came with Goodall's encouragement. "She also reminded us not to expect too much too soon."

One other piece of advice proved crucial. "Jane told me the chimps might need certain things from their past," says Gloria. At first, this seemed like odd counsel. What in their horrible past could they possibly yearn for? But then it occurred to Gloria that many of her charges had lived very differently before being sold into research. "That's when it hit me. Jane suggested I try to find things that would bring back good memories. So we introduced human food."

In the lab the chimpanzees had been fed a joyless diet of water and monkey chow—dehydrated bricks of protein, carbohydrates, and nutritional supplements that would be enjoyable only to the most abstemious of vegans. And at first, in an effort to give the new arrivals something familiar, that is what Gloria fed them, too. But following Jane's advice, Gloria began introducing human foods. Finally, glimmers of hope began to emerge.

Whether in the lab or in human homes, all of the Fauna chimps had been "cross-fostered" to some degree. Cross-fostering is the technical term for removing an animal from the care of its biological mother and having a human surrogate raise it instead. Billy Jo and Sue Ellen, for example, spent the first fourteen years of their lives performing together in circuses. When they weren't onstage or in front of the camera, they were being taught to blow kisses, to use a knife and fork, to ride a tricycle. They ate mostly human food, even though both had had their teeth knocked out at an early age, probably with a crowbar or a hammer and chisel, so they wouldn't be able to bite their handlers. Susie still has fragments of shattered teeth lodged in her gums.

Gloria remembers the first time she brought spaghetti into the chimphouse, and how crazy it made Billy Jo. "That's when we realized Billy wasn't really a normal chimp," she says. "He had a chimp face, a chimp body, some chimp behavior, but his desires and cravings were for human things." Not only did Billy demand a bowl of spaghetti, but he also refused to eat it until one of the Grow sisters gave him a fork. In his youth, Billy used to ride in cars. He went fishing with his owner and even was taken to the local Dairy Queen. When Gloria gave Billy a bowl of spaghetti or the occasional ice cream, she could see the change in him. As he shook with delight, she could tell he was remembering a time before the knockdowns and surgeries began.

Even the chimps who had been born and raised in the lab responded to the new menu. Now they could choose from a wide range of fresh fruits and vegetables for breakfast and lunch, homecooked dinners, and occasional special treats such as yogurt, pop-corn, Jell-O, and, yes, freshly baked muffins. At LEMSIP the extreme deprivation the chimps experienced was mirrored by the austerity of their meals. So by diversifying the foods available to them, Gloria and her sisters took an important first step toward convincing the chimps that Fauna was nothing like a biomedical lab, that it was a place of self-fulfillment as opposed to a prison of self-denial.

"You could see it on their faces," says Linda, about the chimps' gradual realization that this place might not be so bad. "They were like, 'Wait . . . this is yummy. These people are being nice to us.' Sometimes we'd sit and share a fruit juice with them through the caging. Those were amazing moments. But really, really rare."

More amazing moments followed with the ten-year-old Hoodlums, such as Binky and Jethro and Regis, in whom the rambunctious spirit of childhood still survived. After many long months, the kids began engaging with Gloria and her sisters through the caging, inspecting the women's clothing cautiously at first, then trying mightily to remove their rubber boots. Occasionally, after successfully removing a shoe or stealing a latex glove, a young chimp would spin around and present his back to be groomed, an enormously significant act. But at first these grooming sessions were fleeting at best.

So the Fauna team began to focus on these small triumphs, these passing moments of connection, to get them through the days: a faint expression of a unique personality, the pleasure of a happy memory, an act as simple as opening the fridge to a cacophony of hoots and hollers. They had no choice but to persist; there was no turning back now. Somehow, they had to find ways to counter the profound distrust, fear, and anger that each chimpanzee held inside. Through simple acts of kindness and concern, Gloria and her sisters worked to lift, one small corner at a time, the veil of annihilation that had been cast upon these apes the moment they were born or sold into research. There were no guarantees, no expert opinions on the odds of success. The Fauna staff acted on the simple but revolutionary idea that resilience in the face of suffering is not limited to humans but is a trait shared across species lines and perhaps throughout the animal kingdom—that the same persistence in the face of tragedy that keeps Gloria going every day may also be present in the chimpanzee heart and soul.

"In the early years," says Linda, "Gloria just took it and took it and took it. It was like they were initiating her. She was grabbed at, poked at, spat at, barked at, pinned to the caging. Her clothes were torn. But she never took it personally. None of us did. We had all the respect in the world for these guys and what they'd been through. And for all they knew, this place was just another laboratory. For all they knew, the knockdowns and surgeries were going to begin again any second. No wonder it took them so long to figure out they were finally safe."

Rachel's Babies

JANE GOODALL'S advice applied to more than just food. Inanimate objects could also remind the chimps of more comforting times. From the moment she arrived, Sue Ellen derived great pleasure from draping herself in human clothing. The garden hose seemed to have a mysterious sway over many of the chimps. And sometimes the most unexpected object could provide solace for an especially troubled ape.

During her first few years at Fauna, Rachel refused to go anywhere without dragging a car tire behind her. Clearly, the tire that used to hang in her LEMSIP cage had become a surreal sort of security blanket for her, which makes sense when you consider that these tires were the only thing the chimps could hide behind when a lab tech approached with a dart gun. Gloria recalls many times early on when Rachel desperately wanted to go into another part of the chimphouse but couldn't, because she couldn't squeeze the tire in after her.

Luckily, over time, the comfort of that tire was transferred to a pair of old gloves, which were much easier to carry. And today Rachel's security tire has morphed once again, into a matched pair of miniature gorilla stuffed animals. Rachel never goes anywhere without her gorillas and will descend into hysterics if one of them goes missing. The Fauna staffers always refer to these stuffed animals as "Rachel's babies."

Of course, not all objects held positive memories for the chimps. When Donna Rae was presented with a guitar, she immediately went berserk, smashing it to pieces in her enclosure and jumping on top of the shattered remains. Why would a chimp react with such hostility toward a seemingly innocuous musical instrument? The answer lies in her past. James Mahoney later told Gloria that as a child, Donna Rae had belonged to the Elizabeth Hammond Talent Agency. Her "job" was to ride a bicycle and strum a guitar at private parties.

Despite the occasional missteps, and after years of perseverance, Gloria's relationships with the chimps began to thaw. Human food and special objects were part of this gradual transformation, as were the remarkable actions of Tom. And late one night, Gloria had a moment with troubled young Petra suggesting that maybe, just maybe, she was doing something right.

"It was nighttime, a very special time in the chimphouse. The lights were off, everyone had gone to bed. The craziness of the day was over. Every night around this time, Pettie would come down to the corner room and lie on the floor. In the old days, there was a space beneath the doors to slide food inside, and Petra would reach her arm through this space and stretch it out as far as she could. It was as if she needed one part of her body to be completely free. And every time I looked her way, she would jiggle her fingers. I had no idea why she did this or what it meant. This went on for weeks. And then one night when I was so tired and exhausted and alone, I thought to myself, 'I'm just gonna do it. I'm just gonna sit here on the floor next to Pettie and see what happens.' So I sat down next to her, and she touched my knee. She scratched it softly, in the way they do. It felt so good. And then she reached up, her fingers still jiggling, and tried to grab the keys hanging around my neck." Now Gloria remembered some videos that Petra's caregiver at the LEM-SIP nursery, a woman named Nancy, had sent her. In these videos, Nancy always let Petra play with her bundle of keys, which seemed to help calm the little girl's frazzled nerves. "I was still unsure of things, so I took my keys from around my neck and put them in my pocket. And then I let Petra touch the outside of my pocket. She loved it. We must have sat there for an hour, Petra patting my jeans, jiggling the keys inside. And that seemed to be the beginning of something really important for her and me. It was as if she was having a flashback to her childhood, a really good memory of a comforting time."

Although it seemed as if the situation was slowly becoming manageable, Gloria could never stop feeling that invisible forces were constantly pulling at the edges of her sanctuary, threatening to demolish the progress each chimpanzee was making and all that she, her sisters, Richard, and Pat had worked so hard to build. Gloria remembers one morning in particular when, while playing tickle-chase with Regis, the youngster reached his fist through the port-hole and dropped seven industrial-strength screws into the palm of her hand. Regis, ever curious, had secretly been taking the chimp-house apart, one steel bolt at a time.

Harry Harlow

AS TERRIFIED Toby could attest, to negotiate the inner workings of the Hoodlums' world one must first gain their acceptance. Although they sometimes fight among themselves, and Gloria has to split them up, their bonds with one another always prevail. In this way, the Hoodlums behave somewhat like a "natural" chimpanzee family. Faced with this artificial arrangement, Gloria employs a handy motto, which she often mutters under her breath during especially challenging moments: *The only place more unnatural than this is where they came from.*

In *Saving Molly*, James Mahoney writes movingly of the chimpanzee birthing process. "It is like witnessing an exquisite ballet movement perfected without any prior practice," he writes. "Then the mother's attentions [to the infant] begin." But Mahoney knew that for a chimpanzee in his lab, these attentions wouldn't be allowed to last long. "How important are these first maternal interactions to the future normal development of the infant?" he wonders. "What are the consequences if the infant doesn't receive them? I can't help thinking they are profound."

The first trauma in a research chimp's life occurs when she is removed from her mother's care. For the Hoodlums, this happened soon after the ballet of birth. All future traumas, whether physical or psychological, stem from this original one. In humans we take the importance of the mother-child bond pretty much for granted. And in chimpanzee society, this bond is no less crucial to a youngster's emotional and psychological development. Chimps in the wild aren't weaned until the age of five, don't go anywhere without their mother until the age of six, and don't reach puberty until eight or nine; a male chimp is not considered socially mature until he's fifteen or so. A chimp at LEMSIP, by contrast, would be lucky to enjoy a few days with its mother before being whisked away to the nursery.

During these early years with their mothers, young chimpanzees acquire the tool kit of skills they will need to survive and thrive. They learn to groom. They learn the various methods by which chimps reassure and console one another. They learn to use tools. And they experience their first conflict—the battle with their mother over weaning. By the time a youngster is fully weaned in the wild, she has learned the basics of negotiation and manipulation, crucial skills as she navigates the political landscape of a healthy chimpanzee society.

As the baby's relationship with her mother grows, so does her self-esteem. She begins to move through the world with confidence, knowing that should she ever get into trouble, her mother will be there to bail her out. There is no underestimating the developmental value of brimming self-confidence in the young, and there is also no substitute for a mother's touch. "Children need touch for survival," writes Tiffany Field, and although she is referring to human children, her conclusion seems eminently transferable to our fellow apes. Both humans and chimps are profoundly social animals, and as Field writes, "Touch is our most social sense." Positive experiences between mother and child, including plentiful physical contact, have been associated in many mammal species with greater resilience to stress, better immune-system function, healthier and more efficient cognitive development, and even the ability to maintain a healthy body weight. And perhaps most apropos to our story, a positive mother-child bond imbues the child with a heightened ability to empathize with others—in other words, good mothers literally prepare us to care.

As Jane Goodall writes, if a chimpanzee's mother is affectionate, playful, and supportive, "that child is likely to thrive into an individual who plays an important role in his or her community." As young chimps spend time with their mothers, they are learning the very blueprint for all future relationships. "This bond," writes Frans de Waal, "provides the evolutionary template for all other attachments, including those among adults." This sounds a lot like Tiffany Field, when she writes that "a [human] child's first emotional bonds are built from physical contact, laying the foundation for further emotional and intellectual development."

For all these reasons, chimpanzee infancy, childhood, and youth are referred to by scientists as "neuroethologically formative periods"—a fancy way of saying "enormously important times, filled with enormously important experiences." As the old Jesuit saying goes, "Give me the boy until the age of seven, and I will give you the man." The Jesuits could have been speaking for much of the mammalian world.

Not that long ago, infant attachment and the mother-child bond were considered trivial matters, at least by professional psychiatrists. It wasn't until the 1950s, when a man named Harry Harlow conducted a series of famous studies on monkeys, that the world finally had proof of something we have known in our gut for thousands of years.

Working at the University of Wisconsin, Harlow led a team of researchers investigating the effects on infant primates of being deprived in various ways. To explore the mother-child bond, Harlow's team removed baby rhesus monkeys from their mothers soon after birth and placed each one in a small cage with two "surrogate mothers." The surrogates were basically homemade dolls constructed from a variety of materials and designed to resemble an adult female rhesus monkey in size and shape. One of the two surrogates in each cage was covered in soft terry cloth; the other was covered in wire mesh. And either the cloth-mom or the wire-mom was outfitted with a bottle filled with milk.

In his now classic experiment, Harlow recorded how much time the infant monkeys spent in close contact with the different surrogates. His results were breathtaking. No matter which surrogate was providing the food, by the time the monkeys were six months old they were all spending about eighteen hours a day sleeping next to, cuddling with, or clinging to their cloth-mother. In the cages where the wire-mother held the food, the monkeys would occasionally run over to "her" when they were hungry, feed hastily from the bottle, and then return as quickly as possible to the soft cloth-mother. No monkey spent more than an hour a day in direct contact with the mother made of wire mesh.

Harlow's results showed that a mother's reassuring gentle touch —what Harlow called "contact comfort"—is a more important factor in an infant's world than food. The journalist Deborah Blum, in her excellent biography of Harlow, *Love at Goon Park*, summarizes his initial findings: that for a baby primate, "food is sustenance but a good hug is life itself."

Harlow continued his surrogate-mother experiments into the 1960s, all with federal funds, and as they progressed, they provided an increasingly fascinating look at the survival value of motherly love. But the experiments became more and more gruesome. Having determined the importance of the mother-child bond, Harlow then set his mind to seeing if he could destroy it. In a series of infamous experiments, he designed "evil mothers," surrogate dolls that blew pressurized air at the infant or that shook violently back and forth or that were so freezing cold the monkeys would shiver as they clung to them. One of these monster-moms contained a hidden catapult that would send the snuggling infant flying across the cage. The most horrifying model was the one Harlow, ever the scientific showman, called the "iron maiden." Inside it was a rack of retractable brass spikes that could stab the clinging baby at any moment.

No matter what Harlow did to the infants, he couldn't destroy their loyalty to their fake mothers. Even after being stabbed by the iron maiden, once the spikes retracted the infant would return to it, seeking comfort. It appeared that a mother's "love" was more important than just about anything else.

Over the years, Harlow and his team developed countless schemes to test the effects of deprivation on primates. By far the most disturbing ones, and the most applicable to this story, were the isolation experiments. In the most extreme of these, Harlow and his students designed a vertical, funnel-shaped contraption made of polished steel, which he nicknamed the "pit of despair." In the wide bottom of this pit they placed baby monkeys. At first the infants would desperately try to escape, constantly running up the sides and slipping back down. But after a few days, most were resigned to huddling at the bottom and hugging themselves. According to Deborah Blum, "you could take a perfectly happy monkey, drop it into the chamber, and bring out a perfectly hopeless animal within half a week." Harlow left his infants in the pit for anywhere from three to twenty-four months. Each one emerged from this "hell of loneliness" withdrawn, depressed, and essentially psychotic.

While Harlow worked mainly with rhesus macaques, his work inspired researchers to investigate the effects of maternal deprivation and social isolation in chimpanzees as well. Most of this work was conducted at Yerkes in Atlanta. And in a larger sense, Harlow's experiments have been replicated innumerable times over the last one hundred years, on thousands of chimpanzees locked up in biomedical laboratories around the world. The results have been no less troubling than those produced by Harlow's pit of despair. A recent study by Michaela Reimers and her colleagues demonstrates what Gloria and her staff are up against as they try to help the chimpanzees of Fauna learn to live with one another.

Reimers finds that an ex-research chimp's ability to deal with the stress of resocialization (that is, living with others again) depends dramatically upon his history of seclusion and maternal deprivation. "Chimpanzees who were separated from their mothers at a younger age and kept in isolation for more years appeared to be more timid personalities, less socially active, less dominant and more susceptible to stress, as compared to chimpanzees with a less severe deprivation history." From these histories, then, Gloria's attempts at resocializing apes like Toby and the Hoodlums become what Reimers would call "*therapeutic* resocialization." As Robert Yerkes said, "One chimpanzee is no chimpanzee." Every time Gloria opens or closes a door in the chimphouse, she is providing a form of therapy, helping the chimps take another small step on their journey toward rehabilitation.

A Born Mother

ALTHOUGH THE Hoodlums had lost not only their biological mothers but also their human surrogates, at Fauna they found a new mother in the form of a beautiful, softhearted chimpanzee named Annie.

Annie was born in the wild somewhere in West Africa in 1959. Soon after birth, she was caught by a trader of exotic animals, put in a crate, and shipped to America. There she toiled in a circus with a chain and a steel collar around her neck, raised partly as a human child and partly as a slave. She was taught to blow her nose and to drink from a cup, and when she misbehaved, she was spanked. At the age of eight, she had outgrown her adorable phase and was considered uncooperative, so she was retired. But her retirement sanctuary soon ran into financial trouble and started leasing its animals to the biomedical industry. For the next twenty-one years, Annie bounced from laboratory to laboratory throughout the United States until she arrived at LEMSIP in 1982.

As far as we know, Annie was subjected to far fewer invasive surgeries and dart-gun knockdowns than most other lab chimps. This might sound like a blessing, until you learn the reason she was spared: Annie was a member of the LEMSIP breeding program.

Nobody knows just how many babies Annie gave birth to after 1968, approximately when she reached sexual maturity. All we can be sure of is that every one of her children was stolen from her not long after birth, to spend a lifetime in research. Annie also holds the dubious distinction of being the first chimpanzee at LEMSIP to be successfully inseminated artificially.

Annie's medical records from LEMSIP are sparse, but they do allude to her troubles. On November 4, 1982, a lab technician reported that Annie was abusing her infant daughter, named Wotoni. This anecdote, though somewhat lacking in details, is telling. Female chimps who have spent their lives in the laboratory are often unskilled or downright neglectful mothers. Having undergone varying degrees of physical and psychological trauma and having had no chance to hone their maternal instincts by watching and learning from their mothers, sisters, and aunts, female lab chimps are likely to injure or abandon their young. And so it is that lab technicians remove newborn chimps from their mothers' care under the absurd claim that they are doing the babies a favor, while the real motivation—the harvesting of an expensive and potentially lucrative investment—remains conveniently under the moral radar.

When Gloria first met Annie on one of her preliminary visits to LEMSIP, she was immediately struck by the chimp's equanimity. Annie had been removed from the breeding program and was living in a five-by-five-by-seven-foot cage with Rachel, who was so severely traumatized that she spent most of the time screaming and hitting herself in the head and crashing about with all her might. Rachel had been raised like a human child, taught to wear diapers and eat with utensils with a family in Florida. When she was three years old the world she knew was shattered when her owner walked her straight into a laboratory cage.

Each time Rachel lost control in the lab, Annie took it in stride. "She would just lie in the tire with her legs crossed," says Gloria. Other chimps would smack Rachel when she lost control. Not Annie. Somehow, like an experienced mother, she allowed Rachel to express her emotions and then provided comfort once the troubled little girl had calmed down. Perhaps Annie felt a special bond with Rachel because both of them had been cross-fostered. Perhaps Annie understood that her own mind had survived the ordeal much better than Rachel's had.

"Annie made that life [at LEMSIP] look comfortable," says Gloria. "That was Annie's gift."

Annie brought her gift to the gang of variously disturbed Hoodlums running wild at Fauna. She quickly established herself as their matriarch, adopting Binky, Jethro, Regis, Petra, Rachel, and

Chance as if they were her long-lost children, mediating their disputes, consoling them after fights, calming them when their rational minds abandoned them, teaching them the basics of chimpanzee diplomacy and political skills. According to Gloria, Jethro learned everything he knows about conflict resolution, which today is his forte, from Annie. And for Rachel and Chance, who did nothing but scream and panic uncontrollably during those first years at Fauna, Annie's calming presence provided a psychological balm. At one point, Annie invited Chance to share a sleeping nest with her for a few weeks, which is remarkable because in the wild, only a mother and her biological children ever share a nest.

What's most amazing about Annie's renaissance as a mother is that she did it all by herself. In the wild, an adult female usually has a network of other females to rely on for solidarity and support. The females will often band together to face a group of rambunctious juveniles or an overly aggressive male. But at Fauna, aside from two insecure, fearful, and self-mutilating teenage girls (Rachel and Chance), Annie had no group to help her with the youngsters. Because Donna Rae and Sue Ellen, the closest in age and experience to Annie, were HIV positive, they were housed on the opposite side of the chimphouse; Gloria had been warned to keep the HIV chimps separate from the others in case the virus spread — she now recognizes that this directive made it harder to nurture a cohesive atmosphere at Fauna right from the beginning. But Annie showed great resilience with the kids. All were between the ages of eight and sixteen, which can be a difficult period in a young chimpanzee's life. Annie became their leader, their mentor, the calm center in a group of obnoxious, inquisitive, and increasingly powerful acrobats.

"Annie was brilliant," says Gloria. "My lessons from her were the greatest lessons."

All this made Annie's sudden death in 2002 from a gastric torsion so difficult for everyone at Fauna. Literally overnight, everything changed. For the third time in their lives, the Hoodlums had lost a mother. And without their female protector, Rachel and

Chance immediately plummeted in status. Confronted with Annie's body just moments after she died, Binky pounded on her with his fists over and over in a grief-fueled attempt to wake her up.

For Gloria, during a period of her life defined by difficult lessons, Annie's death meant the loss of a great mentor.

War and Peace

So when Toby—a traumatized zoo chimp with nowhere else to go— arrived at Fauna, he found himself in a group of chimpanzees who also lacked the fundamentals, who had also suffered countless traumas. With the support of Sue Ellen and Donna Rae, Toby slowly adjusted to life in his new surroundings, and the rest of the chimps appeared to accept him. But then, five years after his arrival, Toby's outsider status was hammered home in brutal fashion.

Yoko was the first ape to break into Toby's enclosure that day. Though small and unassuming in appearance, Yoko is the most feared individual at Fauna. "Yoko's the tough guy," Gloria tells me. "If Yoko were a warrior in some ancient tribe, he'd be the one wearing the necklace of severed fingers and toes." Despite the peaceful significance of his name, Yoko has bitten off three chimp digits since his arrival at Fauna.

When Kim saw Yoko break through the caging separating him from Toby (Yoko had identified a weak section of new welding that had not yet been double-checked), she immediately called Gloria. Then she opened as many pulley doors as she could, in hopes of giving Toby a chance to escape. But it was already too late. Many of the Hoodlums had quickly followed Yoko through the hole he made in the caging. Now everyone could join in the butchery if they wanted to.

Chimp-on-chimp attacks follow a clear, coordinated script. Attackers go for the victim's fingers and toes first, biting them clean off if possible. In rare cases, they remove a whole hand or foot. With the victim sufficiently hobbled, the attackers move on to the forehead, the eyes, the ears, tearing and scratching and mauling. It is hard to imagine a more intimate version of warfare, the aggressor's breath on the victim's cheek. Then, when the victim is curled up on the ground, comes the coup de grâce, the deathblow: the rectum and scrotum are torn open, and the heavy bleeding begins. In the wild, an ape who suffers the full repertoire of chimpanzee aggression usually limps into the forest to die alone.

"The most horrifying thing about a chimpanzee fight," says Gloria, "is that there is absolutely nothing any human can do to stop it. There is no whistle you can blow or sound you can make that would make them even look up. All you can do is watch and witness. This is by far the most helpless feeling of all."

Led by Yoko and with help from a few of the older chimps, the Hoodlums tore into Toby's hands, feet, ears, and buttocks (only Jethro and Rachel abstained from the carnage). They scratched his eyes and opened a terrible wound on his forehead. One of his fingers was ripped clean off. His head was terribly swollen for weeks. Most disturbing of all, one of Toby's testicles was excised as if with a scalpel.

I do not want to paint the chimps of Fauna as remorseless thugs. But it is no secret that chimpanzees make war, that they maintain hierarchical in-groups, that males are constantly jostling for position and rank, and that violence is a part of their lives. The problem is that ever since the mid-1970s, when Goodall first reported from Gombe on chimpanzees' violent streak, popular culture has fixated on aggression as the species' defining trait. Yes, chimpanzees are intelligent and innovative, and they are savvy politicians. Yes, the bond between chimp mother and child is as profound as it is in humans. And yes, chimps show compassion, they share food, they even show the roots of empathy and morality. But for many people, their violence overshadows all the rest.

The impression persists that chimps are fundamentally cruel and vicious and that therefore humans are, too. This notion has been further embellished by the arrival in the popular consciousness of the bonobo, previously known as the pygmy chimpanzee. The bonobo, as closely related to humans as the chimp, is often referred to as the "other half" of our inner ape, the complete opposite of the chimpanzee, the yin to the chimp's yang. In contrast to chimps, bonobos live in peaceful, female-dominated societies in which sexual contact is preferred to violence in every social scenario. While chimps are often referred to as killer apes, bonobos are known as the hippies of the natural world.

But black-and-white caricatures like these, while useful in fleshing out the full dimensions of our own ape nature, tend to be misleading about the full spectrum of chimpanzee behavior. To me, the most interesting thing about life in a community of chimpanzees is how individuals *mitigate* violence, how they appease each other and often resolve conflicts relatively peacefully. It's true that one of Goodall's major discoveries was that chimps have a dark side, just as we do. But also like us, chimps exhibit a wide range of personalities and persuasions, and they use their extensive cooperative and diplomatic skills to suppress, for the most part, their violent tendencies. It is this interplay of checks and balances, the play of shadows amid the light, that makes chimpanzee society so fascinating to study.

Chimp power structures are maintained through a nuanced political system. To the untrained eye, their methods and machinations may be nearly undetectable. And when a violent dispute does occur, reconciliation afterward is crucial. In chimp society, restoration of peace after a quarrel is arguably more important than the quarrel itself. The intimate rituals of reconciliation are respected by all members of the group, to the point that concerned females who have witnessed a fight will often force the combatants back together to make up. According to Gloria, Annie used to do this all the time with the young Hoodlums.

Although it may seem counterintuitive, social aggression provides an opportunity for chimpanzees to strengthen their bonds with each other—as long as it is followed by compulsory reconciliation. Alliances and friendships are put to the test, and those that survive a violent interlude may actually be the stronger for it. And the rituals of reconciliation allow the pugilists to publicly acknowledge each other's place within the social hierarchy, signaling to their group mates that the dust has settled, that the worst is over. This process gives the whole society an invaluable measure of stability and reassurance; it makes group living possible. In this light, social aggression can be seen not as a knee-jerk, destructive force but as a long-term community-building enterprise. Let's see the pundits spin *that*.

Psychopathic Apes?

WHILE IT would be wrong to ignore the fact that the threat of violence is always lurking in chimpanzee society, the popular image of chimpanzees needs to be recast. Along with making war, they also maintain peace. For the chimps at Fauna, though, the trouble is that peacemaking requires interpersonal skills and intuition that these apes were unable to hone as youngsters learning from their mothers in a natural environment.

The most likely reason for the Hoodlums' attack on Toby is simply territorial instinct. The arrival of the Quebec City Zoo chimps (Spock, Maya, and Sophie) had thrown the chimphouse into great upheaval, and Toby suddenly found himself on the outs with very little support.

But isn't it possible that what happened to Toby is less an expression of innate violence and more an unavoidable consequence of his and his attackers' troubled lives? After all, how did Yoko, who initiated the attack, become such a remorseless bully? What experiences might have caused his inborn group-living instincts to atrophy to such an extent?

A recent study by Martin Brune and his colleagues may provide an answer. Brune makes the case that psychological abnormalities commonly observed in captive apes—self-mutilation, hair pulling, body rocking, and Yoko's extreme and inappropriate aggression—bear a striking resemblance to those commonly observed in humans who suffer from psychiatric disorders. The title of the article—"Psychopathology in Great Apes"—says it all. Although he acknowledges that his field of study is in its infancy, Brune is suggesting that the deprivations suffered by captive chimpanzees may turn some of them into true psychopaths.

Whether Yoko has psychopathic tendencies or not isn't the point. The point is, when you consider how socially deficient the apes at Fauna are and how they came to be this way, we can begin to have compassion for both Toby and his Hoodlum aggressors. Because a chimp like Yoko, who has never learned to control his aggression, might not last long in a wild community of apes. It's quite possible that he would be set upon without warning by a coalition of frustrated group mates in the interest of maintaining the peace. Of course, in that scenario, Yoko would have been raised by his biological mother in the jungles of equatorial Africa. Instead, he was raised by handlers in a Missouri circus, where he drank a shot of whiskey and slept under newspapers every night for the first seven years of his life and then was moved to the Ramapo Mountains, where he underwent at least 144 liver-punch biopsies, often with only a week's break to recover. Perhaps we don't need the work of Martin Brune to understand the difference this unnatural life must have made to Yoko's disposition.

It took Toby almost a year to recover from the wounds he received from the Hoodlums. Without Richard's expert care, he might not have survived at all. In addition to the stumps on his hand where two fingers used to be, Toby will always carry the psychological scars of that attack. Clearly, life at Fauna is not perfect; this is an important lesson to learn about the place. But it's certainly a whole lot better than the alternatives.

Everybody Loves Jethro

ONE DAY, about a week into Toby's most recent infatuation with Maya, Gloria and I take a walk to the islands. Quarreling ducks and the faint drone of Highland cattle are a welcome break from Toby's obsessive hammering. The chimphouse has been echoing with his banging for days now, and all the chimps are becoming noticeably frazzled. Chimpanzee and human ears alike have been ringing nonstop, and Spock and Maya have tried a number of times to grab Toby's fingers beneath the caging—if not to punish him for being a nuisance then simply to scare him quiet.

Gloria recently had Plexiglas walls added to the upper balconies of the outdoor bandstands in hopes that the privacy and protection from the wind might make the structures more appealing to the chimps. Soon we spot Tom on Island One, loping slowly along the boardwalk toward the bandstand. He's already noticed the new feature. When he reaches the staircase, Tom climbs straight to the top and enters the room to investigate. Right away, as if wildly impressed, he runs to the back wall, pounds his fist into it three times, and lets loose an excited scream. Then, perhaps startled by his own enthusiasm, he slumps to the floor and disappears from view.

"Excellent," says Gloria. "He likes it."

Like a nervous schoolboy with an unrequited crush, I admit my fears to Gloria.

"I'm not sure Tom likes me."

"Why?" she asks.

"Because he usually leaves his room when I come near. He never looks me in the eye."

Gloria laughs. "You gotta drop the ego."

"Huh?"

"Tom's been through more than you can imagine. For the first two years, he didn't look me in the eye once."

We watch for signs of the old guy. Nothing. Perhaps he's settled in for a nap.

"It's his choice," says Gloria. "Not yours."

Just then a series of panicked screams emanates from the chimphouse, followed by a crash of bodies against steel and a chorus of howls and banging. Tom's head pops up at the bandstand window. We run back inside, where chaos has broken out.

Two massive chimps are thrashing about on the walkway of the north playroom. They are a ball of flailing limbs, gnashing teeth, and high-pitched shrieks, and all the other chimps in the building are screaming and crashing in their rooms like manic cheerleaders, watching the battle play out. Everyone but Chance, that is. As usual, Chance has locked herself into one of the privacy rooms, where she is spinning in tight circles and punching herself in the gut, the rising tensions having driven her into a minor meltdown.

At first it's impossible to tell who is in the tangle of limbs above us. But then the fighters release for a split second, one of them escapes the other's clutches, and a panic-stricken Toby emerges from the fray, pursued by the enormous and surprisingly agile Jethro. It seems that Jethro has finally had enough of Toby's ceaseless banging. Toby leaps for the top walkway to escape, but at the last moment Jethro grabs him by the ankle and pulls him back down. Now the noise in the chimphouse becomes deafening. To those in the know, this scene is terribly ominous. Jethro now has Toby at his mercy.

Then, curiously, Jethro lets him go. Toby drops to the floor below, tantrum-screaming the whole way, a writhing black blur. He retreats to a dark corner not far from where I'm standing. His screams are sharp and piercing. I have to hold my hands over my ears.

Toby cowers and hugs himself in the half-light, a huge fear face spread wide. There is blood on his lips, and he has lost a tooth. He looks around in stuttering motions, his eyes darting, his chest heaving, his body rocking from side to side. He is searching for something, and I'm suddenly struck by an overwhelming urge to reach out to him. Before I've had time to consciously consider it, my fingers curl around the caging between us. Toby sidles closer but continues to scream. Now I understand what he's looking for. Consolation. Support. Some kind of solace. Unfortunately, in his current living situation, Toby has no one to give him reassurance. Except Rachel, who is up front in a privacy room, pounding her feet and shaking her head like a dervish, joining Chance in a soothing post-traumatic ritual.

Ten minutes pass. Toby has calmed down and stopped screaming. He emerges from his corner and climbs back up to the walkway, the scene of the battle. He sits down, his back to Jethro, who sits heaving in the opposite corner. The wall dividing the playrooms is lined with chimps. Binky, Regis, Petra, and Yoko are watching intently from one side, as are Pepper and Susie Goose from their perch in the opposite window. Everyone is waiting for something to happen, as if the fight we've just witnessed was the precursor to a much more important event.

Gloria and I are looking in from above the crossover walkway. I sneak a peek at Gloria as she grips the steel banister with both hands, watching the moment unfold. Her knuckles are turning white. She is desperate for this to turn out in a very specific way.

Jethro, on all fours, slowly makes his way toward Toby. When he comes within ten feet of his adversary, he sits down. Then, whimpering quietly under his breath, Jethro reaches his arm out, palm up, toward Toby. This is the moment we've all been waiting for; the olive leaf has been extended. All Toby has to do now is take Jethro's hand in his own, perhaps bring it to his mouth, and return the whimpering gesture with one of his own. Then the two of them might come closer and press their lips together, which is the most effective way for two chimps to reconcile after a fight. If Toby can do this, he will have demonstrated to all the chimps that he is beginning to understand how this place works.

But he can't. Instead of reconciling with Jethro, Toby starts screaming again and drops back down to the ground floor. Jethro, his advances spurned, retreats to the sliding door that leads to the other playroom, where his Hoodlum friends await. Gloria slides the door up, Jethro walks through, and is immediately engulfed by a mob of concerned chimpanzees. They crawl all over him, inspecting every inch of his body for bumps and bruises, identifying the open wounds that will require special attention. Then, in a matter of minutes, they are all grooming him, calming him down, reminding him that they are all the friends he needs.

I find Toby downstairs sitting alone, whimpering to himself, his arms wrapped around his body the way a mother might embrace her son. And just when I think the scene can't get any more painful to watch, Rachel squeezes in from one of the privacy rooms. Shaking her head, and with her gorilla babies in one hand, she walks up to Toby and places her other hand on his shoulder. "When are you gonna learn, Toby?" she seems to be saying. "Everybody loves Jethro."

Chapter 7

OPERATION CUCARACHAS

Humanity, I salute you!

— CHEETA, in *Me Cheeta*, by James Lever

Simian Mathematics

IF THERE IS ONE truth about life at Fauna, it is this: you can't keep a secret from a chimpanzee. And today Gloria desperately needs to do just that.

Once a year, to keep the ever-present cockroaches under control, the Fauna chimphouse is fumigated. For one strange week in July, the chimpanzees spend twenty-four hours a day outside, on the islands and in the Sky Walk, while their home is fogged with poison. The preparations for this event are mind-boggling in scale. Over the past week, an army of volunteers has been moving the entire contents of the chimphouse outside. That means everything in the kitchen, the walk-in, the enrichment closets, the medical clinic, the basement — anything that has to be protected from the toxic fumes that are about to be pumped in. Every year it is an immense task, and although it's a break from the everyday routine, no one looks forward to the two weeks in July when, as Gloria puts it, "we take the chimphouse apart piece by piece and then put it back together again." Mario has set up a large party tent outside on the patio, which is now home to a makeshift kitchen and medical dispensary, complete with a working fridge and freezer, a modest pharmacy, and full electrical hookup. The tent is the base of operations for Operation Cucarachas.

But the hardest part of the whole undertaking is convincing (and by that I really mean *tricking*) the chimpanzees to go outside so the fumigation can begin. Like us, chimpanzees are creatures of habit, and the chimps of Fauna are particularly susceptible to stress and anxiety caused by changes to their everyday routines. Gloria knows how disruptive a forced eviction is to their already fragile psyches, so every year she tries to keep the impending event a secret for as long as she can. Considering the prep work required, most of which is performed in full view of the chimps, this is a tall order. And if any of the apes catch even a whiff of conspiracy among Gloria and her staff, they will simply refuse to budge. The show will be over before it can even begin.

And so it happens that at 5:30 P.M. on Extermination Day, we are all standing outside on the patio below the mezzanine. Everyone is here — Gloria, Kim, Linda, Dawna, Mario, Cyndi, a few volunteers — and everyone is utterly exhausted. At the top of the mezzanine stairs, a Disney movie is playing on a black-and-white television. All around us is a sea of empty pop bottles, candy packaging, fruits, and vegetables. A garden hose hangs from the balcony, and a steady stream of water pours down, a flood slowly rising at our feet. On the bench behind us sits a chubby Colombian man, smoking his tenth cigarette since he arrived two hours ago. The man's mood, positively jovial at first, has dropped to within a few notches of full-scale depression.

But no one is paying attention to the television or the mess or the flood or the miserable Colombian. We are all looking up at the mezzanine, where Spock and Maya are causing all kinds of problems. They have figured out Gloria's secret. And they don't like it one bit.

Ten hours earlier, the day began perfectly. Tom went straight outside to his island, exactly where we wanted him. He spent the first few hours of the day snoozing on his back in the bandstand, beneath the new Plexiglas roof.

"OK, that's one outside," said Gloria.

"Twelve more to go," said Kim. "This'll be a snap."

Kim had spoken far too soon.

The first sign of trouble had to do with Pepper. It was midmorning, and Miss Pep had just ambled out onto the island. Pepper is at the peak of her swell. Her rear end is bright pink and engorged with blood, the signal that she is about to begin menstruating. And even though the male chimps at Fauna are somewhat lacking in sex education, females in swell always become objects of fascination to them. Sure enough, soon after Pepper appeared on the island, Jethro and Regis emerged from the chimphouse in hot pursuit.

Pepper walked over to me. As the boys followed, she gave me a look that could mean only one thing: "Men!" On my side of the fence, a few ripe tomato plants hung down from their pots. Pepper reached beneath the fencing to snag a tomato, and as she bent over, Jethro inspected her blossoming hindquarters like a young scientist on the verge of a major discovery. He leaned as close as he could and gently pressed a finger to Pepper's tender sex-skin. Then he brought his finger directly to his nose. Now Pepper gave me a more serious look, meaning something along the lines of "Do *not* lock me out with these guys."

Meanwhile, back in the chimphouse, the tension was slowly rising as the apes realized that something was up. Gloria and Kim met on the walkway upstairs to strategize, fingering their bundles of keys and pointing this way and that, performing the simian mathematics. They needed to figure out who would live with whom, and where, for the next week.

They looked down to Jeannie's Room, where they could see Rachel. The stress was clearly getting to her. She was shaking her head and pounding her feet on the caging. Opposite her, Chance was pacing back and forth and slamming her fist against the steel bars.

"All right," said Gloria. "Let's get this done. Where's Toby?"

"Where do you think?" said Kim.

"Dammit."

"Let's get Maya in here. Toby will follow. Then we'll move Toby over to the other girls."

"Sounds good."

Gloria and Kim called Maya over and took their positions. They fiddled with separate padlocks, which always incites the chimpanzees to start hooting and hollering. Even the snoozing Tom joined in, screaming from his Plexiglas nest outside. But now Petra and Yoko were sitting at the door Gloria was about to open. Moody Maya was nowhere to be seen.

"Where'd she go?"

"She was right here."

"Dammit."

Gloria pulled the door up anyway. Petra and Yoko lumbered into their new quarters. Without Maya, the mathematics had changed, and before making their next move, the women would have to run the numbers again. Gloria and Kim took the stairs down from the walkway. When they reached the bottom, they stopped dead.

"Tommie!" said Gloria.

"Oh no . . ." said Kim.

In the corner of his usual privacy room sat old man Tom. He had four oranges crammed into his mouth and another two in his hand. He looked a little stunned by all the commotion. *What? What did I do?*

"You're supposed to be outside!"

Kim gave a long sigh. Gloria looked as if she might cry in frustration. Tom inspected the oranges in his hand as if someone had just told him they were poisonous. Then came a thunderclap. The chimphouse darkened as it started to rain. Pepper ran in from Island One, followed by Jethro and Regis. Rachel and Chance lost a few more measures of self-control. The anxiety in the building reached a crescendo of screams and crashes.

"Forget it," said Gloria, stomping back through the kitchen.

An hour later, after the rains had passed, Gloria and Kim met on the walkway again for a change of plans.

"OK, Tom can go with the young guys. They'll be fine."

"Are you sure?"

"Yes. Jethro will calm everyone down."

"OK. Let's get them up there right now."

Doors slid open, doors slid closed, padlocks rattled, and in no time Pepper, Sue Ellen, Jethro, Regis, and Tom were locked outside on the covered Sky Walk. Along with Chance, who was still in a daze.

"Wait. Chance is out there."

"Oh."

"Maybe it's fine."

"No, it's not fine."

"She looks a bit better."

"Is Yoko out there, too?"

A quick look around. "No. No. There he is. He's still with Petra."

"OK."

"Good. Fine."

"Poor Pepper."

"Huh?"

We all looked up at Pepper, sandwiched between Regis and Jethro, a look of supreme annoyance on her face.

"Sorry, Miss Pep, but we're running out of time here."

The women moved to the other end of the walkway. Binky immediately appeared at one of the sliding doors, with Petra and Yoko opposite him.

"At least he'll have the new hut Mario built."

"You're right. Binky can sleep in the new hut."

Doors opened, doors closed, and Binky, Petra, and Yoko began their week living together on their islands.

Gloria and Kim were almost there. Just a few more chimps to move. Downstairs, on the other side of Grab Central, the narrow space just off the kitchen, they worked on Toby and Rachel. Gloria went outside with a bowl of fresh rice pudding drizzled with honey. Kim stayed in and tickled Rachel's feet. Miraculously, after five minutes of grooming and cajoling, Toby and Rachel simply walked outside, one after the other, as if they'd heard a whistle no one else could hear. They didn't even touch the rice pudding. Soon they were locked into the outdoor enclosure off Jeannie's Room, the coziest spot of all to spend the week. They could sleep every night within a few feet of a roaring campfire, which I had promised to keep stoked.

Gloria and Kim returned to the kitchen with triumphant smiles on their faces. They had done it. The exterminator would be here any minute, and the show was about to begin. Until, that is, we heard a terrible sound, something we thought was impossible, something that sounded suspiciously like a massive fist slamming against a wall of steel.

"Hey, Gloria?" said Kim. "Where're Spock and Maya?"

"Oh. My. God."

Tag Team

WHILE WE'D been concentrating on the inside of the chimphouse, another drama had been playing out on the mezzanine. For the last six hours, Linda and Dawna had been trying to lure Spock and Maya outside so they could shut the door to the chimphouse. Linda, outside, would coax them with treats, while Dawna was inside, her hand hovering over the door-release button. But Spock and Maya knew something was up, and they were old pros at this particular game.

Before they arrived at Fauna, Spock and Maya had lived together for more than twenty-five years at the Quebec City Zoo. Their outdoor enclosure was tiny, the concrete floor slanted steeply downward, and there was nowhere to hide from the prying eyes of the paying public. But the chimpanzees preferred their outdoor home to being locked up inside the main building. So every night, when the zookeepers arrived to coax them in for the night, Spock and Maya would team up. One would sit just inside the door and take all the treats their keepers were offering as rewards. Then the chimps would switch places. This strategy meant they both got to stay outside a lot longer, and each got a fair share of the delicious treats. More important, it meant Spock and Maya had regained a small measure of control over their own lives.

This daily game at the zoo became an important source of enrichment for the chimps. And now, after refining their methods for so many years, Spock and Maya are experts at manipulating humans, much to the dismay of Linda and Dawna.

In a battle of wills with a chimpanzee, it's very important to remember that you probably don't stand a chance. But you've got to try. This might be the founding philosophy of Fauna. Minds can be changed, laws can be rewritten, and animals can be freed, *but only if you try.* Without this attitude of persistence, Fauna would be nothing more than a tract of fallow farmland or would have been bulldozed long ago for a new subdivision. In other words, Linda and Dawna were not going to back down, and as we joined their efforts to coax Spock and Maya outside, the sisters' resolve seemed to toughen.

As the tallest volunteer, I was assigned to stand on the bench and provide ongoing updates on Spock and Maya's exact location. Dawna gave me my instructions.

"The door takes a few seconds to slide across," she said. "So both of them have to be outside *and* more than ten feet from the door."

"Gotcha. Ten feet."

"Now, we need a code word."

"A code word?"

"A signal for me to close the door."

"Oh, right . . . How about 'Do It!'"

Dawna looked up at me like I was an idiot.

"Do it?" she asked.

"Yeah. What?"

"How stupid do you think the chimps are? I said a *code* word. Spock hears you yell 'Do It!,' and he'll be back inside faster than you can say 'cheese.'"

"So I guess 'cheese' won't work?"

Same look.

"Sorry."

"Look, the most important thing is you don't use their names. So let's use their initials."

"OK."

"S and M."

I return Dawna's perplexed look.

"What?" she says.

"S and M?"

"Yeah."

"They come outside and I yell 'S and M.'"

"Yes."

"Okey-doke."

"Wait. No."

"No?"

"You *whisper* it."

"Right. Of course. I *whisper* 'S and M.'"

"And only if they come *ten feet* outside."

The exterminator would be here any minute now. The sisters had already tried luring the chimps out with sweetened tea, spaghetti, mangoes, and packets of milk. Now it was time for the big guns. Linda disappeared into the tent. The fridge door slammed, and she reemerged with two bottles of ice-cold Pepsi, a coveted treat for the chimps. She climbed the stairs as calmly as possible.

As she did so, Maya eyed everyone down below. When she looked at me, I quickly looked away, pretending I wasn't watching her. I think I started whistling. I've never felt more ridiculous in my life.

Linda knelt on the top step and twisted open a Pepsi bottle. She called to Maya, who slowly inched her way over and leaned her face against the caging. Linda tipped the bottle into Maya's waiting mouth. Meanwhile, Spock, who had heard the fizz of the twist-off cap, was peeking out from the doorway to see what Maya was being given. He took a tentative step outside. Then another. I looked at Dawna, raised my eyebrows. She readied herself at the button. Just a few more steps, Spocker. Just a few . . . more . . . steps. . . .

Then Maya sat up. She looked at Spock, the two shared a silent exchange, and Maya retreated to the doorway. Spock let her back inside, then emerged for his turn with the Pepsi. Linda, shaking her head, pretended to be happy about this development.

"Hey, Spocker!" she said, tipping the Pepsi into his mouth. "You want some too, huh?"

I looked down at Dawna, shook my head. She frowned.

"They're tag-teaming us," she said.

"Pop ain't gonna cut it," said Gloria.

Gloria disappeared into the tent. I heard the rustling of boxes, and soon she emerged with an armload of Maltesers. These malted chocolate balls are a favorite treat. When Spock saw Gloria handing the little red packages to Linda, he began grunting with happiness. This brought Maya a few feet out of the doorway.

Linda quickly gave a package to Spock, who immediately tore it open and upended the contents into his mouth. I could hear his excited crunching from my perch. He finished the pack and reached his hand out to Linda, who reluctantly gave him another one. Then Mario came running out of the chimphouse.

Mario is responsible for all things mechanical, electrical, and technical on the farm. If an engine stops working, or the electric fence goes out, or a water main has burst, it's Mario's job to fix it. He built the islands. He built the south wing of the chimphouse. He used to build retirement homes for Montrealers, and now he maintains one for traumatized chimpanzees.

"I 'ave an idea," said Mario, in his thick Quebecois accent.

"Oh God," said Gloria.

"I will go a-round back."

Gloria followed Mario around the side of the building.

Spock, meanwhile, had finished three packages of Maltesers in about three minutes flat. Linda was looking increasingly anxious (how much sugar should a chimpanzee have in one sitting?), and so was Maya. She was sitting eight feet away from the doorway, eyeing the empty red packages littered around her friend. She wanted treats. It seemed Spock had forgotten about her, and she was about to rectify the situation. Our plan was working. Two more steps and I would give the signal.

Then Maya threw a tantrum. She shoved the picnic table against the caging and pounded her feet angrily on the ground. She wanted malted chocolate balls, but she wasn't willing to be locked outside to get them. Finally, Spock looked up. Chastened, he stood up, returned to the doorway, and let Maya take his place.

Linda and her sisters groaned. Then, from deep inside the chimphouse, a low rumbling sound.

"Is that the pressure washer?"

"Sounds like it," said Kim.

Above us, a faint mist of water drifted through the mezzanine caging. Someone was using the pressure washer on the opposite side of the building.

"Why the hell is someone cleaning right now?" yelled Dawna.

Then a panicked voice rose up, cursing in distinctly Quebecois fashion. "Tah-bear-NAC!" A second later, the washer engine stopped. Gloria came running from the far side of the building, looking angry but also stifling laughter.

"Mario thought the noise of the pressure washer would scare Spock out."

"What?" said Linda.

"Don't worry," said Gloria, allowing herself a hearty whoop of laughter. "Jethro and Regis started throwing tomatoes and water bottles at him. They wouldn't stop until he got down off the ladder."

Dawna came out of the chimphouse carrying a small black-and-white television with a long extension cord. "Cartoons," she said. "Everybody loves cartoons." She climbed the stairs, placed the TV to face the mezzanine, and turned on the French version of Disney's *Cinderella*.

Just then a white van pulled up the driveway.

"Oh no," Gloria said. "He's here."

The van skidded to a stop. The driver's door flew open and out stepped a Colombian man in his mid-thirties with a huge smile on his face. He waved, threw open his sliding door, and lifted a strange contraption out of the van. It looked like a cross between an ancient two-stroke engine and a gramophone set on four wheels. Gloria walked over to bring him up to speed. Soon enough, *el fumigador* Ernesto joined us on the patio.

"*Si, si.* No problem," he said, his smile widening. "I can wait for *las cucarachas*, if *las cucarachas* will wait for me." With that, he sat himself on the bench, lit a cigarette, and settled in to watch the show.

Maya was mesmerized by the TV, her face pressed to the caging inches from the screen, like a toddler on a Saturday morning. Spock struggled to see around her from his spot in the doorway. Down below, Linda was slumped in a plastic chair at the foot of the stairs. "This sucks," she said. "*Cinderella* is so much better in English."

Then Mario reappeared from the other side of the building. He seemed to be limping a bit. "I 'ave a better idea," he announced. "I'll go to the 'ardware store." Like a hobbled superhero, he heaved himself onto Gloria's golf cart and zoomed up the driveway.

Enrichment

AN HOUR later, the smile on Ernesto's face was beginning to wane. Maya had graciously moved to the side so Spock could see the movie from the doorway, and we were nearly out of ideas. As Gloria appeared from the chimphouse waving a bouquet of lit incense sticks, I realized the battle of wills was almost over.

"Do they like that stuff?"

"It's not for them," she said, closing her eyes and scooping the smoke toward her face.

"Let's put in *Beauty and the Beast,*" said Linda, half-asleep in her chair. "No pun intended."

"Wait!" said Dawna. "The hose. They love the hose."

She dragged the hose out and strung it up to the mezzanine caging. "Maybe while Maya is watching the movie, Spock will want to play with the hose." Cyndi disappeared back around the chimphouse. Moments later, the hose came alive with water.

The chimps eyed the writhing hose. Spock took a few hesitant steps outside, but Maya beat him to it. She grabbed the hose, lifted the nozzle, and took a long drink. Then she waved the nozzle through the air. Water rained down on us as Maya played. Spock took a few more steps outside. Maya was having more fun than she'd had in a long time.

Everyone froze. Spock had come within one step of triggering my signal. I could feel Dawna's eyes on me. No one dared speak. Maya continued to play. And then Mario returned on the golf cart. He walked past us without saying a word, carrying a small white canister. As he disappeared into the chimphouse, we all realized at once the terrible mistake he was about to make.

"Mario!" Gloria whispered as angrily as possible. "No!"

But it was too late. Mario hadn't heard her. And if Gloria ran after him, it would break the spell and Spock would retreat. So we all held our breath as Maya continued to soak us with water, as Spock made a few final calculations in his head. Any second now he would lunge for the hose. Any second now the door would slide shut and the extermination could begin.

And that is exactly what would have happened had Mario not chosen that moment to give a single terrifying blast on his brand-new air horn.

It's hard to say whether Spock and Maya are still angry about potentially being locked outside for the week or if they're simply enjoying playing this game with us. It's clear that although the air horn frightened Spock back inside the chimphouse so far we may never see him again, and Gloria and her sisters look to be on the verge of tears, and Mario is out of ridiculous ideas, and we might have to send poor Ernesto home, letting *las cucarachas* live to scurry another day, and it feels like the world is coming to an end, it isn't. It may be small consolation, but this is the most entertainment Spock and Maya have had in a very long time, which is a success in itself. They've had the undivided attention of seven humans for the past five hours. The bright side of this difficult afternoon (which I decide to keep to myself, given how stressed everyone is) is that aside from one moment of abject terror, Spock and Maya seem genuinely happy up there, teaming up and reaping the sweet rewards, taking turns playing with the hose and watching cartoons. There is no question that they've been enriched, however slightly, by the experience.

So here we are at 5:30 P.M., the sun going down on Extermination Day, all of our necks craned so we can watch Spock and Maya take back a small measure of what they've lost. Linda is nearly asleep in her chair. Dawna sits smoking next to Ernesto. Kim, ever vigilant, stands at the bottom of the stairs, while Gloria sits at the top, gently stroking Maya's hand.

"Show me those toe-toes," she says, and Maya sticks her toes up against the caging. "Show me that big butt," and Maya spins around so Gloria can scratch her back. "Hey, Spocky?" she says. "Come on out here, Spocky. Come on out here and play with your girlfriend."

Even Kim has lost interest now. But Gloria keeps talking to the chimps, her voice becoming more and more strained, her "motherese" increasingly cutesy: "Spocky . . . Come on, Spocky. Do it for me, Spocky. Do it for me, big guy." She starts slapping the cement floor with her hand, pleading with the apes. I can hear the frustration welling up behind her words. And I can hear the panic, too, the panic that is always present at Fauna, the constant fear that everything is about to go wrong again for the chimps and that it's all her fault. Everyone else can hear her frustration, I'm sure, but no one takes any notice, probably because they have heard it and felt it themselves so many times before.

And then, as if the pain in Gloria's voice had aroused his sympathy, Spock simply emerges from the doorway and walks right up to her. Maya doesn't move, Gloria's voice goes up another octave, Dawna snaps to attention, and the mezzanine door slides shut. I didn't even get a chance to use my code word, it all happened so fast.

Spock doesn't seem to care that he and Maya are now locked outside. Gloria gives him the hose, which he whips back and forth like a child, while Maya, as if relieved that the show is over, retires to the resting bench halfway up the wall. We all break into a spontaneous round of applause, and Ernesto leaps from his seat. He butts his smoke, pulls his chemical suit up from around his ankles, and howls a mighty howl.

"Look out, *cucarachas*!" he yells. "Ernesto is coming to get you!"

Let the extermination begin.

Chapter 8

TALES FROM THE CAMPFIRE

To live without hope is to cease to live.

— FYODOR DOSTOYEVSKY

Frogs

TWO HOURS LATER, *el fumigador* Ernesto is on his way back to the city. The chimphouse is filled with an ethereal gray fog, and a chemical stench hangs in the air. Gloria and I set up our tents. For the next five nights, she will sleep outside Island One near the main campfire, and I will sleep on the far side of the building, close to the fire beside Island Three. We'll have to get up every three hours to stoke the blazes. I think Gloria is a little surprised that I've volunteered for this job, but I'm looking forward to spending twenty-four hours a day in close proximity to the chimps.

For dinner Mario prepares a feast of stuffed salmon, potatoes, onions, and mango-tomato salad. Soon the garlicky fish overpowers the reek from the chimphouse, and we settle in for a cozy night around the fire. Richard arrives with a case of beer after a long day at the clinic. Gloria's sisters have returned with a two-liter barrel of frozen margaritas. Meanwhile, the Hoodlums sleep soundly in the Sky Walk. All those edgy bodies, now fast asleep and bundled in blankets, their multitude of anxieties finally eased. A chimpanzee's snore is one of the most peaceful sounds I've ever heard.

Like every campfire, this one induces people to pour their hearts out.

"I'm frightened to death of frogs," says Gloria.

"We know," says Dawna.

"She is," Mario snickers. *"C'est vrai, là . . ."*

"I think they're beautiful," Gloria continues. "Their glistening skin, their gorgeous eyes, their beautiful chins, their big smiley lips." She takes a swig of beer, shakes her head. "I just can't go near them." When Gloria was eight years old, she says, her mother put a frog into her bed, thinking it might shock her out of her strange fear. That just made it worse.

As if on cue, the few bullfrogs that live in the island moats begin their evening chorus. Gloria shivers, and Mario snickers again. "I t'ink dey are getting closer, eh?" he says. "Tah-bear-nac. Look out under your chair!"

"You are *so* funny," says Gloria. A few seconds later, when she thinks no one's looking, she takes a quick peek beneath her seat.

Mario is an avid outdoorsman, a hunter and a lover of solitude. He has a cabin in the Appalachians to which he disappears whenever he can. To get there, he must lug his gear for two hours through the bush. The cabin is on a lake in the valley of a high mountain pass. For food in winter he digs ice-fishing holes, from which he pulls "miracle" trout. Sometimes he takes a friend with him, but usually he goes alone. When the heavy snows come, the drifts reach higher than the moose antlers nailed above the cabin door. Mario once spent twenty-four hours hiking through this backcountry. The landmarks he'd always used to find his way to the cabin had been buried by a blizzard, but Mario refuses to say he was lost; he was simply "delayed." He guided himself back to his cabin by "de lay of de land, *ouais?* "

Mario is the sort of person who can chop kindling and set a fire and begin cooking a rustic dinner before I've even located the lighter fluid. He cooks fish on a cedar plank, not because it's trendy but because it's as good a surface as any. He has three young daughters whom he adores. When their pet rabbit died last year, he wept for two days. They had a ceremony for it in the back of the Fauna property, where a small white cross now sits among the trees. The way he tells the story, I'm not sure if his daughters attended the ceremony or if Mario gave the last rites alone.

"I am like Gloria," he says. "I am a very passionate person. Dis is why we fight sometimes."

"Is it?" asks Gloria. "Is that why we fight?"

"*Ouais*. It's like dis fire, eh? We all see seven different fires. But dey are all de same fire."

"That's really deep," says Gloria.

"*Merci.*"

"Hey, why is your English so good right now?"

"Is it? Thank you, *là* . . ."

"Seriously, during the day, I can't understand a thing you say."

"Me too, *là* . . ."

Gloria groans. "We 'ave little communication problem, *là*," she says, copying Mario's accent. Mario spits margarita all over himself.

In addition to his role as project manager, Mario is the only one on the farm authorized to handle a firearm. Occasionally, when one of the farm animals takes ill and Richard can do nothing to alleviate the pain, it is Mario's job to put the animal out of its misery. And if the unthinkable ever happened, if one of the chimpanzees escaped and threatened Gloria or a staff member, Mario would be the one to dispatch it. When I've asked Mario how he feels about this responsibility, he just shakes his head and says, "No. No. No."

Clockwork

TWO BEERS in, Mario recalls a special night three years earlier, when he was working late laying a new floor in the chimphouse. He hadn't been at Fauna very long, and for the first time he found himself all alone with the chimpanzees. Nearing the end of the job, he lay down on the floor next to Jeannie's Room to rest. Jeannie, the most troubled chimpanzee who ever lived at Fauna, was also lying down, and before they knew it, the two had locked gazes.

"It is the t'ing I will never forget," Mario says. "We look at each other for so long, one hour, more maybe. I don't know why. Maybe I am just tired. *J'étais fatigué*, eh? But I don't stop looking into her face. It had a very big effect on me, *là* . . ." Mario gets up and walks to the woodpile. "Sometimes, I t'ink people are just ready for this kind of t'ing, *ouais*? I just had a divorce. Just sold my house. I lied there with Jeannie for hours. We talk to each other, but none of us was saying anyt'ing. After dat I feel much better, better in myself. And the next morning, *pfft* . . . She go."

Jeannie died the next morning.

"When they die, it is terrible," says Mario, walking to the woodpile. "You t'ink, 'ow can I do somet'ing different?'"

Richard says, "You think, what did we do wrong?"

During one terrible stretch beginning in 2005, the Fauna sanctuary lost four chimps in less than four years. All died of complications resulting from prolonged captivity and the invasive lab procedures they'd undergone.

"It was like clockwork," says Gloria. "We lost someone every eleven months."

Every chimp who has died at Fauna has passed away either during or immediately after a big renovation or building project on the grounds. Jeannie died just before Mario had completed a new, more spacious area meant especially for her to enjoy. Now, whenever a big project begins, Gloria is overcome by anxiety. This is part of the reason that extermination week is so stressful. "The Gypsy part of me feels the jinx," she says. "Every time we try to give them something big, something they need, I think we're going to lose somebody."

"It's been a long time now," says Mario, returning with an armload of wood.

A long time?

Gloria polishes off her beer and just nods, doesn't say a thing.

Mario throws wood on the fire. High above us, Regis stirs. With long, languid strides, he lopes to the end of the Sky Walk and lets loose a torrent of urine. Then he returns to his nest and in moments is snoring soundly again.

"Whatever happened with those monks?" Mario asks after a long silence.

Richard and Gloria have many plans for the back forest. One is to invite a group of Tibetan monks to build a mandala in the woods to bless the property. Another involves getting Mario to build a small village of tepees and a traditional sweat lodge, transforming the back half of the property into a sanctuary for local First Nations people. Forty-eight acres of woodland and marsh on the farm's eastern border have already been set aside for wildlife conservation as the Ruisseau-Robert Natural Reserve, and Richard spends many of his weekends planting trees to provide the deer with safe corridors. Gloria thinks the log cabin there would be a perfect writer's retreat. Fauna could have a writer in residence every spring. The visiting scribe's only responsibilities would be a few hours a day of manual labor on the farm.

It is strange to hear about plans for Fauna that have nothing to do with chimps. But the farm will be here long after the last chimpanzee has passed on. As Gloria often says, the chimps are here to retire, but they are also here to die.

Now a rhythmic thumping rises up from behind the chimphouse. We all recognize the sound. An old boat parked in the cattle pasture was originally intended as an enrichment item for the chimpanzee islands, but none of the chimps would go near it, so Mario moved it out back. Now the cattle like to use it as a back-scratcher at all hours of the day and night.

Maybe it's Elsa having a nice, soothing scratch. One morning eight years ago, Gloria found a year-old calf in with her cattle. The new arrival, whom Gloria named Elsa, had a number singed into her butt and a tag in her ear, so Gloria was able to track down her owners in nearby Chambly. Incredibly, this little calf had escaped from her enclosure in the middle of the night, crossed a four-lane highway, scampered through two subdivisions, negotiated her way through Gloria's electric fence, and adopted the Fauna cattle as her new family. Naturally, Elsa's owners wanted her back, but Gloria was not about to return an animal who had made such a harrowing escape to sanctuary. One of Gloria's volunteers bought Elsa's freedom — "the best five hundred dollars she ever spent."

Having demolished the margaritas and the beer, everyone heads for home. Everyone, that is, but Gloria and me. When I get back to my tent, I check on Toby and Rachel, both fast asleep near the fire. As I add more wood, I come within a few inches of Rachel's face as she slumbers. The flickering firelight catches the gray hair around her muzzle and shoots silver down Toby's back. They look like two captive angels put to sleep by some fairy-tale curse. Up in the bandstand, Binky has joined Yoko in the warmer space beneath the Plexiglas. I can see the two sets of shoulders slumped together in the corner of the little room. Looks as if Binky has adjusted to the idea of sleeping with others.

Inside my tent, I set the alarm. I'll get up every three hours for the rest of the night. The frogs in the moat are chorusing. I shoo a fox away from the kitchen tent. The chimps do not stir. As usual, Tom visits me in my dreams. He unzips my tent flap, sticks his head inside, and tells me not to worry. He'll keep the fires going, he says. He'll make sure everyone's warm and dry.

Dostoyevsky's Horse

FOR THE next few days, we manage to keep the chimps comfortable, well fed, and happy from our makeshift setup on the patio. The daylight hours are filled with manic activity, making smoothies in the tent, filling nut bags on the fly, handing breakfast, lunch, and dinner through the Sky Walk caging or slipping it beneath the walls on the islands, chopping firewood. We're all in one another's way. Tensions rise when Petra climbs the caging in front of my tent and grabs the electric fence. We hear a muted *zap*, and with a mighty shriek the big girl falls backward off the fence, a look of pure terror on her face. Petra was already frightened at being locked out of her home. She wasn't trying to break out of sanctuary but rather to break back in. She spends the next couple of days hiding in the hut.

In the late afternoons, as the chores wind down and the pace begins to slow, the whole operation takes on a serene, magical air. The chimps, their bedtime approaching, are much calmer. The fires are brought to full strength, the day workers go home, and we're left with the full-timers — Gloria, her sisters, Mario, and me.

Late one evening, while we all indulge in more of Linda's homemade margaritas, I ask Dawna when she first learned of Gloria's decision to rescue chimpanzees.

"She called me from Ellensburg at three in the morning," says Dawna, a big smile on her face. Ellensburg, in Washington, is where Roger and Deborah Fouts run the Chimpanzee and Human Communication Institute. That's where Gloria blurted those fateful words thirteen years ago. "She said she'd met some chimps. She said she wanted to rescue chimps."

The Grows grew up in a working-class suburb of Montreal called Croydon, now part of Saint-Hubert. Their father, Rudy, was born in Canada, but his parents had emigrated from Romania to escape the war. Their mother, Agnes, stayed home to raise the three daughters and one son. They lived in the house Agnes was born in, one of the first little houses on the South Shore. The family were known as the eccentrics of the neighborhood.

Their house was home to a menagerie of wildlife. "Everyone in town knew," says Dawna. "You want to go see animals, you go to the Grows." Each of the animals was a rescue, and many required some rehabilitation. "We had cows and chickens and ducks and pigeons and raccoons," says Dawna. "We were the family that bought the duck for Easter, and instead of eating it we just kept it. We used to take the ducks camping with us. Daddy had built this box, and I can still remember their little heads sticking up. We're going camping! We'd take them up to Jackson's Creek, where we spent a good part of every summer. The ducks just lived with us."

The girls get their love of animals from both parents. Every few days Rudy would come home from work with an injured animal in the back of his van. Then Agnes would take over, nursing it back to health. One event is particularly vivid in Dawna's memory.

"Sometime in the late seventies we had a real bad drought. The St. Lawrence Seaway is a major breeding ground for seagulls, and as the water dropped lower and lower, the mother seagulls couldn't find enough food for their young, so thousands of fledglings began to starve. Some of them began floating across the canal in search of food, and then they'd walk up onto the highway and get smooshed. One day Daddy was driving across the Victoria Bridge, and no kidding, there were birds everywhere. Lots were already dead, but some were OK, so he started throwing as many as he could into his van. For two weeks straight, Daddy would come home with a van full of baby seagulls. Beautiful ones, with speckles. He'd put them in the backyard, and my mother would feed them, and once they were healthy Daddy would pile them back into his van and drive them a little further down the Seaway and release them."

I ask Dawna why her father loved animals so much.

She sniffs. "He got it from *his* father. But not in the way you might think."

When Rudy was young, he witnessed his father whipping a horse who refused to cross a bridge. In a scene seemingly pulled straight from Dostoyevsky, the horse had been spooked by a car—a rare sight back in those days. Dawna's grandfather had laid into the horse with such ferocity that Rudy Grow never forgot it.

"Daddy told us that was the worst thing he ever saw in his entire life. And it changed him. Our whole family, we've all been through this. We've rescued animals since day one."

• • •

The next morning, as if Dawna had conjured it with her words, an equestrian catastrophe strikes the farm. Jethro, the old calèche horse, has collapsed in his stall.

When I arrive at the front paddock, the gorgeous chestnut named McLeod is anxiously pawing the ground with his hoof. Gloria, Richard, Mario, Linda, Dawna, and the handyman, Andre, are all inside the stable, so I hop the fence and run to help. But before I get close, Eeyore the donkey appears and runs straight for me.

I try to dodge him, but he's surprisingly agile for a sixteen-year-old jack, and he almost nips me in the side. I lose my footing, stumble in a panicked semicircle, try to redirect my flailing body toward the stable, and fail miserably. Eeyore keeps nipping at me until I complete my retreat and vault back over the fence. Everyone in the stable has witnessed my pathetic display, and no one is laughing. Linda later tells me I screamed like a little girl as I went airborne, but I think she's probably exaggerating.

Soon Gloria's brother, Glenn, and Linda's boyfriend, Chris, show up in their pickups. Then the local big-animal vet arrives. Eeyore allows all three men to pass unmolested to the stable. For some reason, he has his eye only on me.

Along with Mr. Puppy, Jethro and Eeyore are talismans of Fauna's early days. Until Gloria and Richard intervened, Jethro had been destined for the glue factory as punishment for dragging his carriage up and over a taxicab in Montreal. Eeyore arrived as an abandoned baby and spent the first few years of his life click-clacking through Gloria and Richard's house. Both animals are getting on in years. Jethro has collapsed like this three times in the last two years.

I decide to make another attempt at donkey evasion. Armed with a carefully selected stick, I mount the fence and gingerly lower myself into the paddock. Eeyore immediately turns to face me. His ears twitch. His tail swishes. He pretends to munch on something, but I know he's faking. When I take two steps toward the stable, the donkey grunts and starts running at me. I wave my weapon at him, but with its first pass through the air the branch snaps weakly in half. Now I can do nothing but run, and the donkey has already worked up a pretty good head of steam. Then, just as Eeyore bares his buckteeth and prepares to bury them in my side, the young woman who feeds the horses every morning steps between me and the overly protective ass. With a commanding sweep of her hand, she brings Eeyore to a dead stop. With her next gesture, she sends the donkey off to join McLeod in the pasture.

There is no time to dwell on my embarrassment. I join the team in the stable, where everyone is trying to lift Jethro to his feet. The old guy is conscious, but the nerves in his hips are shot, which means we're in a race against time. A horse cannot lie on his side for very long, because the weight of his body on the rib cage makes it very difficult to breathe. No one knows how long Jethro has been in this position, but his breathing is already beginning to sound labored.

With great effort, we all try to heave the horse onto his haunches. Linda and Dawna yank on his harness, while everyone else pulls or pushes on his backside. We try three times, but it's not working, so Mario and Andre run over to the garage and return with a drill, some planks, and a winch. Mario attaches a wooden brace to the roof timbers. Chris loops a length of chain over this brace and hooks it to the leather belt wrapped around Jethro's midsection. The vet injects the horse with anti-inflammatories, pain relievers, and glucose, while Gloria gives him some water and an apple. When the winch is ready, we all bend down and search for purchase on Jethro's massive body. Outside, McLeod lets loose a panicked whinny and takes off on a frantic lap around the paddock.

We lift, Mario cranks the winch, but Jethro doesn't budge. The wooden brace begins to split, the chain threatens to fly loose. We stop lifting. Chris unlatches the winch. I look at Gloria, who is caressing Jethro's muzzle. I wonder if she is secretly saying goodbye.

We decide to give it one more try. Ten pairs of hands search for a suitable grip, and on the count of three, we throw our backs into it. Nothing happens. But then, incredibly, Jethro's left back leg shoots out beneath him, searching for purchase. Chris and Glenn quickly leverage the opportunity, Gloria calls out for Jethro to make one last effort, and suddenly the old horse is standing again, breathing long and fast, Gloria kissing his muzzle, Mario removing the brace and chain, everyone rubbing Jethro's quivering back and sides. I want to clap, but no one claps, because there is nothing to celebrate; this could happen all over again tomorrow.

McLeod pokes his head inside the stable to check on his friend. The vet slips another needle into Jethro's neck. And soon the Grow family is standing outside in the sun, watching Mario walk Jethro around the pasture, swatting horse flies, and chatting about the old woman who took care of their mother, Agnes, during her decline last year. That woman was so tough that she once took a bus to the hospital when her water broke. This story might be apocryphal, but the way the Grows nod their heads as they discuss the old woman's resilience makes me think I should quit standing around and get back to the chimps. Eeyore follows me out of the pasture. He seems happy to see me go.

A Second Kick at the Can

JUST AFTER sunrise the next day, I find Jethro and McLeod grazing lazily together. Jethro seems to be doing much better.

Petra, meanwhile, has emerged from the hut and appears none the worse for wear. The chimps seem to be on their best behavior, as if they know their current living arrangement is only temporary. Aside from a small squabble in the Sky Walk, when Sue Ellen lashed out at Regis for stealing her chemise, there have been no real fights or cause for alarm.

In the evening, while Gloria sweeps up thousands of dead cockroaches and hoses the chimphouse clean of Ernesto's toxins, Dawna tells me about her first trip to LEMSIP with Gloria twelve years ago.

"We left at three in the morning so we could be there when the chimps woke up, and it was pouring rain. I was driving, and I couldn't see a thing." Gloria spent the whole time folding pieces of paper into makeshift envelopes and filling them with nuts and seeds. She planned to give these to the chimps as rudimentary loot bags.

"LEMSIP was in such a beautiful spot," says Dawna. "You're in the woods in a valley in the mountains. You don't see anything. You don't hear anything. It's absolutely friggin' beautiful. It's so hard to believe what these guys went through there. Jim Mahoney met us at the gate. Inside, it was just a bunch of ugly trailers. A main building, the office building, and these ugly portable trailers. In the middle of the most ideal campsite you'd ever want to be in! Mountains right there—like you could touch a mountain."

Dawna will never forget the first time she entered a chimp unit. "That's when I met Pepper," she says, as if that's explanation enough. "I don't know what our connection is. Well, actually, that's not true. I do know what our connection is." She takes a drag on her cigarette. "I think Miss Pep is our father."

Dawna pauses to let this revelation sink in. I give her a look, the only look one can give a recent acquaintance who has raised the topic of reincarnation around a campfire while holding a cup brimming with tequila.

Dawna laughs. "Oh my gosh, oh my gosh, oh my gosh," she says, taking another drag. "When I went in there, Pep was the first chimp I saw on my right. Petra was there, Chance was there, Annie was there. Jim was trying to get a group together for us to take."

Mahoney had used a forklift to move some of the chimps bound for Fauna into a single trailer to introduce them to one another. Most had heard the others' screams for years, but they had never met.

"Something automatic happened when I saw Pepper," Dawna says. When the sisters started handing out the envelopes of seeds, Pepper stayed where she was, in the back of her cage, terrified to come closer. Petra also ignored the envelope, but she tried to grab the women through the caging. Annie took the envelope, removed each seed one by one, and carefully placed them on the ledges between the bars of her cage. She was soon surrounded by seeds, but she didn't eat them right away. As if enjoying the mere presence of new and interesting food, Annie sat for more than an hour before eating the seeds.

Eventually, Pepper worked up the courage to take an envelope from Dawna. She opened it and begun munching away on the nuts. And then she did something entirely unexpected — she presented her back to Dawna for grooming.

"Mike, the lab tech, had told us not to touch them. Do *not* try to touch the chimps, he'd said. But Mike had gone outside for a bit. And when Pep presented to me, Gloria whispered: *She wants you to scratch her back. Just be careful, stick your fingers in, and scratch her back.* So I did."

Dawna stops again, lost in her thoughts. She takes a long drag and smiles to herself.

"Our father had passed away about a year before, and there was something about the nape of Pepper's neck that looked like his. The way she turned her head. That's what pulled me to her. I was like, 'Oh my God. Daddy's there.' These days, the way she looks out for me when I visit, it's him. It's just him. A reincarnation. Part of his spirit. A second kick at the can. He's talking to me through her. It's the best feeling I've ever had."

When Mike walked back into the unit and caught her grooming Pepper, Dawna thought she was in big trouble. But Mike wasn't angry. Instead, he was amazed. "I'll never forget what he said," says Dawna with a strange smile. "Pepper had been in that cage for fourteen years and she'd never, ever been touched."

Mario's Last Laugh

ON THE last night of Operation Cucarachas, I am awakened by the sound of a pig snorting. I unzip my tent and shine my flashlight out past the island, but I see nothing out of the ordinary. Rachel and Toby are unconscious. The fire is still going strong. At sunup, I report what I heard to Gloria, but she says it's impossible. "You dreamt it," she says abruptly, a degree of annoyance in her voice.

Once breakfast has been served to the chimps, the crew begins to take apart the kitchen tent and ferry the contents back inside the chimphouse. At about eleven o'clock, Gloria and Kim open the doors to the islands and the Sky Walk, and the chimps race back inside to inspect their sparkling, roach-free home. For the next hour they put on a simian symphony of howls, screams, and percussive blasts, as old friendships are reestablished, new social groups are formed, and various hierarchies are reinforced. By midafternoon, everyone is either napping or grooming as the week's anxieties dissipate in the humid air. Everyone except Sue Ellen, that is. Susie has dragged her nesting blankets along the Sky Walk to the roundabout overlooking the pond. There she will spend a starlit night all by herself.

While I'm putting together the dinner trolleys, Kim busts me for leaving plastic wrap on a head of lettuce. "Hey, Trolley Boy," she says, "what's this all about?" And that's when I make my biggest mistake since arriving at Fauna. In front of the entire staff, I defend myself by saying that Gloria leaves the plastic wrap on the lettuce all the time.

"What?" Gloria yells. "What did you just say?"

"I said that sometimes you leave the —"

Gloria gives me a look that could melt cement. Everyone else starts to laugh, but not Gloria. She walks right up to me, her hands on her hips.

"Why do you have to be so weak?" she says, and the laughing stops. "Why couldn't you just apologize?" she continues, loud enough that even Sue Ellen out near the pond can hear her. "It was your mistake, not mine."

"I know. I know. I just thought—"

"You are such a man," Gloria says with a note of triumph, as she stomps out of the kitchen. "You're slitting my throat here!"

Apparently, I have one hell of a surprised look on my face, because once Gloria has left the building, Linda quickly provides damage control. "She's stressed and sleep-deprived," Linda says. "She doesn't mean it, she's just got a lot on her plate." Embarrassed, fuming, I go outside and begin to take down the tents.

When I consider what I've learned about the Grow family this past week, I realize a peculiar truth: that in order for people to commit themselves fully to fighting injustice, they must first witness an extreme example of it. Gloria and Dawna had to see the horrors at LEMSIP for themselves before they could commit to rescuing the chimps. Their father had to see a horse being mercilessly flogged before dedicating himself to helping animals in need. These experiences lie at the root of their passion, a passion that sometimes overwhelms them and causes them to lash out for no apparent reason. This play of opposites makes me think Gloria's plan to invite a bunch of Tibetan monks to bless the sanctuary might not be a bad idea.

With the tents sprayed and drying in the sun, I am tempted to sneak off to my apartment for a quick nap when I hear a great commotion from the chimphouse. From my vantage point, the chorus of alarm barks and angry shrieks sounds bottled, as if I'm listening to a recording of thirteen furious chimpanzees. They continue for about three minutes. I can see many of them displaying through the second-floor windows that face the cattle fields. Soon it is only Jethro who continues to bark, making sure that whoever has spooked his family is heeding his powerful warning.

Then I hear a familiar, high-pitched beacon—and the chimps go off again, shrieking and pounding on the windows. I wonder whether that glass really is shatterproof. And then I spot the cause of their fear. Almost on the horizon, Mario is running through a field. His eyes are on the ground in front of him, but his arm is raised high above his head. He holds a familiar white canister in his outstretched hand.

Apparently, the best way to corral a family of escaped pigs is with a few well-timed blasts on an air horn.

Chapter 9

THE PRESSURE WASHER

> Only to the extent that we expose ourselves
> over and over to annihilation can that which
> is indestructible be found in us.
>
> — ANCIENT BUDDHIST SAYING

Smoothie Boy

I HAVE A NEW NICKNAME on the farm. The women used to call me Trolley Boy, but today it seems I've been promoted. At least I like to think of it as a promotion. Now I'm known as Smoothie Boy.

Of all the daily rituals in the chimphouse, the preparation of afternoon smoothies is the one that the apes anticipate most. Kim arranges the ingredients on the counter—soymilk, bananas, frozen strawberries and blueberries, nutrient supplements, and protein powder—and before she even takes the lid off the blender, Binky, Regis, and Spock appear in their privacy rooms to watch. I position thirteen empty water bottles on a trolley, and Kim writes a chimp's initials on each one. Then she throws a cupful of berries into the blender, unpeels the first banana, and Binky yelps his encouragement—*Aow! Aow! Aow!* Spock grips the caging in front of him as if he might explode with excitement.

"The smoothies can't be too green," yells Kim over the blender. "If they're too green, they won't drink them."

For the next half-hour, under the watchful eye of Kim and a growing gallery of expectant chimpanzees, I blend up a storm, filling thirteen bottles with a nutritious purple-green sludge. I make sure to leave about an inch of space at the top so that Kim can add the final "supplements." Smoothies may seem like a luxury item, but they are the most reliable delivery mechanism for the cornucopia of medications the chimpanzees have to take.

Over the years, the chimps' meds have changed frequently. These days Regis gets pills for diabetes, Spock gets heart meds, Yoko gets thyroid pills, Tom gets antiparasitic and antidiarrhea meds, Rachel gets a small dose of diazepam to ease her extreme anxiety, and Susie Goose gets meds for her bum hip. As the chimps get older and their decades in research take a larger toll, this list is sure to grow. New symptoms will emerge, and new medications will be added to their smoothies.

When the bottles are full, the meds in, and the caps screwed tight, I follow Kim through the chimphouse as she makes her deliveries. The walls echo with excited pant-hoots. Binky, Regis, and Jethro are first to the portholes, as usual. They greedily take their smoothies and disappear. The more reserved individuals, like Pepper and Sue Ellen, wait until the boys have left.

Kim slips the bottle labeled "SE" through the porthole toward Sue Ellen, who quickly glances over her shoulder to ensure she's safe. Then the old girl grabs the bottle, lets loose a few muffled food grunts, and turns to go. But suddenly Jethro reappears right in front of her, his own unopened smoothie gripped tightly between his front teeth. Susie gives Jethro a broad grin in an effort to appease him, but no luck. With hardly a peep from Susie Goose, Jethro deftly relieves her of her smoothie and turns to make a quick escape.

"Jeffie!" says Kim. "You've got yours, Jeffie. That's Susie's." Jethro stops, turns back around to face us, and gives Kim a strange look. Susie continues to grin at her amiable thief. Kim decides to strike a deal.

"You give that back to Susie, and I'll get you a muffin, OK?"

I can almost feel my eyes rolling. There's no way Jethro is going to make that deal. He's got all the leverage. And we're talk-

Another day begins at the Fauna chimphouse. Sue Ellen and Pepper love to sit and stare out the windows on the left.

The author's tent during Operation Cucarachas. Binky and Yoko are playing together up in the bandstand.

All photos courtesy of Frank Noelker and Howard Yezerski Gallery unless otherwise noted.

Binky may look tough, but he's actually a very sensitive and loving chimpanzee as well as the resident practical joker.

Regis loves to paint and listen to music. He sometimes gets very anxious, but hanging out with his best friend, Jethro, makes him feel better.

Jethro is the peacekeeper at Fauna. An enormous male, he is well loved by all the chimpanzees and lives happily with each of them.

Before being abandoned by her human owner at the age of three, Rachel enjoyed taking bubble baths and wearing frilly dresses. Now she is very fragile.

The smallest chimp at Fauna, Yoko more than makes up for his size with his intense loyalty and passionate personality.

Petra, a highly intelligent chimpanzee, quietly watches and learns from others. She and Chance are half sisters.

Spock had been raised with Maya as a human child at the University of Montreal. Today he prefers female companionship and likes to drink from the garden hose.

Maya adores the treat bags at Fauna. She will spend hours peering into the bags, slowly investigating the contents and eating the treats one by one.

Chance, or Chancey-Pants, is very nervous and cautious. She doesn't like hot peppers on her pizza.

Though he is Fauna's most famous resident, Tom keeps to himself. He can fit five apples in his mouth at once.

Sue Ellen, or Susie Goose, Fauna's senior citizen, makes exceptionally intricate sleeping nests.

In the lab, Pepper barely saw the light of day for twenty-seven years. Now she loves eating fresh kale and picking tomatoes from the planters outside.

Toby never misses an opportunity to groom his best friend, Rachel. He enjoys chasing geese and wearing a scrunchie around his wrist like a bracelet.

ing about smoothies here. But to my astonishment, Jethro stays put while Kim runs to the kitchen and returns with an oatmeal muffin.

"OK, give Susie her smoothie, and I'll give you the muffin," says Kim. Jethro doesn't hesitate. He drops Sue Ellen's smoothie at her feet, and Kim rewards him with the muffin.

"Thank you, Jeffie. That was very nice of you."

Jethro ambles off with his afternoon feast. When the coast is clear, Susie retrieves her smoothie—and her meds.

Over the next half-hour, through a mixture of lucky timing and hard-nosed negotiations, we manage to deliver every smoothie into the proper hands. And a half-hour later I'm back at the blender, making another batch.

"Come on, Smoothie Boy," says Kim, failing to disguise her annoyance as she labels thirteen new water bottles. "Not so green this time." Apparently, the chimps took one sip of my first attempt and poured the rest out on the floor.

Skinny Reege

WITH MY new batch of sufficiently purple smoothies delivered, I wander down to the south playroom to collect the lunch trolleys. As I gather up the spilled paper cups and toppled vegetables, I feel a presence right in front of me. Raising my eyes slowly but staying in a crouch, I lock gazes with the Hoodlum Regis. He is no more than two feet away. I expect a ball of chimp spit to explode on my forehead any second, but Reege just opens his mouth and flicks his tongue out at me. His long, drawn face—usually the picture of fatigue—seems brighter. There is a spark in his sunken eyes I've never seen before.

Not long ago, Regis was diagnosed with diabetes, but unfortunately, he refuses to volunteer his arm for insulin injections. He has always been suspicious of needles—by the age of three he had been knocked unconscious forty times at LEMSIP, and every time it was by dart gun.

Regis was born at LEMSIP and taken from his mother only a few days after birth. He spent the first six months isolated from other chimpanzees, in an incubator and then in a cage, being reared by human caregivers. As a result, Reege has always been a nervous wreck. In the lab he was treated repeatedly for depression and anorexia, and even today he is prone to panic attacks that often leave him whimpering and choking in the corner of his room. Gloria is currently researching alternate ways of getting insulin into an uncooperative chimpanzee, because without daily injections, Regis's health will continue to decline. Although he is the same age as his veritable brothers, Binky and Jethro, Regis looks twenty years older than them, his body wan and withered, his gait slow and loping. He is the only chimp at Fauna whose hair is still sparse enough that the identification tattoo he was given in the lab — 645 — is still visible on his chest.

Today, though, something is different about skinny Reege. When I rise out of my crouch, he throws his arms up above his head, grips the caging, and playfully nods his head at me. I do the same, trying to imitate his grunts, and then he lets go of the caging, runs past the porthole, and takes up the same stance on the other side. I follow. Again I expect the spit to fly any second. But then Regis pushes back from the caging, turns, and takes off for the far side of the playroom. There is a youthful bounce to his gait, and as he rounds the play-fort near the far wall, his buddy Jethro emerges from the shadows, skipping along on all fours behind his friend as if Reege were the Pied Piper. I can hear them huffing at each other now, their feet slapping the floor, their shoulders dipping in unison as they round the fort again. Soon Reege is back in position, hanging languidly from the bars in front of me. Jethro sits behind him, his legs splayed, his chest heaving, waiting intently for whatever is about to happen.

Perhaps it was Operation Cucarachas that loosened them up, a week of prolonged exposure to their strange new caregiver. Or perhaps it's just that I made a mean smoothie on my second try. Whatever the reason, Reege and Jeffie have sought me out to play. In the chimpanzee world, this is a pretty significant act. They have chosen to strike up a relationship with me. Now I have no choice but to blow their simian minds.

Slowly I open the sliding door that leads to the inner courtyard. Regis pulls back from the bars, a look of intrigue on his face. Then, as quickly as I can, I disappear outside, run along the outside wall of the chimphouse in an awkward crouch, and pop my head up in the playroom window. Regis is still looking out the door, wondering where I went. But Jethro spies me immediately. His huge body erupts in excited convulsions, his great belly shaking with delight. Arms flailing, feet bobbing, head going in circles, Jethro tries to push himself up onto all fours, but his enthusiasm proves too great. As if tethered to the floor by his tremendous size, he falls backward into the caging with a crash. Regis looks over at his floundering friend, but Jethro is too excited to direct him my way. For one glorious moment, Jethro the chimpanzee is completely speechless.

Regis figures it out soon enough. And for the next hour or so, we play an exhausting game of now-you-see-me, now-you-don't. Every once in a while, the two chimps will take off and march around the fort again, one behind the other, but they always return to the porthole and to me, their new playmate. Ever since I arrived at Fauna, I've felt like an outsider. Although Sue Ellen, Pepper, and Binky were receptive to me almost from the start, I've been craving a sign from the other chimps that my presence here is OK with them—that instead of making them more anxious, I might make them less so. Now, more than six weeks into my stay here, it appears we've had a breakthrough. It seems as if this game is never going to end.

Until, that is, we hear a thunderous roar coming down the driveway—the unmistakable brattle of a Harley-Davidson motorcycle. The front door of the chimphouse opens and slams shut, a baritone voice rumbles through the building, and Tom howls a passionate pant-hoot greeting from somewhere near the kitchen. Reege and

Jeffie forget about our little game and disappear into a privacy room to see what the commotion is about. In the kitchen I find a man of about fifty who is doing everything he can to squeeze his substantial body completely inside Tom's room.

Where's My Kiss?

THE MAN wears a plaid shirt, blue jeans, and black leather boots. He is gruffly handsome, with thinning hair and a robust belly. So far he has managed to get both of his arms entirely through Tom's porthole, and he is tickling Tom with abandon.

If Tom's reaction is anything to go by, the man is hitting all the sweet spots. Tom is shaking with happiness. When the man stops for a moment, Tom claps his hands three times, a signal to continue. Soon the tickling devolves into light play-fighting, then all-out wrestling. Finally, when the man opens his arms wide and Tom leaps from his resting bench into the embrace, I realize who he must be.

"Where's my kiss?" asks the man. "Where's my kiss, big guy?"

At this, Tom leans out of the bear hug, huffs with pleasure, and plants a big, wet kiss on Pat Ring's cheek.

Pat Ring is the retired rancher who used to own this farm. When Richard and Gloria bought the land from him in 1990, Pat agreed to stay on for a while to help bring in the hay, clear the snow, and generally manage the place. Back then no one could have imagined just how deeply he would be affected by what Gloria and Richard eventually made of his old farm; Pat wasn't exactly an "animal rights" kind of guy.

"Used to be," he tells me, "if I didn't like the look of you, I wouldn't give you the time of day. If you looked different from me — or worse, if you looked gay — just forget about it."

Gloria is even more blunt when she describes the rancher in the days before the chimps arrived. "Pat was a redneck," she tells me.

"And I don't think he'd mind me using that term. He was a cowboy, a hunter, and a homophobe. And he was terrified of AIDS."

When Gloria told Pat that she was planning to rescue chimpanzees, he was a little taken aback, but he pledged his support nonetheless. When he heard that some of the apes would be HIV-positive, however, he balked. "When this all first started," he says, "I told Gloria we didn't need none of them chimps with HIV. No way I was going near no chimp like that. I was scared of getting the HIV from mosquito bites. You could call me totally ignorant back then."

On one of Gloria's early visits to LEMSIP, she met Tom the chimpanzee for the first time. Something about Tom—his strong personality, his tough exterior—reminded her instantly of Pat. "I came home from that trip and I just said, 'Pat, you've *got* to meet this guy. He's just like you!'"

So Pat accompanied Gloria to LEMSIP on her next visit, and the journey changed his life. He had been to the lab before, but this time, when he followed Gloria into the biohazard unit, he found a team of lab technicians trying to get a middle-aged male chimpanzee to move from one cage to another. This chimp looked different from the others Pat had met. He seemed more worn out, the gray hair around his protruding jaw giving him a grizzled appearance. And the way he was stubbornly refusing to do what the lab techs wanted struck a chord with Pat. If Tom refused much longer, he would inevitably get knocked down with a dart gun. So Pat Ring walked over to the empty cage next to Tom's and bellowed, "Tommie! Come here, big guy. Come on over here, big guy!" And to the utter amazement of the lab techs, Tom stood up at the sound of Pat's deep baritone, ambled through the crossover walkway into the new cage, and sat down next to this abrasive, straight-shooting stranger as if they'd been friends forever.

"It was an instant connection," says Gloria. "Something just clicked between them." And their relationship blossomed at the Fauna sanctuary. Tom and Pat became inseparable, and Gloria began to see sides of Pat she had never imagined he had. "Chimps can see things in us we just can't see," says Gloria. "It was as if Pat had found his soul mate. He became best buds with an HIV-positive chimpanzee." Now, more than seven years after Pat retired from Fauna, he still visits Tom and his chimpanzee family at least once a month.

Pat admits he has softened a lot since meeting Tom. He is much more accepting of different sorts of people and more sensitive to the troubles others are going through. And he's learned to see his own human failings.

"Someone like Tom, the things that have been done to him by us . . . and he can still forgive? I'm telling you, that's an amazing animal that can do that. Put me through half of what Tom went through, and I'd spend the rest of my days looking for you. I'd track you down. I'd want revenge. But not Tom." Pat reaches in to tickle Tom again. "Not you, right, big guy?" Tom huffs, and Pat does the same. "They're better than us, the chimps," he says. "That's what changed me."

Dr. Tom

TOM ARRIVED at the Fauna sanctuary with a serious injury on his foot. Just before he was scheduled to leave the lab, he got into a vicious fight with Billy Jo, who bit Tom's foot badly. James Mahoney kept Tom at LEMSIP for a few extra weeks to give his foot a chance to heal, but when he finally arrived at the sanctuary, the skin on his foot was still very fragile. He was constantly catching it on something and opening up the wound, so he had to be given antibiotics to combat infection. But the last thing Gloria wanted to do was use a needle on a newly arrived lab chimp. That would give Tommie the wrong impression of his new home. So how could she get Tom to take his meds?

Pat Ring had the answer. Whenever Pat was in the chimphouse, he would make himself a cup of tea with lots of milk and sugar.

Tom was always curious about this ritual, and he'd always ask Pat for a sip. So one day, with Pat's approval, Gloria laced his tea with antibiotics. Pat took a few sips, then handed the cup to Tommie, who quickly took a sip and was immediately a tea aficionado.

Soon the tea-drinking ritual spread throughout the chimphouse. Aside from Gatorade and Pepsi, which are rare special treats, tea is now every chimp's favorite drink. Some of them like it piping hot, others let it cool before drinking it. The more inventive chimps, such as Yoko, like to pour a bit of bottled water into the steaming cup to cool it down.

Unfortunately, the antibiotics in the tea gave Tom terrible diarrhea, so Gloria and Pat had to stop dosing him. The infected wound on Tom's foot was soon seeping. It needed to be cleaned and a topical ointment applied. But how would Gloria and Pat do this without knocking Tom unconscious?

When they called Richard at the clinic, the vet gave it to them plain. "Tom's just gonna have to do it himself."

The duo set to work. Gloria locked down the enclosure next to Tom's and put a child's chair and a big bowl of water on the floor. Then they let Tom into the room.

"Pat asked Tommie to sit on the chair and stick his foot in the bowl," says Gloria. "It sounds crazy to say it now. And we were completely shocked when Tom just did it, no questions asked. Then Pat asked Tom to give him his foot. And Tommie lifted his leg. It was incredible. All Pat had to do was reach through the bars and pat the foot dry with a paper towel." Pat smeared a glob of antibiotic cream on Tom's hand so the chimp could smell and taste it—this is an important step in introducing a new substance to a chimpanzee. Then Pat dabbed some of the cream on Tom's foot, rubbed it in a little, and they were done.

"We were bursting inside," says Gloria now. "Bursting with love for this amazing, intelligent, sweet, and gentle soul who was doing everything we asked, who was helping *himself* to heal and saving us the stress of having to do it for him. Never in my wildest dreams did I think a chimp would ever cooperate like that."

Pat and Tom continued their cleansing ritual for three days, and Tom's foot began to improve. But then Tom started asking for the materials himself. "He wanted the spatula with the medication on it," says Gloria. "And then he started applying the stuff to his own foot. So we made him a tray with everything he'd need—paper towels, tissues, the spatula, the ointment in a Dixie cup. We even gave him the iodine sponge, which people warned us he might try to eat. He didn't. He just started to treat his own wound, the way he'd learned from Pat."

Apparently, Tom was a very conscientious nurse.

"Thorough, thorough, thorough," says Gloria with a laugh. "Scrub, scrub, scrub, scrub, scrub. Rinse and dry. Then apply. We could see how serious he was about it. He moved his mouth like he was concentrating real hard. He made sure the cream got into all the little cracks and crevices in his foot. Soon we'd put the cleaning stuff on the food trolley for him, and he'd treat himself."

Tom's foot eventually healed, and today the only sign of the injury is a patch of light pink skin. But the impact of that time is still felt in the chimphouse. Because while Tom was learning how to heal himself by watching Pat, the other chimpanzees were learning something else by watching Tom. The chimps witnessed Tommie submit to medical attention offered by a human, and over time a few brave individuals began following his lead. "Without Tommie showing his trust in Pat," says Gloria, "who knows if the others would ever have started trusting the rest of us?" Chimpanzees learn by watching others. Tom has always been the sanctuary's greatest teacher.

Tom reminds me of a chimpanzee Jane Goodall once knew, a distinguished fellow named David Greybeard. While the other chimps at Gombe remained aloof in the early years of her research, David was always less afraid of the strange white woman. He allowed

Jane to approach his family closer than the others did, and he was the first to let Jane touch him. David also gave her the first glimpse of what would eventually be hailed as one of the greatest discoveries in twentieth-century science, when she witnessed him fishing for termites with a blade of grass. David Greybeard served as an enormously important bridge between chimpanzees and humans. Fifty years later, in the Fauna chimphouse, Tom has become a similarly important go-between.

With one small additional feature: Tom also acts as a doctor now and then.

Not long after Tom learned to clean and dress a wound, Regis and Yoko got into a small tussle, from which Regis emerged with a bad bite wound on his head that quickly became infected. Reege grew lethargic, his condition made worse by his diabetes, so Gloria went inside a few times each day to give him antibiotics, food, and Gatorade. As Regis slowly recovered some of his strength, Gloria no longer felt comfortable going in with him. But the wound still needed to be cleaned. Gloria had noticed that Tom kept inspecting Regis's head, occasionally wiping the wound for him with a blanket. So she decided to see if Tom, given the proper tools, would be willing to treat Regis.

"Every day," says Gloria, "I put the bowl of iodine soap, the paper towels, and the ointment on the trolley, and Tom would go to work. He walked right up to Regis, sat down in his usual way, with his legs out and his arms by his side, and Regis dragged himself over and lay down between Tom's legs. Tom cleaned and treated Regis like this for a whole week. He even sucked the pus out for him. How's that for a resident doctor?"

Shotgun

MY DREAMS with Tom continue. Tonight he and I are in the Fauna pickup truck, taking turns driving. I don't think we have a particular destination in mind. All I know is, we are desperately trying to get the truck down the driveway and off the property. Once we reach the road, we know we'll be safe. But safe from what?

The pickup is notoriously cranky, with a clunky gearbox and whiny brakes. I've been driving it to shop for groceries in Chambly for the past six weeks, and I've only recently mastered the shift from second to third. But in the dream, I am completely useless. When I am behind the wheel we lurch down the driveway, and it seems we'll never make it off the property. Tom sits as calmly as possible in shotgun, politely waiting for me to get the hang of it, but inevitably his fear takes over and he starts pounding on the window and screaming. Then he reaches over, puts his hand on top of mine, and looks me square in the face. He nods and I nod back. This is the signal for us to switch places.

With the truck in neutral, we both climb out and run around the vehicle. Then Tom gets in and drives. Each time he takes over, I feel greatly relieved. But it isn't because he's any better than I am at the wheel. Far from it. Tom is a terrible driver. He can handle the gearshift, but he can't keep the truck heading straight. Once he almost hits a llama who's broken out of her paddock. Another time Pepper comes running up to the edge of the driveway with something really important to tell us, but Tom can't line up his open window with Pepper's face.

But it doesn't matter. In fact, it makes me quite happy to see Tom doing such a terrible job. Neither of us knows what to do. And as long as Tom is behind the wheel instead of me, my feelings of desperation are gone.

My two white swan guards, Jekyll and Hyde, eventually rescue me from this dream. I awake to their honking and pecking at my basement window.

Trespassing

GLORIA MUST have heard about my breakthrough with Regis and Jethro, because it seems I'm up for another big promotion this morning. It's Wednesday, Cleaning Day again, when the chimp-house gets washed top to bottom. Instead of my usual post at the sink, washing mountains of urine-soaked toys and poop-stained musical instruments (with gloves on, of course), this morning Gloria has outfitted me with my very own plastic broom and shovel and an industrial-size garbage can. Kim and Linda are excited about my new responsibilities, because they won't have to do so much of the dirty work. Today my recurring dream of crossing boundaries will become stark reality.

This morning I'm going in.

"It's time you see what it's really like to work here," says Gloria, leading me through Grab Central and around to the north playroom. "You're gonna shovel shit like the rest of us."

The chimps hate Cleaning Day, because they are forced to cede control of their territory to the humans. For an animal as territorial as an ape, this is upsetting. Even worse, while the humans are shoveling, sweeping, and bagging the very things that make the enclosures feel like home—the enrichment items and sleeping nests that give the captive chimpanzees a sense of ownership and belonging—the residents are forced to participate in what amounts to a long and arduous game of Musical Rooms. Through a combination of experience, luck, and simian mathematics, Gloria and Kim are able to shuffle the chimps around the building and onto the islands so that each enclosure can be safely cleaned. Needless to say, Wednesdays are stressful for everyone involved.

With little ceremony, shovel and broom in one hand and trash can in the other, I enter the chimpanzee world. Within seconds Binky howls from the opposite playroom and Jethro appears on the high walkway, staring at me through the caging. I try to ignore them as I set to work. I've been instructed to begin at the top and work my way down. As I climb the metal staircase, Jethro gets up and stomps his feet, his hair on end. Someone else lets loose a deafening scream.

I start sweeping. Crushed water bottles, overripe fruit, and half-chewed musical instruments crash to the floor far below. When the walkway is swept, I go back over it with the shovel, chipping hardened feces from the grating and sweeping it away, slopping piles of still-warm poop over the edge. My job is to prepare every surface in the playroom for the pressure washer, which Gloria wields all day long. "If I get hit with one piece of dried poop," she warned me, "you're really gonna get it."

With the walkway finished, I descend the stairs. I spot Tom up in the walkway above the privacy rooms. In his usual way, he is watching me out of the corner of his eye. Then Binky screams for the third time, Tom disappears from view, and a great commotion ensues. Through the crosshatched steel I glimpse Gloria and Kim racing through the kitchen. I leave the playroom, hurry back through Grab Central, and find quite a vicious chimpanzee skirmish playing out in one of the privacy rooms. The muscular Binky has been cornered by the much smaller Yoko and his friend Petra. The three haven't lived together in a while, and it appears they have some scores to settle. Binky, in self-defense, flails out at Yoko, and when the two make contact, the chimphouse erupts. Yoko turns to flee, but he runs into Petra, who is less agile. The two of them struggle to squeeze up into the walkway, with Binky chomping at their backsides. Binky chases them out onto the Sky Walk and then returns to nurse his wounds. Gloria runs outside and reports back that Petra's arm is cut and Yoko's eye is swollen shut.

I can't help but feel responsible for these heightened tensions — I am, after all, a relative stranger trespassing on their territory. But when I mention this to Gloria, she shakes her head.

"This happens every Cleaning Day."

"But are you sure I should go back in?"

Gloria smiles impatiently. "Binky's not getting you out of this."

"Smoothie Boy!" yells Kim in faux-encouragement as I traipse back to work.

• • •

For the next hour, I shovel, sweep, and bag a surreal cornucopia: yogurt cups, urine-soaked hay, torn cardboard, soiled tambourines, mini-pianos, plastic xylophones, baby bath toys, Lego people, stuffed animals, paper bags, peanut shells, pistachio and walnut shells, hollowed-out pumpkins, lettuce leaves, lettuce hearts, apple cores, mango pits, empty water bottles, full water bottles, half-empty water bottles with a hole toothed in the cap, children's magazines, adult magazines, young adult novels, crayons, markers, necklaces, bracelets, headbands, socks, gloves, dress-up dolls, wide-brimmed sun hats, cotton cardigans, faux-silk scarves, paintbrushes, painting palettes, paintings by a Chimpson Pollock. More banana skins than I can possibly count. Blankets are strewn across the seven-day landscape as if a village of sleeping people had evaporated beneath them.

I am pouring sweat. It's running into my rubber boots and soaking my socks—at least, I think that's sweat. Everything around me is drenched in either old smoothie, old pee, old diarrhea, or all three. The concentrated stench makes me gag, but I manage to stop the reflex when I realize that trespassing on another animal's private world is bad enough. Vomiting on it would be an even worse insult.

Occasionally I come upon an oasis among the week's worth of filth: a chimpanzee sleeping nest. Constructed from intertwined blankets, these circular beds resemble the mattresses wild chimps construct from branches and rainforest foliage, and they are models of neatness and planning. Up in the highest walkway, I find a nest that surely belongs to Sue Ellen. When I pick it up, countless bracelets, necklaces, and sports socks tumble out, along with shells and rinds from various midnight snacks. I have to bag the blankets for the laundry, and it takes me more than ten minutes to unravel them, so tightly has Susie woven her nest. From this spot the Goose would have had a wonderful view of the driveway, the bridge, and the pond in the distance. Tom's nest must be somewhere nearby.

Perhaps out of friendship or because they share the same nightmares, the two oldest chimps at Fauna love to sleep next door to each other.

As I bag Sue Ellen's nesting materials, Jethro reappears across from me, his hair still on end. He grabs onto the caging and displays at me with all his might, pounding his feet against the steel wall over and over. I am reminded of how strange I felt last night when Gloria called to tell me that someone would be cleaning my apartment today. Before I left it this morning, I spent a few extra minutes tidying up, putting my private things away in the closet, readying the place for a stranger to come in and nose around. If I were to go home tonight and find this stranger in my living room, I guess I'd be a bit annoyed. But imagine if I had to sit there all day long and watch this intruder tip my whole world upside down?

Not only am I trespassing, but I'm trespassing on sacred ground. Every dramatic episode in the last twelve years of the chimps' lives has occurred within these walls. This sanctuary was built by humans, but it no longer belongs to them. Every inch of this place hums with significance. When I sweep the high walkways of the south playroom, I can almost see Yoko lying prone, his legs mysteriously numb and useless, Pat Ring courageously climbing up there with Tom as his chaperone and throwing Yoko over his shoulder to take him to the clinic; Yoko eventually regained the use of his legs, but no one ever figured out what had caused the paralysis.

When I bag the mountains of garbage down below, I can picture the claustrophobic Pepper wading through five weeks' worth of refuse, because that's how long it took for her to find the courage to explore the rest of the chimphouse for the first time. And when I shovel muck from the mezzanine, I can imagine the incorrigible Binky sitting up there all day long, waiting for the wind to blow at just the right angle so he could grab the two flags, one Canadian and one American, that used to fly above the chimphouse door in honor of the chimps' dual citizenship. According to Gloria, moments after Binky tore the flags down, the fashion diva Susie

Goose ambled out onto the Sky Walk proudly draped in the Stars and Stripes.

These rooms are where their lives play out, but it's also where their lives are destined to end. The air is thick with spirits of the living and the dead. Take the Apartment, for example, the small living area just behind Tom's privacy room, where especially troublesome chimps are sometimes housed. Chimpanzees mourn their dead in ways that are remarkably similar to human rituals. When Donna Rae died of kidney failure, Gloria had her body placed on the ground floor of the Apartment for a "chimp visitation." Pepper, Susie, Rachel, Petra, and Chance gathered around Donna and spent the next three hours preparing her for her final journey. They groomed her fingernails and toenails, tried to feed her water, occasionally tickled her to make sure she wasn't just sleeping. Then Binky came in. As the Bub had done with Annie, he dragged Donna's body around the Apartment, flipping her over, trying to wake her up. In the process, Donna's face became bloodied, but Rachel quickly took care of that. She disappeared for a few minutes and then returned with a handful of paper towels. Rachel dabbed every spot of blood from Donna's face. "When they were finished with Donna Rae," says Gloria, "she was immaculate. She was perfect, ready to go." And then, in a slow procession, her friends left the Apartment one by one.

With every step I take and with every garbage bag I fill, I sink deeper into the difficult histories of my new friends. I begin to see the world through their eyes. Squeezing myself down into Jeannie's Room, I finally understand why Rachel loves it there so much — full of sunlight at dawn, dark as a cave in the late afternoon. I crawl on hands and knees through the high walkways and realize Tom has made the absolutely right choice — there is no other place I would consider building my sleeping nest.

On the second floor above the kitchen, where the laundry machine hums, I take a break from bagging the entrails of a smashed pumpkin to duck beneath the resting bench, sitting in the only place in the building where it is physically impossible for a human to spot me. I feel the serenity that must come over a chimpanzee in this hidden corner and can imagine the lifetimes of bad memories that have surely been exorcised in this spot.

Just Beneath the Blueberries

NEAR THE end of the day I slip into privacy room no. 6, where Grab Central begins and ends, the locus of one of Tom's worst memories. I can almost see the old man panicking in here back in October 2001, the day death came to the Fauna sanctuary for the first time.

Tom was locked in room no. 6 when his best friend, a chimpanzee named Pablo who was three rooms over, suddenly lost his breath and couldn't get it back. Pablo was said to be an angry, aggressive chimp who held most humans in utter disdain. This is understandable when you read the header on his LEMSIP research file: HARDCORE RESEARCH ANIMAL. None of the other chimps had "hardcore" written on their files. Apparently, Pablo had suffered even more than all the others.

Pablo had the stocky build of a powerlifter and a tense, prickly personality that made it nearly impossible for a human to build a relationship with him. He was, in Gloria's words, "a chimp's chimp," preferring the company of his own species, especially Tom's company, to that of the naked apes who had ravaged him for so long. An ex–lab worker once told Gloria a story that speaks to what Pablo had been through. During one especially fraught knockdown, he was shot with five separate darts. He pulled the first three from his torso with ease, but the fourth hit him in the gum line, which is not surprising, considering that a chimpanzee expresses fear by peeling back his lips and exposing his gums in a broad, ghoulish grin. The fifth dart got Pablo in the head.

"When Pabbie started throwing stuff around the room here," says Gloria, "we were all like, 'Gotcha, bud. We hear you.' None of us ever questioned Pabbie's anger." Even Pat Ring had to work extra hard to make headway with Pablo. Ultimately, it was Pat's relationship with Tom that unlocked the old bruiser's heart.

But Pat was off on a hunting trip that awful day in 2001. And all Tom could do was watch the human drama play out in front of room no. 3. He watched as Gloria, Richard, and Dawna tried to diagnose Pablo from their side of the bars, as Richard ran to the phone and called James Mahoney for advice, as Richard assembled six needles with the drugs Mahoney had recommended. Until then, the chimps had considered Richard persona non grata, since his presence meant that someone was sick, or dying, or in desperate need of medical attention. Richard's relationship with the chimps has always been strained by his role as chief vet.

In his four years here, Pablo had never willingly accepted a needle. But he submitted to Richard right away, presenting his forearm as he struggled to breathe. It was as if all of his righteous anger toward humans had been swept away by his panic, as if some part of him had always known that the humans at Fauna were there to help.

Time passed as everyone waited for the drugs to take effect. But Pablo became weaker and weaker, and soon his chest was barely moving. So Gloria did something she thought she'd never have to do with an adult male chimp: she opened the front door to the privacy room and walked inside. She climbed up to the resting bench, where Pabbie was lying, and she lifted his arm in the air. "And that was it," she says. "I was in the room with him, and I was screaming at Richard, 'Do something! Do something! You've got to do something!' And Richard just said, 'He's gone.' And he walked out of the chimphouse and left me there."

Richard's day job as a veterinarian has inured him to death. He has to see it and sometimes dish it out every day. Over the years, out of sheer necessity, he has erected a surprisingly efficient emotional wall in order to deal with an animal's passing. "Richard has a great love for animals," says Gloria. "People may think he doesn't care, because he walks away afterward, but he cares so much. It's just that he deals with death all the time."

Everyone knows that Richard is available twenty-four hours a day, seven days a week. Local people are always bringing their dying animals to Fauna. A few weeks before, Gloria's brother, Glenn, had brought his sick cat over for Richard to euthanize, as did another Fauna staff member on the same day. And that afternoon, a guinea pig on the farm passed away. With nowhere to store the corpses before burial, Gloria wrapped them up and put them in the only place she could think of. "In the freezer. Just beneath the blueberries. We had to throw out so much food after that."

At times Fauna can seem equal parts morgue and sanctuary. And as time passes, more and more of the farm becomes a graveyard. Today there are about one hundred animals—pets or rescues or strays—living aboveground at Fauna, and perhaps double that number buried below.

Unlike Richard, Gloria has erected no walls between herself and what she witnesses. She survives a traumatic ordeal by sinking as deep inside the emotional turmoil as possible. So after Richard left the chimphouse that day, Gloria and her sisters lifted Pablo's dead body down to the floor of the privacy room, and for the next few hours they watched the chimps visit one by one. Jethro and Regis weren't all that close to Pablo, and they didn't spend much time saying goodbye. But Yoko, who along with Tom was one of Pablo's closest friends, couldn't bear to come into the room. He just stayed in the back, pacing back and forth, seemingly unable to cope.

And then it was Tom's turn.

"Tom had been locked in room six the whole time," Gloria tells me. "He was going crazy with fear and anxiety. And when I finally unlocked his door, he flung it open in anger, sprinted through the crossover walkway, and zoomed down the ladder into Pabbie's room. I've never seen poor Tom move that fast. He got down on the floor, hovered over Pabbie to check if he was breathing, and that was it. That was all it took. He stood up, turned around, and slammed his fist into the wall four times. Then he let out this call, this awful scream. It was a scream that said 'My friend is dead.'"

The Pressure Washer

FOR THE rest of the afternoon, I struggle to reconcile the spirits that inhabit these enclosures. Sometimes, as when I stumble on a forgotten children's toy in a remote corner, I am overcome with a sense of lightness, the conviction that this might be the happiest place on Earth. After all, the youngsters, like Binky, Jethro, and Regis, have been living at Fauna longer than they lived at the lab—surely good memories have begun replacing the bad. But other times, such as when I'm picking through a mountain of stinking refuse to salvage reusable bottle caps, my thoughts turn dark and brooding. How messy their lives are, how weighted with consequence everything is in this false, invented home. And then I think about my own life and how free it is from mess and consequence. In addition to dreaming about chimpanzees, people who work with them inevitably begin to see their own lives in unexpected ways. As if peering into a long-hidden mirror, I realize for the first time that I have never lost anyone close to me. I have never grieved the way Binky and Jethro and Regis and Tom have grieved.

When the rooms are swept and shoveled and the garbage bags are hauled outside, I find Gloria in the north playroom, where my day began ten hours ago. She's going over the room one last time with the pressure washer. High above us sits Sue Ellen, peering in from the opposite playroom, where Jethro displayed in anger at me earlier. It appears the Goose has already ransacked the week's worth of enrichment goodies that Kim left for her in the freshly cleaned room. Susie is looking very demure, with a long plastic necklace wrapped across her shoulder like a Miss America sash, and a white sports sock pulled tight over her left hand.

Gloria always does the pressure washing on Cleaning Day. The sound upsets many of the chimps, so Gloria figures it's best if she's the one responsible for all the commotion. Also, no one else does the job quite the way she likes it to be done. But the main reason

Gloria prefers to do the pressure washing herself is that the work is like a meditation, a rare chance to clear her mind.

As I follow behind her with a floor squeegee, Gloria tells me about her friend Carole Noon, the founder of Save the Chimps in Florida, who recently passed away. Save the Chimps, the largest chimpanzee sanctuary in the world, is where the research apes from the notorious Coulston Foundation are slowly being retired, ever since Coulston went out of business in 2002. "Carole was known as the 'mad hoser,'" Gloria says. "She had so much to do and worry about, moving hundreds of chimps all the way from New Mexico to Florida, but she always seemed to have a hose in her hand." Gloria grabs the squeegee from me, shows me how to use it properly. "Men sit on the toilet. I do the pressure washing. It's where I do all my best thinking."

When the gutters in the floor finally run clear, Gloria releases the trigger on the washer, and the chimphouse falls eerily quiet. I climb up to the high walkway. Sue Ellen sees me coming and presses her puckered lips up against the caging. I sit with her for a while, coo a variety of meaningless, meaningful things into her Yoda ears. Through the far window, I glimpse Tom and Spock sitting next to each other on the boardwalk, a pair of war vets swapping stories. High on the tall risers next door Binky, Jethro, and Regis sit in a circle, quietly grooming each other. The floor below me sparkles. The contents of Susie's tickle trunk are strewn about, as if a village of happy children had stumbled upon a dream come true. Order has emerged from chaos. Light has won out over dark. And a week from now we'll do this all over again.

Binky Will Be Binky

OVER THE next week or so, my relationships with the chimps turn several interesting corners. Regis and Jethro increasingly seek me out for play. Pepper and Sue Ellen now routinely offer to groom me. Spock—who caused such a commotion the day I arrived, throwing his furniture and pounding on the walls—now greets me every morning with a quick juke of the shoulders and a request for more tea. From him this is high praise. Binky seems to consider me just one of the crew. We play with shovels and skipping ropes through the bars every day, and although he still throws fruits and vegetables at me, I suspect he could be doing so with a lot more precision—these days the tomatoes and cucumbers usually whistle past my head. Petra, who used to leave the room whenever I came near, now stays put and gazes directly into my eyes. Sometimes she lets out a long sigh, as if needing to make a confession. Yoko, her excitable sidekick, watches calmly from his usual spot in the windowsill.

Late one Friday afternoon, after delivering my smoothies, I sit in front of Jeannie's Room, face-to-face with troubled Rachel. She has a vacant expression on her face and is blowing spit bubbles through her lips. Her babies lie at her feet. Only the smallest fraction of her being seems to be conscious of my presence. Then Yoko and Petra climb down from upstairs and approach Rachel from behind.

When I arrived at Fauna, Gloria warned me to always remove myself from a one-on-one interaction when another chimpanzee appears. I have broken this rule only once before, when Regis and Jethro asked me to play, but this time the outcome seems much more unpredictable. Gloria explained that at a certain point in my friendships with the chimps, I become a very powerful member of their social dynamic. When the chimps finally show interest in spending time with me, it becomes much more likely that one of them will become jealous or overexcited and redirect these powerful emotions onto an innocent neighbor. One of the great ironies of this place is that although it was designed by the chimps and belongs to the chimps, the human caregivers still have considerable power over them. We serve them, we entertain them, we ultimately decide where and with whom each chimp is going to live. Gloria is the first to admit that although Fauna is a sanctuary, it is also a prison. And as in any prison, the inmates have many reasons to cozy up to the warden.

As Petra and Yoko approach, I back up from the caging and turn to leave. But it appears my fears were misplaced. Petra sits down beside Rachel and starts grooming her shoulder. Yoko climbs to the resting bench above us, lies down, and sinks into a deep sleep. The only excitement in the building at the moment is coming from Toby, who's been watching Rachel and me for the last twenty minutes from room no. 5 and is going nearly around the bend with anticipation. For Toby, the mere sight of a relative stranger interacting with two of his friends is enough to make him extremely anxious, perhaps even a bit jealous. So Gloria sits with Toby for a while, and I stay with Rachel. Petra continues to groom, then lies down on the floor to join Yoko in dreamland.

Soon Binky joins the party. He is in a playful mood, so I grab a wooden spoon from the kitchen and poke him with it through the bars. He spits at me, playfully, over and over. I dodge each spit, and when he finally runs out of saliva, he just sits and watches me, watches the spoon, seemingly racking his brain for his next practical joke. I think back to the first day we met, how instantly comfortable he was in my presence. It seems his extended family is beginning to feel the same way.

Then a contorted look comes over Binky's face, as if he's got terrible heartburn. I hear a small gurgle from deep inside him, then a muted gurgle-bark, and then a liquid gushing sound like a washing machine filling. I lean closer, wondering if he's unwell. Binky's cheeks begin to swell. And before I can bring my hands up in defense, I am struck square in the face with a perfectly aimed bolus of purple, strawberry-flavored smoothie-vomit.

The day Jim Mahoney began seeing the LEMSIP chimps as individuals was the day his world began to turn upside down. For me that day is today. As Binky gallivants around Jeannie's Room in triumph, I pluck my goopy glasses from my nose and wipe them on the hem of my shorts. I hear Gloria's laughter and Toby's excited huffing, and I realize that Binky will always be Binky. Petra will always be Petra, Rachel will always be Rachel, Tom will always be Tom. But this understanding comes with an unexpected consequence. As much as seeing each chimpanzee as a distinct being fills me with happiness, it also fills me with dread. Because real empathy has two sides, the joyful one and the grieving one. Everything that has happened to these apes, for better and for worse, is now a lot more personal to me. They have welcomed me into their world, and with this new citizenship comes a responsibility I'm totally unprepared for.

As if summoned by these thoughts, old man Tom appears on the far side of Grab Central. He saunters up to the bars to get a closer look at the mess Binky has made. Then he claps his hands three times. The hairs go up on my neck. Tom pushes himself up from his seated position, stands on all fours, and bounces up and down on his knuckles. He's looking directly at me. If this was one of the other chimps, I would immediately know what he was telling me. But this is tough old Tom. I look to Gloria for confirmation.

"Come and get me," she says with a smile. "He wants to play with you."

I stand up and walk over to Tom. At the red lines on the floor, I crouch down to his level, then bounce up and down a few times on my knuckles. For a surreal split second, I worry that I'm not doing it right, that my performance is lacking some essential chimp-ness and that Tom will see right through me. But Tom is an endlessly generous soul. He watches me bounce for a while, encouraging my amateur display by opening his mouth wide and huffing at me—*Huh! Huh! Huh!* Then he pounds his fist on the caging between us, turns on his heel, and quickly lopes out the back door of his room. He wants me to chase him. I begin to run. Finally, a moment of connection with Tom.

But then I stop myself. I'm not allowed to follow Tom around to the playroom, where he is now waiting for me at the porthole, because to do so I'd have to walk through Grab Central, breaking one of Fauna's most strictly enforced rules. I look over at Gloria, hoping she'll make an exception. Sadly, professionally, she refuses to budge.

"Tom will figure it out," she says, nodding. "He'll come back and play with you once he figures it out."

I wait until the lights go down. Tommie never returns.

Chapter 10

INNER SANCTUARY

Resilience is about abandoning the imprint of the past.
— BORIS CYRULNIK, quoted in *The Guardian*

A Thousand Bees

RACHEL IS ATTACKED on a Sunday.

It begins the way things usually begin in the chimphouse, with an otherworldly sound. I am standing in the walk-in fridge, struggling to load as many zucchinis as possible into my arms, when I hear a rhythmic clanging, like the bell of a distant buoy. When I return to the kitchen, the sound grows louder and Gloria whisks past me, her eyes fixed on a faraway spot near the roof. Her rubber shoes squeak faster than usual, so I fumble the vegetables to the counter and follow.

Rachel is slumped beside the door to the Sky Walk. Gloria had just locked this door—she needs the chimps to stay inside for a while so Mario and his crew can do some work on the islands—but Rachel is not happy with this arrangement. She is trying to get out, shoving the door handle methodically back and forth—*CLANG! CLANG! CLANG!*

"Maybe she left her babies outside," I say.

"Ah-ha!" Gloria runs up the spiral staircase to the top of the upper walkway and peers into the back playrooms. "Nope. Her babies are here."

Now Rachel is incensed, shaking the door nearly off its hinges, then pounding it with her fist. Gloria descends the stairs. Realizing that her demands are not going to be met, Rachel finally gives up, lets go of the door, and retreats to her walkway.

Gloria returns to the kitchen and breathes a long sigh. She flicks the kettle on for tea, and I go back to stocking the food trolleys. And then Rachel starts to scream.

The others join in briefly. Binky gives a haunting howl from the far side of the building. So does old man Tom. But as the chorus dies down, Rachel's screams change. Her voice grows more ragged and strained and desperate with every breath. Her wails become those of a banshee, bloodcurdling, deafening. I look up from the trolleys, fear running up my spine, and glimpse Gloria disappearing down the hallway toward the medical clinic. Up in the corner of her walkway, Rachel appears to have lost her mind.

She shivers wildly, as if being stung by a thousand bees. She grips the cage with both hands and lunges back and forth, jinking like a maniac. Her face is spread in a fear grimace, her eyes wide and darting, her lips pulled back to expose her teeth and gums. Although withered from decades of trauma, her body seems suddenly enormous, her hair on end, her chest and shoulders ballooning. A steady stream of urine splatters to the floor.

But none of this is as disturbing as what is happening to the chimpanzee hand curled around the caging in front of her. As she screams, Rachel feverishly gnashes the fingers on this hand with her fierce canines. When she bites down, her shrieks intensify and the hand pulls away. But a moment later the hand and fingers return, as if to taunt her, and the carnage continues. Soon the knuckles turn crimson. Rachel's lips are flecked with blood.

I've already seen that chimpanzees can be terribly violent with each other. But this scene is different from any other I've witnessed. No chimp is anywhere near Rachel right now. Those fingers are Rachel's fingers.

Imanishi

EVER SINCE research on wild primates began in the early 1950s, scientists have battled their own conclusions about them. The first shot in this battle was fired by the founder of Japanese primatology, Kinji Imanishi, when he suggested to his students that they give the monkeys they were studying individual names. This idea was met with fierce opposition and ridicule in American universities. Until then field researchers had always identified their animals using numerical or alphabetical codes. Naming the animals, claimed the critics, would humanize them in the eyes of their observers, which would risk the objectivity of Imanishi's results. Imanishi had committed the most heinous crime a biological anthropologist could in the 1950s: he had *anthropomorphized* his study subjects.

To a modern scientist, this argument now seems rather quaint. Any primatologist worth her salt names her animals. In the jungles of Suriname, we named more than one hundred monkeys as a matter of course. It made our jobs infinitely easier. By giving them names like Agnes or Banana or Mignon or Bruce, we were able to conjure up a much more immediate image of each monkey when we discussed or wrote about them. Agnes was old and frail. Bruce was a massive alpha. Their names reflected these qualities much more accurately than a numerical code ever could.

Eventually, Imanishi's ideas revolutionized the practice of primatology. His influence goes well beyond the mere naming of animals. And since the 1950s, countless scientists have removed countless more bricks from the wall erected by Western culture to separate humans from the rest of the animal kingdom, in particular from the great apes. In addition to the well-publicized discoveries of Goodall and others in the 1960s and '70s, we now know that chimps possess at least a rudimentary "theory of mind," a relatively advanced mental ability; they understand that their own thoughts, desires, and intentions may differ from those of their peers. We know that chimp communities have distinct cultures, a development first hinted at by Imanishi himself when he reported on the potato-washing traditions of Japanese macaques on Koshima Island. And perhaps most apropos to this story, we have learned that chimps can be altruistic and can show compassion, sympathy, and empathy toward others.

These are just a few of the more dramatic discoveries from the past half-century that illustrate how similar humans and chimpanzees are. With each breakthrough, a trait once thought to be uniquely human has been shown, instead, to be uniquely animal. Yet still the prohibition on anthropomorphism persists. So the question arises: if scientists agree that humans and chimpanzees are profoundly alike, do they contradict their own findings by insisting that a certain distance between humans and apes be maintained whenever we talk about them? Chimpanzees are not humans. They are a distinct species, and no scientist would argue otherwise. But we are closely related to them; according to one genetic analysis, about 99.4 percent of our functionally important DNA is the same. Humans and chimps are genetically closer than rats are to mice. In a pinch, if the blood type is a match, a chimp's blood can be safely transfused into a human.

Frans de Waal suggests that the continuing prohibition on anthropomorphizing chimpanzees smacks of something he calls *anthropodenial*, "a blindness to the humanlike characteristics of other animals, or the animal-like characteristics of ourselves," a blindness that emerges from our subconscious need to promote human exceptionalism at all costs. If a chimpanzee appears to be suffering grief or providing solace or experiencing happiness, why shouldn't we use these terms? After all, the science of neurology tells us they are likely the most accurate terms available.

So what does this have to do with Rachel attacking her own fingers? One of the most recent discoveries about human and chimpanzee similarities — the latest brick to be removed from the wall separating the apes from the apes — has to do with our ability to recover from extremely traumatic experiences, a topic about which Rachel knows a thing or two. In addition to Martin Brune's study on psychopathology in great apes (which might suggest that Yoko's vicious attack on Toby had more to do with Yoko's suffering in the lab than with Toby's outsider status), a recent paper in the *Journal of Trauma and Dissociation* demonstrates what lab workers and sanctuary staffers have long known: that the psychological distress exhibited by captive chimpanzees (including fear, depression, and self-mutilation) resembles very closely the distress of humans who suffer from trauma-related psychiatric disorders. This paper, entitled "Building an Inner Sanctuary," by Gay Bradshaw of the Kerulos Center, Theodora Capaldo and Lorin Lindner of NEAVS, and Gloria Grow, concerns two chimpanzees who spent more than a decade in a biomedical laboratory. It concludes that both chimps exhibit psychological symptoms of complex posttraumatic stress disorder (PTSD) consistent with those of humans who have suffered torture and imprisonment. In other words, the experiences chimpanzees go through in a typical biomedical laboratory render them as psychologically compromised as human victims of domestic violence or political and war prisoners.

Rachel was one of the two chimpanzees diagnosed with complex PTSD by Bradshaw and her colleagues. When Rachel mauls her own fingers, she is exhibiting something called "floating limb syndrome," in which traumatized animals mutilate their own limbs, believing them to be foreign objects.

The other chimpanzee was named Jean.

The Heart of a Chimpanzee

GLORIA MET Jean—or Jeannie, as she was better known—on her first visit to LEMSIP. Gloria, Richard, and Pat had already met the kids in Junior Africa, but now it was time to meet the adults. James Mahoney escorted the three past the biohazard signs and into the HIV units. Among the warnings he gave before they entered were a few requests: please don't react to the chimps, please don't mention the size of the cages, and please try not to cry.

What Gloria saw when Mahoney opened those doors haunts her to this day.

"To be honest, I couldn't have reacted if I'd tried," she says. "I was speechless. It felt like I was frozen in time." Gloria was seeing firsthand what she'd seen before only on video. A long, windowless trailer, the walls pockmarked with the impacts of countless anesthesia darts gone astray. And two rows of cages suspended a few feet off the floor like gigantic birdcages, each one with a large, panicking chimpanzee inside. In the first cage on the left was Jean.

"The moment the door opened, she started to spin," says Gloria, "and she just kept spinning and banging herself into the sides of the cage. She was screaming and urinating and defecating and frothing at the mouth, and saliva was shooting out. She was beside herself. Her eyes were literally rolling back in her head."

Mahoney asked everyone to back out of the unit quickly. Then, over the intercom, he called for a technician named Mike. When Mike arrived, he went into the unit by himself. Gloria peeked through a small window in the door to see what was going on.

"What I saw through that tiny window will always be with me. Mike walked over to Jeannie's cage and wrapped his arms around it as though embracing her entire world. She wasn't a small chimp, and she was out of control. She could have seriously hurt Mike. But she didn't. He reached his hands in as far as they would go and pressed his whole body against the bars. And then Jeannie pressed her body right back into him. Mike was comforting her. And that gesture of love completely broke my heart."

After about fifteen minutes, a strange calm came over Jeannie, and Mahoney allowed the visitors back into the unit. The moment she got inside, Gloria removed her mask, goggles, and gloves and pulled the hood off her Tyvek suit. Then she crouched next to Jean's cage, and the two of them locked gazes. "That was the first time a chimpanzee ever looked at me directly," says Gloria. "She looked so exhausted, and there was no doubt in my mind that her eyes were screaming, 'Help me! Help me get out of here!' I knew right then that Jeannie would become one of the great loves of my life."

Although Gloria didn't know it at the time, Jeannie was not on the list of lucky chimps destined for Fauna. She had been removed from research protocols at LEMSIP two years earlier because she'd suffered a full-blown nervous breakdown during an HIV study. Over more than twenty years in three different labs, Jeannie had seen it all. In her nine years at LEMSIP, she underwent countless invasive procedures, including vaginal washes; cervical, liver, and lymph-node biopsies; infection with multiple strains of HIV and hepatitis C; and more than two hundred knockdowns by dart gun. By the time Gloria met her, Jean was in appalling health, suffering from pelvic pain, asthma, autoimmune and upper respiratory issues, undiagnosed seizures, and tremors in her hands and feet. She was a completely dysfunctional, withdrawn individual who could suddenly snap into violent spinning episodes and self-mutilation. Her physical, emotional, and behavioral instability led to her removal from research. It also made Mahoney very hesitant to place Jeannie in a sanctuary, for he feared she would never be able to live comfortably in a social group. He was leaning toward euthanasia as a humane way of ending her misery.

When Mahoney told Gloria of his fears about Jean, however, Gloria wouldn't stand for euthanizing her. "How could I let that happen?" she asks now. "I was already in love." She begged Mahoney to release Jean to Fauna, promising to build a special private space in the chimphouse that would give Jeannie solitude and comfortable places to hide. She would also have ample opportunity to interact with humans and even other chimps if she wanted to. Ultimately, Gloria tells me, it was the lab technician Mike who convinced Mahoney to spare Jeannie's life. But Gloria followed through on her promise and built the place now known as Jeannie's Room.

"I believe we can make miracles happen every day if we just help someone in need," says Gloria. "I think that's why we're here on Earth. We need to be of service, or our lives will be empty. God put us here for a reason, and I believe that reason is service."

That was the only time Gloria mentioned God in our discussions. And it makes sense to me that she would speak about the divine only in reference to Jeannie. Because Jean's transformation after arriving at Fauna, although slow and far from perfect, was miraculous. In the lab, Jean had had prolonged bouts of anorexia, but within a few months at Fauna she began eating regularly and putting on weight. Over the years, the frequency of her dissociative outbursts decreased from several times a day to perhaps once a month, and eventually she was taken off tranquilizers. Although the old Jeannie became extremely anxious when another chimp touched her, after many years at Fauna she began seeking out other chimpanzees for solace when she was frightened or angry. These interactions were usually very awkward, given that she and her housemates were so lacking in social skills, but the fact that Jeannie would do something so naturally chimplike as seek physical reassurance from others was an uplifting sign.

As with many of the most troubled research chimps, Jeannie's favorite interactions were with humans. After just one year at Fauna, she allowed Gloria to touch her toes through the caging. A year later, Gloria was able to touch Jean's fingers, which held huge significance, because Jeannie used to attack her fingers uncontrollably. Eventually she came to enjoy human touch so much that she would pull Gloria's hand right into her enclosure, place it over her heart, and then clasp her own hand on top of it, as if she were about to share her most intimate thoughts with her best friend.

It only took Jeannie three days to work up the courage to go outside, and she loved it. After more than twenty years indoors, once she felt fresh air on her skin, there was no turning back. Most mornings she'd grab a bunch of bananas and a cup of hot tea and amble outside and sit with her arms in the air, her face tilted to the sky, and the cool breezes off the St. Lawrence soothing her body and mind. She took great pleasure in simple things like drinking her tea or arranging the enrichment items in her room just so, or being chased around the caging by a human. Gloria recalls how challenging it was to pretend that Jean was a fast runner. Jeannie seemed to think of herself as a world-class sprinter, when in actuality her health issues and numerous phobias meant she moved slower than a sloth.

In the lab and at Fauna, Jean would often slip into a serene, self-soothing trance. First she would methodically arrange her peanuts, raisins, monkey chow, and other small pieces of food in a perfect circle on the floor around her. Then she would lie down on her side in the middle of this circle, carefully pick up a piece of food, then place it slowly in her mouth and begin chewing. She did this unconsciously, systematically, like a Buddhist practicing a koan. Gloria would often watch Jeannie soothe herself like this for more than an hour.

Many of the most traumatized apes at Fauna dissociate from reality when they feel extremely anxious. After a stressful episode, Rachel, Petra, and Chance all go into a trancelike state, an inner sanctuary to which they escape when the world becomes too much to handle.

Jeannie's partial recovery and the rehabilitation of all the Fauna chimps began with something very simple: for the first time in their lives, they had choices. In the lab or the zoo, every aspect of their existence was imposed on them. Now they could choose what to eat and where to eat it. They could choose where to sleep, what to sleep on, whom to sleep next to, and whether or not to sleep in. To some extent, they could choose whom to live with and where to spend their days. They could be inside or outside or both. They could be alone or with friends. They could be with friends and choose to leave at any time. These may sound like trivial choices, but such small decisions lie at the very heart of what it means for an ape to live a full and dignified life. It may sound paradoxical to speak of dignity for an animal who has technically been "liberated" but is still behind bars, but there are many landmarks on the long journey toward self-determination, which has to start somewhere. Dignity begins when an animal feels that she is the chief instrument of change in her life.

Jeannie's troubles never fully disappeared. But slowly, by reading her body language and becoming familiar with her cues, Gloria began to understand what would trigger her outbursts. Certain times of the year were more difficult than others. Jean had a really hard time during the short days of February and March, when the shadows were long on the chimphouse walls. Gloria wonders if those months might have been when new studies, and therefore new surgeries, began in the lab. Making such discoveries took years of careful observation, as Gloria spent more and more time in communion with each individual chimp.

Gloria often says that her primary job at Fauna is to listen to the chimps. This might seem like a banal comment, but it is actually quite revolutionary. Gloria has become so knowledgeable about each chimpanzee, so sensitive to the mixture of moods and memories that are continually reshaping the emotional atmosphere of the chimphouse, that she has become much more than a caregiver. Among humans, this level of intimacy is usually found only in the relationship between trauma victims and their therapists.

Gay Bradshaw's paper on PTSD in chimpanzees is part of an emerging area of study, founded by Bradshaw herself, called trans-species psychology. The core message of this field is that human and animal minds are not distinct, as conventional wisdom holds, but are inextricably linked by our shared evolutionary history. The trans-species psychologist seeks to translate the latest scientific understanding of animal consciousness into human ethics, law, and culture. The goal? To usher in a new paradigm for the way humans relate to animals.

Bradshaw and her colleagues suggest that if trauma symptoms

are so similar in humans and chimps, then the methods we use to treat a traumatized person might also be useful in treating a troubled chimpanzee. "Discussions have shifted from *if* ape psychotherapeutic treatment is reasonable," writes Bradshaw, "to *how* it might be effected." Gloria has been intuiting this idea for years in the chimphouse.

Trans-species psychology has been called the "science of the heart." It involves listening to what an animal is saying, however the animal is able to say it. Therapists agree that a basic stage of recovery in a traumatized human is the reconstruction of the "trauma story," the narrative of what she went through and how those experiences still affect her. And even though the chimps of Fauna can't speak to Gloria in words, they have other ways to tell her their stories — through gestures and sounds, through rage and calm.

"Knowing, loving, and caring for chimps means not only getting into their mind," Gloria once told me, "it also means getting into that sacred place, the heart of a chimpanzee." When she said this, I wasn't really sure what she meant. But now, having been at Fauna for almost two months, I think I get it. The long and difficult process by which Gloria came to understand Jeannie and her trauma was the same process by which Jeannie began to heal. This is a very powerful idea: that the act of empathizing with a troubled animal may be a fundamental ingredient in her recovery. It suggests that healing and rehabilitation, at least for animals as social as apes, depend upon the health of our relationships.

The Rain Dance of Chancey-Pants

SOME RELATIONSHIPS are more demanding than others. Take my budding friendship with Chance, who, like Rachel, is one of the most disturbed chimpanzees at Fauna. If I didn't know better, I'd think Chance hated my guts, because she is always trying to scare me. Whenever I approach her room or simply walk past it, Chance makes a loud puckering sound with her lips and jukes her shoulder at me as if she's about to charge. Even though there is heavy caging between us, until very recently her aggressive feints and angry noises always made me jump. But as I've learned more about her personality and her awful childhood, I've come to understand that when Chance tries to frighten me, she is actually trying to reach out to me. Chance is desperate to have others acknowledge her existence, and she has been this way since the day she was born.

Chance was born by cesarean at LEMSIP in 1983, to a mother who had been infected with, and tested positive for, hepatitis B. Babies born to infected mothers stand a fifty-fifty chance of getting the disease, which can take up to five years to show up in blood tests. So in order to protect the other infants in the lab from accidental infection (which would ruin their scientific value as "clean" test subjects), it was decided that the new infant would be housed alone, in a separate room from all the other chimpanzees, for the first five years of her life. The staff decided to name her Chance, a reference to her odds of being infected.

Those first five years were torture for Chance. Taken from her mother immediately after birth, she was whisked away to live by herself in a tiny baboon cage, with almost no contact with other members of her species. The only interactions she had were with the lab techs who were usually either refilling her food or water or knocking her unconscious with a dart gun so that her cage could be cleaned. If it was traumatic to be shot with a dart gun while surrounded by nine of your friends, imagine what it must have been like to go through it completely alone.

Chance's cage was in a room next door to the LEMSIP cage-washing machine, which apparently operated nearly twenty-four hours a day and made a terrible racket. Even today, Chance hates Cleaning Day at Fauna. The splash and howl of the pressure washer always sends her spinning in her cage, as if memories of her lonely childhood were suddenly flooding her mind.

At the age of five, Chance emerged from solitary confinement completely broken. She'd become intensely neurotic, aggressive, and, to put it lightly, uncooperative. She was psychotic, biting her fingers, pulling her hair out, unable to reconcile her terrifying new surroundings—a windowless trailer filled with nine other manic chimpanzees—with the deprivation she'd suffered for so long. The ultimate irony of Chance's story is that she was born lucky—blood tests eventually proved she hadn't caught hepatitis from her mother. Her cruel incarceration had been totally unnecessary.

Chance was used in only four studies during her fourteen years at LEMSIP. She was eventually retired from protocols because of her psychological instability. She spent her last six years at LEMSIP sitting in her cage and waiting for the next lab tech to enter her unit, when her next bout of insanity would begin.

Chance looks different from all the other chimps at Fauna. Her hair has a beautiful silver tinge, which makes her body seem to shimmer when she sits outside in the sun. Chance also sounds different from the others in a quite adorable way. She hasn't quite mastered the Bronx cheer, which Binky uses to perfection: when Chance wants to get your attention, she makes a strange blowing sound, like a child learning to whistle, as if she's unable to press her lips together firmly enough. It is a sound all her own, and now it is just as effective at getting our attention as Binky's mighty *pwbbt!* or Tom's clapping.

Now that I know what she's been through, when Chance tries to scare me, I try to ignore it or laugh it off, and I stay right where I am. When I stick to my guns like this, Chance eventually stops acting out and starts to relax. Once she realizes I am not here to hurt her, Chancey-Pants begins to lower the wall between her and me, the wall she's been building, as a matter of survival, ever since she was born.

I've recently discovered that Chance loves to play with tennis balls. When I approach with one, she'll stick her arm through the porthole as if she wants to play catch. When I throw it to her, she'll usually catch it and bring it inside her enclosure, claiming it as hers. But then she'll reach the ball out through the porthole, and the real game will begin. She'll throw the ball as far away from me as she possibly can, usually aiming for the storage room next to the kitchen or the hallway leading to the observation room. The farther she can throw it—that is, the farther she can make me go to retrieve it—the happier she is. We do not play catch, in other words. We play fetch. When she makes an especially good shot—as when she bounces a left-handed curveball into a bucket of wash water in the storage room—she will almost collapse in excitement, huffing her chimp laugh and shaking her head, taunting me the way only a chimpanzee can. But as quickly as her excitement arrives, it is over. Chance does not like to feel overwhelmed, even by happy emotions. She always seems to be holding herself in check, not letting her enthusiasm boil over lest she lose control again.

One day not long ago, I had prepared a trolley full of tea for the chimps, and Gloria decided to give Chancey first dibs in an effort to cheer her up. Chance had had a couple of tough days. She'd been living in a large group of chimps for almost a week, and the stress was beginning to wear on her. Gloria sometimes offers Chance the opportunity to live with a larger group to see if she can manage to get along and perhaps achieve a small measure of social standing. But this time it wasn't going well. Even the calmest individuals, like Tom and Pepper, had displayed at her through the caging just the day before, sending Chance into a tizzy. Now she had closed herself into a privacy room. Jeannie used to do this regularly. It signaled that she needed some solitude, a break from the relentless social obligations of living in a large group.

Gloria rolled the trolley of carefully balanced cups of tea over to Chance's porthole. And just as Gloria realized her mistake, Chance reached out, grabbed the trolley by the corner, and gave it a violent shake. Hot tea went everywhere. Cardboard cups clattered to the floor, and Gloria jumped back, just missing a scalding. "Chancey!" Gloria roared, her emotions overcoming her usual control. "Why would you do that?" Unperturbed, Chance simply let go of the trolley and dropped to the floor to inspect the river of tea flowing into her room.

Gloria returned to my side of the counter, clearly infuriated. But as she flicked on the kettle to boil more water, I could hear her muttering, over and over under her breath, "She's in control. She's in control. She's in control." Among the many mantras Gloria relies on to get through difficult moments, this is one of the most important. Because it doesn't matter how frustrating her day is or if any of her plans actually reach fruition. Her goal, above all, is to make the chimps feel, every single day, that they have some control and agency over their own lives. Chance had the opportunity to spill a trolley full of tea that day, and she did so, much to her amusement. The fact that Gloria and I then had to mop the floor and remake the tea is inconsequential.

Gloria eventually returned to Chance's porthole, this time with a single cup of tea on the trolley, and Chance happily took it and placed it on the resting bench to cool. Then she and Gloria spent the next fifteen minutes playing tickle-chase together.

Last week, on a particularly humid afternoon, I noticed Chance pacing back and forth in her privacy room. Her mood was even more anxious than usual, and every time she passed a particular spot she would sit down, position her body so she could see out onto Island Three, hook her fingers through the caging, and start swaying back and forth. After about thirty seconds, she'd get up and resume her pacing. This sequence went on for about a half-hour. Just as I was about to call Gloria over to make sure Chance was all right, a flash of light filled the chimphouse, followed by an earsplitting boom, and I realized what was causing her upset.

In the wild, when a thunderstorm approaches his territory, the alpha-male chimpanzee will often perform an elaborate ritual known as the rain dance. He will sway back and forth, almost in slow motion, as if prostrating himself to some higher power. Then, when the thunder and lightning reach a crescendo, he will begin a powerful dominance display, throwing branches, screaming and charging as if possessed. Although Chance is no alpha male, she seems to have her own version of this rain dance, complete with her own rituals of surrender. As the rain clattered onto the chimphouse roof that muggy afternoon, Chancey-Pants continued pacing and swaying, as if submitting to some of her own invisible demons.

Like Jeannie, Chance also has a unique way of checking out from reality after a stressful episode. Her eyes roll back in her head as she sits cross-legged in the lotus position, and her consciousness appears to entirely leave her physical body. Then she begins a surreal pantomime. With her right hand, she lifts an imaginary weight from the floor and passes it in front of her body, then lowers it back to the ground with her left hand. She'll do this over and over, for up to an hour at a time.

As I watched Chance that rainy afternoon, I realized that my affection for her had grown unexpectedly strong over the past few weeks. She is such a difficult chimp, but such a resilient survivor. After everything she's been through, it is ultimately up to her to overcome her trauma. Gloria, her sisters, and Kim can help, but no matter how hard they work, everyone knows it is the chimpanzees themselves who are doing the real heavy lifting here.

Gloria worries that Chance will become as mentally unstable and antisocial as Jeannie was or as Rachel is today. Ever since her mother-figure, Annie, died all those years ago, and with the recent addition of the zoo chimps, Chance has been on a slow downward spiral. But Gloria is under no illusions that every research chimpanzee can be rehabilitated to the point that they can live comfortably in a large group. Jeannie never could, nor could Billy Jo. Although she continues to hope that Chance will find the strength and confidence to make group living work for her, Gloria is becoming resigned to the likelihood that Chance will spend most of her time alone.

"Every time Chance goes into a group, she starts something," says Gloria. "Either screaming or fighting. She gets terribly anxious. And we've only recently started to realize that every time she does this, she's actually asking to be put in a locked room. And if she's always asking to be alone, then we need to pay attention to that. Let her be alone. Let her be alone. Let. Her. Be. Alone."

The Meaning of Freedom

CHANCE'S STORY provides a window onto another common misconception about animals in captivity. Many of us assume that the animal wants nothing more than to be freed from its cage. But for most, after years and years behind bars, that is not the case. Routine is of the utmost importance, giving them a sense of order and predictability in a world in which they are relatively powerless. And routine for them means life behind bars. For an animal in a cage, especially for a chimpanzee in a biomedical laboratory, an enclosure is actually the safest place he knows.

Gloria learned this lesson firsthand from Chance. A few years back, when only one of the islands was finished, Chance was outside exploring when she managed to slip beneath the electric fence. Suddenly she found herself on the next island over, with the other chimps screaming in a mixture of excitement and fear, while her human caregivers pleaded with her to go back under the fence.

Chance wasn't sure what to do. She began walking nervously all the way around the chimphouse on all fours. Gloria and her staff followed as closely as they could, and soon Chance was running along the patio toward the front door of the building. But instead of trying to open the door to return to her enclosure, Chance did something unexpected and completely heartbreaking. Back then the old LEMSIP cage was on display just a few feet from the front door. In her hysterical state, Chance ran right up to this cage, gripped the door with one hand, and yanked as hard as she could. The door was locked, but that didn't stop her—she just kept yanking and yanking. All she wanted was to get inside that cage.

This was the moment when Gloria realized how institutionalized her chimps are. To the humans at Fauna, that cage represents suffering and injustice. But to the panicked Chance, it was the only place she could feel truly safe at that moment.

For severely institutionalized animals, freedom is far from absolute; it is more a state of mind. The goal at Fauna, then, is to change the concept of freedom that each chimp holds in his head. When they first arrived at the sanctuary, the Fauna chimps were terrified by their new surroundings. Now that fear is gone. When the islands were first opened, many of the chimps took weeks to venture outside, and when they did, they avoided the grass because they'd never felt anything but concrete beneath their feet. Now the islands are simply another part of their world, and many of them love the grass. Although outdoor enclosures are every sanctuary director's dream — what better expression of freedom is there than fresh air and sunshine on the skin? — some lab chimps take a while to warm up to them. When Gloria's friend Carole Noon opened her impressive island complex at Save the Chimps in Florida, she quickly realized that some of her chimps would never get to enjoy them. Her most troubled individuals refused to go anywhere unless they could hold on to steel caging the whole way. After living at the infamous Coulston Foundation for decades, they needed the feeling of steel between their fingers for reassurance — a surreal twist on the notion of a security blanket. So Noon built a winding trail of steel fencing leading from the indoor enclosures out onto her islands, ensuring that even the most cautious chimps could experience the nourishing Florida sunshine while still holding onto their "cage."

If the image of an elderly chimpanzee carefully inching her way along an absurd stretch of fencing seems incongruous with the idea of freedom, you are beginning to understand the difficulties of working in a chimpanzee sanctuary. Gloria knows her chimps will never be free in the truest sense of the word — to return them to the jungles of Africa upon retirement would be a cruel death sentence. But she also knows that freedom is relative, and it comes in all shapes and sizes. When Chance locks herself into a privacy room

for some quiet time, or when Rachel carries her gorilla babies outside with her, or when Sue Ellen obsesses over arranging her nest
just so, or when Petra fiddles with her key chain, Gloria remembers
her real role at Fauna. Although the rest of the world views her as a
savior to these chimps, she doesn't see it that way: "The only way I
could be their savior is if I had prevented what happened to them in
the lab." Instead, Gloria considers herself their custodian, the person responsible for ensuring that the chimps get whatever definition
of "freedom" they can handle on any given day. Be it fresh air or
sunshine or permission to disappear deep inside an inner sanctuary
of their own making, it is up to Gloria to give them what they need.

For a profoundly troubled animal, real freedom may come only at
the end of life. Gloria has never provided this sort of liberation to
any of her chimpanzees, but she has witnessed it blow onto her farm
a number of times over the years. Although she is loath to make dis-
tinctions, her most difficult such moment occurred on New Year's
Day of 2007.

For two months that winter, Gloria had spent every evening at
Jeannie's side, trying to comfort the love of her life. She watched
as Jean's breathing became labored, as her body weakened, as her
spirit grew dim. Jeannie had been refusing her usual cups of tea
since before Christmas, so Gloria knew what was coming. But
knowing didn't make it any easier when, just after dawn on January 1, Gloria heard old man Tom let loose a heart-rending howl as
she was walking the boardwalk to the chimphouse. She knew right
away that her Jeannie was gone.

Ever since my arrival at Fauna, Gloria has avoided talking with
me about Jeannie. She made it clear from the start that the death of
a chimp, and especially Jean's death, were subjects she would rather
not discuss. The irony is that these are the very stories that have the
power to move the public, the stories she feels great pressure to tell
when speaking to reporters, television crews, or large audiences.
"People need to know the truth," she told me when I asked what in-

spired her to allow me, a writer, to come and live at Fauna. But the more of the truth I learn, the more I understand why Gloria avoids it so deftly at every turn. The truth can devour you. The truth is why she does what she does. Maybe that's all we need to know.

"Chimpanzees have a way of stealing our hearts," Gloria told me the night after we watched Rachel maul her own fingertips, as we sat in my little apartment with enough wine in our systems to loosen some truths from their moorings. "They give us their hearts. They break our hearts. They forgive with their hearts. They are all heart. And then, their hearts are the ultimate sacrifice." Gloria was speaking as directly as she ever would about Jeannie.

Days after that dreadful morning at the start of 2007, Gloria stood over Jean's eviscerated body, holding her best friend's heart in her hands. The failed organ was terribly damaged, the stress from untold rounds of hepatitis and HIV infections, biopsies, and decades of psychological trauma having turned it into an exhausted, fatty, shapeless mass.

Perhaps there is no sanctuary, either in the Quebec countryside or deep inside the soul, that can compare to the one Jeannie was finally retired to. But Gloria will always believe that even the most troubled animal deserves a second chance at life. Jeannie almost didn't make it to Fauna—hers was a narrow escape. And the years she spent here were unquestionably her best. When death finally swept her away, Jean was better off in every sense of the phrase.

An Ancient Ritual

THREE DAYS after Rachel attacked herself, I am in the kitchen restocking the nighttime bags when Rachel appears in Jeannie's Room. She grabs the caging and gently pounds on it with her foot. Then she climbs up to the resting bench and does the same thing. She wants my attention, so I push my trolley of nuts and monkey chow out of the way and slowly approach her.

When I get close, I spot a mischievous look in Rachel's eye, and sure enough, she quickly jumps down from the bench, grabs the caging with her hands, and flips her body over backward like an Olympic gymnast on a set of rings. "Look at you!" I say, encouraging her. "Look at you!" And at the sound of my voice, she drops to the floor, spins around to face me, and starts bouncing up and down on all fours. I do the same, crouching and bouncing my six-foot-three frame up and down. She starts to laugh, and I do my best to impersonate her huffing. And then she takes off, ambling next door into the wake-up room (usually reserved for chimps recovering from general anesthesia), where a large hammock is hung. By the time I get there, she has disappeared behind the hammock. But a moment later, she punches the wall in excitement and moseys out of the room again, ending up back where she started, in Jeannie's Room. She pulls herself up to the resting bench, we peer into each other's eyes, our noses less than an inch apart, her breath like compost, her lower lip hanging open—and then the whole routine begins again. The rings, the bouncing, the chase, the hammock, back to the bench, the stare. We do the circuit four or five times. My back begins to ache from all the bouncing. And then, just as I expect Rachel to take off again into the wake-up room, she does something entirely different. She spins around, pushes her back straight up against the caging between us, and sits down. I think I know what this means, but I don't dare assume. Then Gloria appears at my side.

"Use this," she says, handing me a wooden back-scratcher. I am stunned. A little nervous. I take the back-scratcher, reach out, and touch it to Rachel's rigid back. A satisfied breath escapes her nostrils, and her shoulders relax. Gloria backs off. She's been watching us the whole time, keeping an eye on me, making sure I didn't break her no-touching rules. But she's also been enjoying watching Rachel, who reminds her so much of her Jean, interact with someone new.

When I realize that Gloria has been watching us, I suddenly feel ashamed for how I reacted a few days ago, when we both witnessed

Rachel attacking herself up near the Sky Walk door. My first feeling was one of utter sadness; Gloria didn't see it, but I quietly began to weep. Gloria, on the other hand, just stood there stoically, a Dixie cup of juice mixed with antipsychotics in her hand.

For the next half-hour, with Gloria observing from afar, I sit in front of Jeannie's old room and groom Rachel with the back-scratcher. In no time, she is directing me to where she likes it best: behind the ears, along her shoulders, in the small of her back. Sometimes she spins around and I use the back-scratcher to pick at her fingernails with her, tend to the scabs that have grown over her most recent self-inflicted wounds. Then she turns around, bends over, and pushes her impressive buttocks against the caging, her tender sex skin just beginning to swell. I poke her bum as gently as I can, the way I've seen Jethro and Regis do it. Rachel leaves it up there until she's sure I'm finished.

It seems a mockery of life that one consequence of extreme psychological trauma can be the turning of the body against it-self—that after being devoured on the inside, you might be left with an appetite for your own flesh. That is how it was for Jeannie and how it still is, on occasion, for Rachel. It is horrifying to watch an ape lose its immunity to itself.

But it also seems a triumph of life that primates have evolved the capacity, through the grooming process, to console and soothe a fellow group mate, to put another's mind at ease, to reassure her and even help her heal. This is the first time I have ever groomed a chimpanzee. I am participating in an ancient custom, an age-old healing ritual, even if by wooden proxy.

Chapter 11

WAR MEMORIALS

Every great movement must experience three
stages: ridicule, discussion, adoption.

— JOHN STUART MILL

How to Repair Your Self

GLORIA AND I SIT in the departure lounge of Montreal's Trudeau
Airport. We have an hour to kill before our flight to Washing-
ton, D.C., so I've brought a book to read, *The Darling,* by Russell
Banks. But it looks like I'm not going to get any reading done.

"I think one of the veins in my forehead is going to burst," says
Gloria as she struggles to liberate a three-day-old airport sandwich
from a thick shroud of military-grade plastic wrap.

Gloria is feeling a little more anxious than usual today. Tomorrow morning she will give one of the most important speeches of
her life. Tomorrow afternoon she will attend some of the most important meetings of her life. And the day after tomorrow, Gloria will take part in a historic gathering of movers and shakers in
the movement to free all chimpanzees from biomedical research in
America. After years of struggle to have the bill put on a committee
agenda, the U.S. Congress is finally ready to be briefed on the Great
Ape Protection Act.

But there may be another reason for Gloria's feelings of anxiety. Three years ago, she was sitting in this same departure lounge,
waiting for another important flight, just hours after Billy Jo died.

• • •

Of all the chimps who have lived at Fauna, Billy Jo had the most difficult time rediscovering what it meant to be a chimp. Before he was sold into research, Billy was forced to work in the circus, and when he wasn't under the big top he was taken on car rides, fishing trips, and regular excursions to Dairy Queen. Raised by humans since infancy, having contact with just one female chimp, Sue Ellen, in childhood, Billy was dependent on humans for all his social and emotional needs. According to Gloria, Billy thought he was more human than chimp.

In the lab he was hostile, uncooperative, and aggressive. One day, while recovering from surgery, Billy chewed both of his thumbs off. At Fauna his troubles continued. He rejected the other chimps, much preferring to interact with humans, and eventually the others rejected him. In attacks similar to the one on Toby, they severely beat Billy a number of times. That is why he usually chose to isolate himself.

Billy was a huge chimp, and his aggressive displays were frightening to witness. Like Sue Ellen, Billy had had his teeth knocked out when he was young, and as he charged toward an unsuspecting human on the other side of the caging, Billy would peel back his lips to reveal pink, lumpy gums, conjuring up the image of a lunatic middle linebacker, mouth guard in place, about to lower the boom. According to Gloria, however, Billy had a heartbreaking way of negotiating with his human caregivers in lieu of violence. "He would start doing handstands or lip flips, just like in the circus," she tells me. "As if he were saying, 'If I entertain you, will you not hurt me?'"

A recent study by Gay Bradshaw and her colleagues, "Developmental Context Effects on Bicultural Post-Trauma Self Repair in Chimpanzees," published in *Developmental Psychology*, analyzes the effects of trauma and captivity on a chimpanzee's identity. This work makes a convincing argument for why Billy Jo had such a hard time in the lab and at Fauna. While many of his group mates exhibited the classic symptoms of PTSD, Billy's psychological issues fit a different but no less debilitating diagnosis. According to Bradshaw, Billy was probably suffering from "a severe, recurring major depression," the result of a species-identity disorder caused by his being cross-fostered as a youngster. "It should be noted," writes Bradshaw, "that much or all of his distress derived *externally* from the social context—chimpanzees who rejected him for who he was . . . The perennial 'mismatch' between internal and external contexts resulted in prolonged psychological distress."

The real topic of this study by Bradshaw is resilience, or the ability to recover after traumatic experiences—something psychologists refer to as "self-repair." Bradshaw compares Billy's inability to deal with anxiety and stress to the psychological struggles of two other Fauna residents, Tom and Regis. She concludes that Tom has been able to deal with stress more easily than Billy and has built relationships with both humans *and* chimpanzees because he was raised by his biological mother in an African jungle for his first three years. These experiences "formed the basis for a resilient self . . . that permitted psychological survival after 30 years of traumatizing procedures, including isolated living and other deprivations."

In contrast to Tom, Billy showed compromised resilience. By force of circumstance, and despite all that Fauna provides, Billy was not able to rebuild a healthy sense of self. And how could he, really, when he probably didn't know which self—human or chimp—was the one that needed rebuilding?

"I stayed with Billy as long as I could," says Gloria, her eyes shut as she chews her airport sandwich, recounting the day Billy died. "I held him, hugged him, gave him a kiss goodbye. Then everyone told me I had to leave." The next day, Gloria's friend and mentor Carole Noon was moving a group of chimpanzees from the Coulston Foundation in New Mexico to her sanctuary in Florida. Gloria had promised to help her Sanctuary Sister, so she made a difficult decision, one that still haunts her. Instead of staying with her stricken family and saying a proper goodbye to Billy, she left for the airport and spent the next hour sobbing by herself at the gate.

And then something strange happened.

"I saw a monk," says Gloria, opening her eyes.

"A monk?"

"An older gentleman wearing brown robes. He sat down directly across from me." Gloria smiles as she sinks deeper into her chair and takes a big bite of her sandwich. "He was the spitting image of the Dalai Lama."

Gloria tells me this monk was carrying a small satchel. Moments after sitting down, he stood up, placed the bag on his seat, and gave Gloria a questioning look. Anxious to mask her grief in the presence of such serenity, she nodded in agreement as best she could, and the monk walked away. Then Gloria took a closer look at the satchel, and her breath caught in her throat.

"I always knew monks loved animals. But this guy was special. His bag was covered in pictures of dogs and cats. I mean totally covered. And all I remember thinking was, oh my God, oh my God, oh my God. This is a sign. This is a message. A monk just asked me to look after his animals."

Gloria realizes there are more responsible ways to react when you see someone abandon a bag in an airport departure lounge. She doesn't care. "I'm allowed my spiritual side," she says. And that's not the end of the story.

The monk returned and gave her a warm smile for watching his bag. At the preboarding announcement, he stood, draped his bag over his shoulder, and got in line.

Now Gloria narrows her eyes and raises her index finger like an amateur sleuth. "I watched him at the gate. I watched them check his ticket. I watched him walk into the walkway. I needed to know where he was sitting. If there's ever a time to sit close to a monk, it's the day you lose a great love in your life."

So when Gloria boarded, she looked for the bald man in a brown robe. When she got to the last row of seats and still hadn't found him, she turned around and walked the length of the plane again. Then she checked the bathrooms and the common areas. Her monk, her messenger, was gone.

Gloria turns to face me, shakes her sandwich accusingly. "You ever lose someone on a plane like that?"

"Nope."

"Me neither. Monks are very important people. You've heard of Eckhart Tolle?"

"Yes. He helped a good friend of mine once."

"He's helped me a lot over the years, too. I once drove to Toronto to see him speak. Normally, I only drive that far to see one of two things."

"Two things?"

Gloria nods and chews. "Chimpanzees and Bruce Springsteen."

Two Percent

OUR FLIGHT is announced. We get in line, check our tickets, board the plane. As we taxi to the runway, Gloria continues where she left off.

"I read somewhere that only two percent of the population is truly conscious. I mean truly aware. Sensitive to things. Two percent. Do you know what that means? It means every time I lead a tour at Fauna or give a speech like the one I'm giving tomorrow, the chances that I'll make a real connection with someone is around two percent."

Gloria fiddles with her seat belt. She is growing more and more anxious. We're hurtling down the runway now, but I don't think that's the reason for her nerves. The engines howl. We lift off. Gloria launches into a restless monologue.

"Two percent. That's pretty bad odds. Back when I started talking about the chimps, I never imagined it would become a sales pitch. I always figured I'd show people the tiny cage, or I'd tell their stories, or I'd show some videos, or they'd meet the chimps, and that would be that. They'd learn what the chimps have been through, and their lives would be changed, just as mine was. Because how do you walk away from that knowledge? I was sure no one could walk away from that.

"So how do you make a lasting moment? How do you improve on two percent? God, I wish I knew. Sometimes when you say something, you catch them. You see it happen, and you think, OK, let's work on that. I take people around the farm. I show them the trees, the flowers, the turtle laying her eggs, the goslings, the baby ducks, the pigs, my dogs. *Come on, come on. Where am I catching you?* You have to keep trying until you find that one thing. And then I take them to see the chimps."

The Fauna sanctuary receives a small amount of financial support from some nongovernmental organizations. But almost all of Gloria's operating budget, which is more than $250,000 a year, must be met by donations from the public. Gloria recently started the Fauna Lifetime Care Fund, which she hopes will eventually provide a more reliable income stream for the sanctuary. Not only does she have to act as a lobbyist now and then, she is also Fauna's primary fundraiser.

"So maybe we watch Tom in the Sky Walk," she continues, "and I tell the story about when Tom first met Pat. And then we go to the mezzanine, where they meet the amazing Pepper, my love Sue Ellen, and poor Rachey Rach. And then maybe someone will start screaming and Pep will come over and hug Sue Ellen, and that might be it. *Ah ha! Did you see that? They hugged each other!* So then you tell stories about love, about relationships. And bang! They make a connection. Those people will never forget. But it's so hard. And it's only getting harder. I can always express myself well when the chimps are there, but it's very different when you're somewhere else. Like in Congress. We're using the chimps to save the chimps. It makes me sick sometimes. How do I expand that almighty two percent?

"Or maybe I'm talking to someone on a plane. We've just taken off, and the captain has turned off the seat-belt sign, and everyone is waiting for one thing: the drinks trolley. So I make the analogy with life in a laboratory. Because waiting for the drinks on an airplane is a lot like waiting for feeding time at the lab. Everyone is anxious, agitated, angry, bored. Everyone is eyeing their caregivers, or flight attendants. *When are they going to feed me? Are they going to ignore me? Are they going to forget me? Are they going to cure my boredom? Look at me! Don't forget me! I have important needs!*

"I've lost some amazing loves, some amazing ambassadors. Pablo, Billy, Jeannie, Donna Rae, Annie. No one wanted to hear their voices, and now they're gone. And now we're running out of time. That's the point. Time is running out. That's why Tom is so important. His story. His life. Everyone needs to know about Tom. And Pepper. And Susie Goose. And Yoko. The first HIV-positive chimpanzees to ever breathe fresh air."

Gloria stops talking. The plane levels out and the seat-belt sign goes dark. The drinks trolley arrives. We both order beer. Gloria sighs as she snaps open her can of Bud.

"How monklike," she says, taking a long swig. "I'm not even freakin' thirsty."

What Would Archaeologists Think?

"I'VE DONE the math," says Rob Shumaker, the director of orang-utan research at the Great Ape Trust in Iowa, triumphantly. "We each take 125 chimps, and Bob's your uncle!"

It's the morning after our flight, and we're sitting in the back of a sweltering shuttle bus bound for Capitol Hill. It's seven A.M., wiltingly humid, and the inbound traffic from Crystal City is snarled. The other passengers laugh nervously at Shumaker's joke. Today promises to be a historic day, and everyone in this bus has a critical role to play.

If something were to happen to this vehicle on its way into D.C. — if we were T-boned by a tractor-trailer, say, or if the air conditioning suddenly gave out and the windows jammed — the movement to free chimpanzees from invasive research in American labs would stand to lose a significant portion of its senior leaders. Many of the biggest names are here: along with Rob Shumaker, there is Theodora Capaldo, president of the New England Anti-Vivisection Society (NEAVS); Patti Regan, director of the Center for Great Apes; April Truitt, cofounder of the Primate Rescue Center; Jen Feuerstein, director of Save the Chimps; Linda Brent, president and director of Chimp Haven and the National Chimp Sanctuary System; Kathleen Conlee, director of Program Management and Animal Research Issues at the Humane Society of the United States (HSUS). And, of course, Gloria Grow, the only Sanctuary Sister from north of the border.

As we inch toward the Capitol, the passengers grow quiet, and Gloria shoots me a quick glance. She is the epitome of a calm urban professional in her charcoal power suit, black-rimmed glasses, and three-inch heels, with perfectly done hair and makeup. But I can sense her growing unease. She has thirteen troubled souls on her mind—no, nineteen souls. The closer we get to the Hill, the louder and more insistent their voices become.

After going through security at the Rayburn House Office Building, we walk some of America's most iconic hallways, the marble floors and vaulted ceilings made famous by countless Hollywood political thrillers. We reach Rayburn Room 2247, home of the House Energy and Commerce Committee. As Gloria and the rest of the team prepare to deliver the first-ever congressional briefing on the Great Ape Protection Act (GAPA), I flip through the latest *Roll Call*. Apparently, the buzz on Capitol Hill today is that the actress Emily Deschanel has written to her congressman asking him to cosponsor GAPA. These days, such an endorsement might be a big help. Clearly, the minds behind GAPA understand a powerful truth about politics in America: that the ties between Hollywood and the Rayburn Building extend far beyond the lens of a camera.

• • •

An hour later, Room 2247 is filled with supporters, campaigners, and congressional aides. It is the aides, many of whom are just a few years out of college, who hold the real power here. If they are sufficiently moved by the case put forth by HSUS, NEAVS, Gloria, and the rest, they will return to their offices in the Rayburn Building and urge their bosses—the congressmen and congresswomen of America—to become cosponsors of GAPA. As a first-time visitor to Capitol Hill, I am shocked at the youth of these power brokers. Many of the young women sit together, giggling and gossiping. Many of the men look as if they're wearing their fathers' suits.

Soon the briefing is standing room only, and Wayne Pacelle, president and CEO of HSUS, opens the proceedings by outlining the goals of GAPA: to phase out the use of chimpanzees in invasive research in America, to make the current ban on the breeding of chimpanzees permanent, and to retire all federally owned chimpanzees to sanctuary. Then he takes a moment to dedicate the coming presentations to the primatologist and activist Carole Noon. "We hope we can advance this issue in her memory," he says, at which point the packed room becomes impossibly quiet. The crusading creator of Save the Chimps was not just a mentor and friend to Gloria; she was one of the founding members of this movement, and since her death, her stature and influence have only grown. In primate circles, Carole Noon is spoken of with the same reverence as Goodall, who was one of Noon's close confidantes. All of the presenters today and many of those in the crowd either knew Carole as a friend or colleague or admired her courage and generous spirit from afar.

Pacelle goes on to speak about HSUS's recent undercover investigation of the New Iberia Research Center (NIRC) in Louisiana, home to more than three hundred chimpanzees and six thousand other primates. It is the largest chimpanzee research facility in the United States and the largest colony of captive primates in the world. Over the course of a nine-month sting operation, an HSUS camerawoman posing as an NIRC laboratory assistant secretly filmed hours and hours of footage inside the primate units. The resulting real-life account of life in a modern primate research center has become, in the few short months since its release, a public relations nightmare for the facility.

By the Humane Society's tally, the footage shows at least 338 individual violations of the Federal Animal Welfare Act. Some of the most disturbing sequences from the investigation appeared in an exclusive ABC News *Nightline* report in March 2009, which resulted in a firestorm of public outrage.

Pacelle asks for the lights to be dimmed. For the next six minutes we sit transfixed by the graphic video. I remember watching the original *Nightline* report back in March. But sitting here in the dark, deep within a stronghold of American power, the footage seems even more disturbing. Young monkeys scream with terror as unidentified substances are shoved down their throats. An unconscious chimpanzee slips off a table and lands on the cement floor with a sickening crash. Psychotic monkeys spin in their cages and mutilate themselves. Technicians wielding dart guns shoot hysterical chimpanzees in their cages like fish in a barrel. Newborn monkeys are torn from their panicking mothers. Sedated chimpanzees are flung like bags of garbage onto surgery tables. Bloodied rhesus macaques have gaping self-inflicted wounds on their arms and legs. With requisite force, a technician performs a liver-punch biopsy on a sedated chimpanzee. A shrieking, terrified monkey is held down by two people while a needle is passed into its tender groin. Lab techs wrestle wide-awake monkeys out of their cages with Ketchalls and then force them into medieval-looking restraint chairs, where their shivering, sensing bodies are subjected to all manner of horrific-looking procedures. A magnificent adult male chimpanzee — slack-jawed, limp, and seemingly lifeless — has a feeding tube thrust down his throat.

The most horrifying footage, without a doubt, is the short segment that shows a researcher smashing a defenseless monkey in the teeth over and over with a pipe, apparently because the monkey refused to open its mouth and submit to whatever it was about to endure.

The video ends with a shot of Sterling, a twenty-one-year-old male chimpanzee, huddled in the corner of an empty room. Sterling has been permanently removed from research protocols at NIRC. Why would a research facility that has spent hundreds of thousands of dollars feeding, housing, and studying this chimpanzee suddenly remove him from protocols? The answer is simple, a matter of scientific practicality: Sterling is useless to the biomedical community because he has begun the long, torturous descent into madness.

Sterling suffers from stress-induced psychosis brought on by years of captivity in a research facility, just as Jeannie did and as Rachel and Chance still do. Sterling is a haunting reminder of where Jethro, Regis, and Binky might have ended up had Gloria and Richard not built Fauna; he is only a year younger than the boys, and although he is slowly wasting away, his beautiful, majestic frame is eerily reminiscent of the Bub's. Unless GAPA is passed, Sterling will likely spend the rest of his life—which could be forty more years, but will probably be much less, considering his history—spinning, screaming, and mutilating himself in solitary confinement.

"The federal government is not being consistent or scrupulous in adhering to the standards it has adopted and espoused for many years," says Pacelle as the video ends and the lights come up. He is referring to the amendment to the Federal Animal Welfare Act that was passed in 1985, which stipulates that research facilities using primates must create environments for their animals that promote their psychological well-being. This amendment was hugely controversial in 1985, and it still raises the ire of animal rights groups, because nowhere in it was the critical term "psychological well-being" defined. For more than two decades now, biomedical laboratories have been allowed to decide for themselves what this term means and, therefore, what level of resources they are required to commit to the animals' welfare. According to many observers, this legal loophole allows the more unscrupulous labs in America to skirt the very spirit of the Animal Welfare Act. "Twenty-three years later," says Pacelle, "we see no evidence that this lab, the nation's largest for primates, was adhering to any standard that took into account the psychological well-being of primates." The law, he says, is so poorly articulated that it is simply being ignored.

In response to HSUS's complaints regarding NIRC, the U.S. Department of Agriculture (USDA) conducted its own investigation, which resulted in the USDA alleging that the New Iberia facility, and by proxy the University of Louisiana at Lafayette, was indeed guilty of violating the Animal Welfare Act. Instead of litigating the case, however, the USDA offered a settlement, allowing the university to pay a fine without admitting or denying that any violations took place. The fine was $18,000.

Moving on from NIRC, Pacelle invites one of GAPA's lead sponsors, Congressman Roscoe Bartlett, from Maryland's Sixth District, to address the audience. Before being elected to Congress in 1992, Bartlett worked for twenty years as an engineer and research scientist in the U.S. military and at NASA. Long ago he worked with chimpanzees in a laboratory setting. Now he is one of Congress's leading animal protection advocates and a fierce proponent of GAPA. As he steps to the front of the room, the congressman looks visibly shaken by what he has just witnessed on the television screen.

"When I was looking at that film, I was thinking about archaeologists," he says, "and the evidence they look for to see if a society has reached some level of civilization. They judge that by how well they took care of the sick and infirm. If they find a skeleton with advanced arthritis, someone who couldn't have walked on his own, well, they judge that there must have been some reasonable level of civilization in that culture." Bartlett takes a moment to compose himself. "I was wondering what archaeologists of the future, looking back at our generation, would think about *our* level of civilization if this DVD was made available to them."

In the Year 2041

OVER THE next hour, a tag team of experts (Kathleen Conlee from HSUS, Linda Brent from Chimp Haven, and Theodora Capaldo from NEAVS) carefully lay out the case for the Great Ape Protection Act. Their argument is a mixture of economics, ethics, science, and overwhelming public opinion.

Today approximately one thousand chimpanzees are locked up in six biomedical research facilities in the United States. The federal government, and therefore the American taxpayer, owns just over half (517) of these apes, while the remaining 450 are owned by the labs themselves. Chimpanzees account for less than 0.005 percent of the more than 25 million rats, mice, pigs, dogs, and other animals used by the American biomedical research industry every year.

Over the last fifty years, chimpanzee populations in Africa have declined sharply, from an estimated one million in 1960 to less than two hundred thousand today. The chimpanzee is extremely endangered, mostly because of habitat loss and the bushmeat trade, and some scientists say the species could go extinct in about ten years if dramatic steps aren't taken to protect them. It might seem strange that a species threatened with extinction is still being used in biomedical laboratories across the United States. Wild captures stopped with the signing of the international agreement CITES in the mid-1970s, and there has been a moratorium on breeding since 1987, so some people might reasonably assume that these labs are skirting international law. But thanks to some impressive legal maneuvering by the U.S. Fish and Wildlife Service, they are not. Since 1990 United States law has classified chimpanzees in two very different ways: a chimp in the wild is considered *endangered*, but one that lives in a cage in America is only *threatened*. This clever "split-listing" allows the biomedical industry to continue using chimps in research with a clear legal conscience, though one could argue that doing so contravenes the spirit of the Endangered Species Act of 1973 and other international treaties.

Of the one thousand chimps in research today, more than 90 percent have been living in a laboratory setting for more than ten years, and an astonishing few have been inside for nearly half a century. One chimp at New Iberia, a grizzled old lady named Karen, has been in captivity since 1958, when Dwight Eisenhower was president. Generally speaking, 60 percent of the total population is considered middle-aged, and about 35 percent is deemed elderly. Experts estimate that 50 percent of the current population will still be alive in 2026. It is estimated that the last government-owned chimpanzee in the United States will die sometime around 2041.

Over the last twenty years, the use of chimpanzees in invasive research has declined dramatically around the world. The United States is the only developed nation that still subjects chimpanzees to invasive research and testing. During the 1990s, several significant U.S. biomedical labs housing chimps closed, LEMSIP among them, and since 2000, spending on research protocols involving chimpanzees in America has dropped 47 percent. If GAPA were passed today, only three research grants in the country would be affected. There are more than three active grants involving chimp research, but only three fund invasive work, as opposed to housing and maintaining the chimps or conducting noninvasive research like cognition and behavior studies.

This decrease is due in no small part to the astronomical costs of maintaining a captive chimp colony. According to HSUS, the federal government currently spends between $20 million and $25 million annually on chimpanzee maintenance and experiments, and most of this money covers the costs of housing and feeding the apes ($36 to $60 per chimp per day), not the research itself. Chimpanzees are easily the most expensive of all research animals—Linda Brent estimates that a lab chimp who lives to the age of fifty-two might cost the government as much as $1.4 million over its lifetime. If current contracts are extended for the foreseeable future and with 3 percent annual inflation, the federal government will be on the hook for a whopping $312 million for ongoing care of its captive chimps.

According to researchers themselves, no more than 5 to 20 percent of the remaining captive chimpanzees will be subjected to scientific procedures. The rest are considered unsuitable because of advanced age, chronic health conditions, or a history of infectious disease exposure. Over the course of the nine-month HSUS investigation at New Iberia, only twenty individuals were actually used in protocols. The rest, more than three hundred chimps, were simply being warehoused.

At first this seems like good news; the fewer chimpanzees being knocked down, infected with viruses, and subjected to invasive surgeries, the better. But this line of thinking reveals a common misunderstanding about the realities of animal research. Captivity in itself can be just as destructive as being used in a scientific protocol. Indeed, prolonged confinement — whether in a cage or simply within a lab facility — is often the experience that destroys not only the chimpanzee body but also the heart, the mind, the spirit, and the soul.

The mental breakdowns of Jeannie, Rachel, Chance, Sterling, and countless other chimpanzees should be all the proof we need of this, but thanks to eyewitness accounts and undercover videos like those shot at New Iberia, much more evidence is available. It shows clearly the uncontrolled aggression, the constant fear and anxiety vocalizations among lab chimps, innumerable episodes of self-mutilation, individuals spinning in their cages, proven cases of PTSD, self-hugging and self-rocking, signs of progressive psychological deterioration. A chimpanzee housed in a lab is in a constant state of physical, mental, and psychic agony, no matter how few scientific procedures she undergoes.

Capaldo, who is a psychologist in addition to being president of NEAVS, reminds the audience at the hearing that human prisoners of war held in isolation in Vietnam consistently reported their visceral need for physical movement, which manifested as repetitive self-rocking, identical to the stereotyped rocking of captive chimpanzees. When asked why they rocked themselves so much, the POWs responded that it was the only way to remember they were still alive.

According to HSUS and NEAVS, opinion polls show that a majority of the American public supports the goals of GAPA. Ninety percent of U.S. adults believe it is unacceptable to confine chimpanzees in government-approved cages, and more than 70 percent of Americans believe a chimpanzee who has been living in a lab for more than ten years should be retired from research—that covers more than 90 percent of the current captive population. Most tellingly, in 2001, 54 percent of Americans, up from 30 percent in 1985, were opposed to research that causes pain and injury to dogs and chimpanzees, *even if this research leads to breakthroughs in human health*. One can logically assume that without the stipulation of "breakthroughs in human health," the numbers opposed to such research would be significantly higher.

This brings us to the final argument in support of GAPA. While the decrease in chimpanzee experiments over the last few decades has had a lot to do with growing public distaste for the practice, as well as the prohibitive cost of housing great apes and the unavoidable ethical issues, there is another reason that HSUS, NEAVS, and many other groups believe chimpanzees should be released from their bondage to invasive science. The science, they say, has been marred by widespread failure.

The use of chimpanzees in HIV-AIDS research is now recognized as having been an ethical, financial, and scientific disaster. By 1997 an estimated 198 chimpanzees had been infected with one strain or another of HIV, and not one showed symptoms of AIDS.

This is a particularly serious ethical problem because the surplus of chimpanzees languishing in labs is a direct result of the breeding push that began in 1986 in response to HIV-AIDS. Today AIDS research on chimpanzees is very nearly dead, and in a recent paper in *Alternatives to Laboratory Animals,* the NEAVS science director, Jarrod Bailey, hammers the final nail into this particular coffin.

Bailey compares the results of AIDS vaccine trials in chimps with the results from the same trials in humans and finds no correlation. Vaccines that had an effect in chimps had none in humans, leading Bailey to conclude that "claims of the importance of chimpanzees in AIDS vaccine development are without foundation, and a return to the use of chimpanzees in AIDS research/vaccine development is scientifically unjustifiable." Here Bailey is echoing the conclusions offered by Thomas Insel, then the director of the Yerkes National Primate Research Center, in an interview more than a decade ago. "I can't tell you what it is that those studies have given us that has really made a difference in the way we approach people with this disease." In a rather more blunt response a few years earlier, when Insel was asked to reflect on the scientific community's decision in 1986 to begin breeding hundreds of chimpanzees for AIDS research, he said simply, "I think we blew it."

Bailey has also written a paper on the use of chimpanzees in human cancer research, and his conclusions are similar to Insel's. He writes that it "would be unscientific to claim that chimpanzees are vital to cancer research. On the contrary, it is reasonable to conclude that cancer research would not suffer if the use of chimpanzees for this purpose were prohibited in the U.S."

In a 2007 paper entitled "The Poor Contribution of Chimpanzee Experiments to Biomedical Progress," Andrew Knight randomly selected 95 of the nearly 750 reports on experiments on chimpanzees that appeared in the scientific literature between 1995 and 2004. In order to determine the importance of these experiments to biomedical research, Knight scoured the literature to see how many of the 95 were cited by subsequent studies. Only 49.5 percent of the 95 chimp studies were cited by others, and less than 15 percent were cited by papers investigating methods for curing human diseases. This last point is crucial, because the main argument always put forth by proponents of chimp research is that their work is critical to saving human lives. Upon closer examination of these human disease studies, Knight discovered that alternative technologies such as in vitro studies, human clinical and epidemiological studies, molecular assays, and genomics actually contributed the lion's share of the reported advances. "No chimpanzee study made an essential contribution, or, in most cases, a significant contribution of any kind," he wrote. Another paper based on the same data set, by Jarrod Bailey and Jonathan Balcombe of the Physicians Committee for Responsible Medicine, offered an even more strident conclusion: "Far from augmenting biomedical research, chimpanzee experimentation appears to have been largely incidental, peripheral, confounding, irrelevant, unreliable and has consumed considerable research funding that would have been better targeted elsewhere."

Today the majority of invasive research studies on chimpanzees involve the hepatitis-C virus (a smaller number of studies focus on hepatitis A, malaria, Alzheimer's, and other age-related illnesses). But in the summer of 2005, reports emerged that researchers had successfully grown the hep-C virus entirely in vitro, in human-cell culture. In contrast to studies involving chimps, which have yet to produce a workable vaccine after decades of trying, this study is a genuine breakthrough in hep-C research. It means we are one step closer to being able to study the virus in its natural human environment as opposed to an entirely unnatural one — that is, the bloodstream of a chimpanzee.

The balance of evidence as laid out by Bailey, Balcombe, Knight, and many others over the last decade or so suggests that the chimpanzee is not a good model for studying human physiology and disease. More and more scientists are coming to the conclusion that the ways in which chimpanzee physiology differs from that of humans are not, in the end, all that subtle and that extrapolating results from chimps to humans requires a hefty leap in logic. Although it would be wrong to suggest that we have learned nothing from research on chimps over the last sixty years, the disaster of the HIV-AIDS research is certainly a cautionary tale worth heeding.

Here again is the curse I spoke of at the beginning of this story. Like Chance, who spent five years in isolation for a disease she never contracted, chimpanzees are only now emerging as the sum of their differences from humans as much as the sum of their similarities. They are like us and they are unlike us—this has always been their great misfortune.

The Aboveground Railroad

So what should be done with all the chimpanzees languishing in American labs? If they are so expensive to house, and they spend every day suffering, and the result of all their suffering is, for the most part, either useless or reproducible through other techniques, and the National Research Council deemed mass euthanasia out of the question back in 1997, what should become of them?

You may have already guessed the answer: the chimps should go to sanctuary.

Using HSUS numbers, if GAPA were passed tomorrow, and all federally owned chimpanzees were retired to sanctuary in 2012, the cost to the American taxpayer to take care of these apes for the rest of their lives would be approximately $88 million. Given that the status quo scenario (leaving them in the labs and continuing research) will cost about $312 million over the same period of time, sanctuaries represent an enormous savings for the U.S. government. Even if you throw in an extra $50 million to build brand-new sanctuaries instead of retrofitting existing lab buildings, GAPA will save the taxpayer about $173 million. In these times of extreme financial constraint, says Wayne Pacelle, sanctuaries are the only fiscally responsible course of action.

In 2000 the Clinton administration enacted the Chimpanzee Health Improvement, Maintenance and Protection (CHIMP) Act, which mandates the retirement and lifetime care of "surplus" chimpanzees—that is, those not currently involved in active protocols at national primate research centers. Although the CHIMP Act doesn't outlaw invasive research on chimpanzees, it is a response to the widespread recognition by the scientific community that the breeding push that began in 1986 in response to the AIDS crisis was misguided and that far too many chimps were born into research in America. By providing for the retirement of some of these apes, the CHIMP Act also makes a critical philosophical point. It is the first legislative acknowledgment that along with the financial costs of invasive research, keeping all those chimps behind bars with no scientific justification carries a significant moral cost, one that we can begin repaying by building sanctuaries for them.

So far, Chimp Haven, in Keithville, Louisiana, is the only federally funded retirement sanctuary for surplus research chimps. This flagship facility is a direct result of the CHIMP Act, the first step in what supporters hope will become the National Chimpanzee Sanctuary System (NCSS), a collection of refuges across the United States where surplus chimps can live out their lives in peace.

"With the right kind of care program," says Linda Brent, Chimp Haven's president and director, "and the right kind of environment, all research chimps can be rehabilitated to live with purpose and dignity." Gloria sometimes refers to the NCSS as the "aboveground railroad," alluding to African Americans' escape from slavery, without batting an eye.

Chimp 411

With the economic, scientific, and ethical arguments laid out, the first congressional briefing on GAPA is nearing its conclusion. It is Gloria's turn to speak. As she stands, the television blinks to life again. The screen pauses on a familiar pastoral scene from south-western Quebec.

"First of all, thank you for listening to this," Gloria says. "Some of it is very difficult to hear and process, and I respect and admire all of you for being here. You are the type of people who will make a difference." She takes a moment to compose herself. For a split second I worry that stage fright is getting the best of her.

"Twelve years ago," says Gloria shakily, "I walked into a laboratory unit on the same afternoon that a certain chimpanzee was soon to be returned to his cage. The chimp, known only by the code CH-411, had just been through an invasive surgery. This would be the first time I would meet him." Gloria explains that the scene at LEMSIP at the time was much like what we'd just seen happening at New Iberia—the screaming, the banging, the clear and present suffering. The cages were the federally mandated size, five by five by seven feet, and were hung from the ceiling.

"All of a sudden," says Gloria, "I heard this anxious cry over the intercom. A human voice. It was yelling, 'He's waking up! He's waking up!' Chimp 411 was supposed to be asleep, but he wasn't."

One of the most often told anecdotes about life inside primate laboratories is that of the chimp who wakes up too soon. Even with humans, anesthesia carries risks; it is never an exact science. But anesthesia becomes even more inexact and risky when the patient is not a human but an adult male chimpanzee.

Chimp 411 was transported as quickly as possible from the operating room to his cage in a long plastic box fitted with a lid. To Gloria the box looked like a coffin. The pallbearers—four lab techs dressed all in white—came rushing into the unit and hurried toward the cage. And right then all hell broke loose. The lid of the box popped off, and 411 sat straight up, a simian resurrection, his withered arms flailing, his skinny legs kicking, his eyes still dopey, but his body coming vigorously back to life.

"That was the first time I met Tom," says Gloria.

When the five other chimpanzees in the unit saw their friend Tom come crashing back to consciousness, they went berserk. According to Gloria, the noise was deafening, and the lab techs panicked. They grabbed Tommie by the arms and legs, lifted him out of his coffin, and heaved him into his cage as quickly as they could. The cage was filthy—when a chimpanzee is knocked down with a dart gun, as Tommie had been hours earlier, the fear and stress often make them urinate and defecate profusely—and the techs hadn't had time to clean up the mess. So Tom landed in his cage with a sickening thud, face-down in his own shit and piss.

For the next half-hour, Tommie threw himself around his cage as if drunk, slammed his body into the bars as if being thrashed by some invisible demon, climbed up to his tire, and then crashed to the ground as if trying and failing to fly. Tommie always had violent reactions to heavy sedation. The techs knew this, and they were yelling at him, pleading with him from the other side of the bars to calm down. But they could do nothing from where they stood, and soon Tommie's face was bleeding freely. Sue Ellen, his longtime friend, happened to be caged next door to him. Upon seeing his wounds, she collected the few "enrichment" rags she had in her cage and tried to squeeze them through the caging toward Tommie. Alas, she couldn't reach him.

"This is a typical day in the life of a chimpanzee in a lab," says Gloria. "It's heart-wrenching and painful as anything to witness. But today . . ." Gloria's voice begins to quaver again. "Today Tom is a different chimp. He is a serious connoisseur of vegetables—will it be romaine lettuce today or iceberg?—and pistachios are his new favorite food. He has friends, some of the same friends from the lab. He is loving. He is loyal. He is a nurturer. He cares for his family. And, most importantly, he gets choices every day. Tom likes to rise with the sun every morning and give a big, loud call. He's the first chimp I hear from my home every day. And by the time I arrive for work at eight A.M., he already wants to go back to bed."

For the first time since the briefing began, the room fills with laughter. Then the lights dim again, and we turn our attention to the television, where another video starts to play.

This one, the final scene of Allison Argo's excellent documentary *Chimpanzees: An Unnatural History*, was shot at Fauna on a very special day. Argo had timed her shoot to coincide with the completion of the island habitats in April 2006. The cameras were rolling when Gloria opened the doors of the chimphouse that lead to the islands for the very first time.

What Argo captured that day was pure cinematic magic. Tom had been feeling unwell for a few days, but the moment the island door slid open, Tom went straight outside and started running through the grass. This was the first time in more than thirty years that Tom had seen the world without his view being mediated by steel and caging. As if he understood the significance of the moment, Tom then did something extraordinary. As the filming continued, and with Gloria and Pat Ring begging him to be careful, Tom ran to the base of the only tree on the island and began climbing it. When he reached a major fork in the trunk, he decided to stop. He sat back, his arms bracing his body as if he were an old hand at tree climbing, as if he'd been doing it every day since he was born. As Tom surveyed the farm below, Gloria exclaimed, "I would think that would confirm he's a wild-caught chimp!" From the camera's vantage point on the ground, Tom looks like a perfectly normal chimpanzee.

The lights come up in the hearing room, which feels strangely warm. "These are happy stories and happy endings," says Gloria. "Tommie, previously known as Chimp 411, has a new life, a life he's completely deserving of. So on behalf of all Fauna's residents and the hundreds of chimps still in research today, I'm hoping and trusting that you'll hear their pleas and do what's right for them. Thank you very much."

As soon as Gloria stops talking, the room erupts in applause. Many people stand for the ovation, and nearly everyone is either dabbing eyes or reaching for a handkerchief. Gloria has just proven herself wonderfully wrong. Only two percent of us may be truly conscious and fully aware, but at the sight of Tommie climbing that tree, every single person in this room snapped to life.

And that's why, her speech finished and her nerves calming, Gloria decides to keep the rest of the story to herself. The truth is, it took Tom the entire day to work up the courage to come down out of that tree. Like a strung-out housecat, he sat up there until sunset, too petrified to move.

The Real Question

GLORIA WILL spend the rest of the day being shuttled from room to room in the Rayburn Building, meeting with countless representatives, lobbying them to support GAPA. To pass the time, I leave the Rayburn and spend the afternoon wandering the National Mall.

As I write this, GAPA has 157 cosponsors and is considered one of the more popular bipartisan bills currently in committee on the Hill. But numbers and opinions aren't politics, and until the full House votes on the bill, its passage isn't certain. Politics will always be a fickle friend of public opinion. The majority of bills in committee never make it out, and this is the second time GAPA has been introduced in Congress (the first time, in 2008, the congressional session ended before GAPA came up for debate). This time around, nine months into the global financial crisis, it is hard to claim that GAPA is a national priority. To illustrate this, one of GAPA's lead sponsors, Representative Edolphus Towns of New York, couldn't attend today's briefing because he was chairing the Committee on Government Oversight and Reform, taking testimony from a certain government official named Ben Bernanke, chairman of the Federal Reserve.

GAPA is not without its opponents, and as the bill gains momentum, these groups are sure to become more vocal. The National Association for Biomedical Research (NABR) is a nonprofit lobbying group that advocates on behalf of public and private universities, medical schools, and the pharmaceutical and biotech industries. NABR, which calls itself "the voice of the biomedical research community," is undoubtedly a force to be reckoned with; *Nature Medicine* magazine chose it as one of the fifteen most influential lobbying groups in Washington. NABR has registered its dismay over GAPA and has published a fact sheet outlining "the chimpanzee's critical contribution to biomedical research." Another group on *Nature Medicine*'s top-fifteen list is the Federation of American Societies for Experimental Biology, which is also on record as opposing GAPA, having sent a letter to the House of Representatives.

Some scientists are also in opposition to the act. One of the most notable opponents is John VandeBerg, director of the Southwest National Primate Research Center in San Antonio, Texas. Southwest is currently home to approximately 166 chimpanzees and is one of only six biomedical facilities in the country still housing chimps. "It would be a great tragedy for humanity if research with chimpanzees were stopped," VandeBerg recently told Voice of America, referencing the potential he sees for future breakthroughs in human medicine. VandeBerg's facilities at Southwest are respected for their relatively high standards of animal care, their enrichment programs, and the fact that most of his chimps live in social groups with access to outdoor enclosures when not involved in protocols. Nonetheless, it is difficult to determine who would suffer the greater tragedy—all of humanity or just VandeBerg and his colleagues—were invasive research on chimpanzees made illegal, and large chunks of federal grant money suddenly stopped arriving. By raising the specter of "a great tragedy" should chimp research be ended, VandeBerg is unconsciously holding a fun-house mirror up to Raymond Corbey's classic line from *The Metaphysics of Apes:* "Our fascination with apes is only rivaled by our rebuff of apes."

VandeBerg is not alone in publicly supporting the use of chimpanzees in research. His most vocal colleague, Stuart M. Zola, is the director of Yerkes in Atlanta, the only other National Primate Research Center that still houses chimps. Yerkes, of course, also relies on federal money to keep the lights on. VandeBerg and Zola coauthored a controversial paper in *Nature* in 2005 calling for increased funding for chimp research. In "A Unique Biomedical Resource at Risk," they write that chimpanzees "continue to play a vital role in our efforts to discover and understand the mechanisms that underlie a wide range of infectious diseases" and that "many advances from biomedical research with chimpanzees have been published in the past one to two years, demonstrating that rapid medical progress pertinent to a wide range of human diseases is being made through the use of chimpanzees." These statements are at odds with the literature reviews performed by Bailey, Balcombe, and Knight, as is the authors' contention that chimpanzees "are still important for testing vaccines aimed at preventing HIV-1 infection."

One of VandeBerg's colleagues at Southwest, the virologist Jonathan Allan, admitted the misgivings of many scientists about studies on chimps. "If you talk to a lot of primate researchers," he told *Science* in 2007, "they're not comfortable with it. You *shouldn't* be comfortable with it. You should have to search your soul as to the balance between the research and the good that comes from it and the bad part, which is what happens to the animals . . . If you're comfortable with it and you don't have any problem with it, *that's* a problem." In the same article, another virologist, Beatrice Hahn, claimed that "95% of the experiments done with [chimps] are not necessary."

One of the main arguments in support of using apes in invasive research is that because chimps have been marginally involved in past breakthroughs—in the development of the hepatitis-B vaccine, for example, in which chimps were used merely as living test tubes to grow the virus, a feat that can now be accomplished entirely through in vitro methods—researchers have an ethical responsibility to continue using them. This sentiment was stated most firmly by Louis Sullivan, then the secretary of Health and Human Services in the late 1980s at a press conference cosponsored by NABR. Sullivan said that "it would be evil to forsake vital animal research when lives hang in the balance." But a closer look at this line of reasoning demonstrates that it is entirely specious. If the grounds for deciding whether a species should be subjected to invasive research were simply the *significance of the results*, then we should be doing invasive biomedical research on human subjects. We should be performing liver-punch biopsies on humans or injecting them with HIV or malaria or hepatitis and then testing vaccines on them, because the best model for human physiology is, of course, the human body. Imagine the results. Imagine the breakthroughs that might come from testing these things on ourselves.

In this day and age, we would never subject humans to such violations. We might have in the past—consider the Fernald School experiments of the 1950s (in which institutionalized young boys were fed radioactive oatmeal) or the Holmesburg Prison study of 1960 (in which convicted criminals were exposed to radioactive isotopes and chemical weapons) or the Tuskegee experiments that ended in 1972 (in which hundreds of impoverished African American men suffering from syphilis were denied treatment). But today, thankfully, Western culture prohibits the abuse of humans in the name of science.

A society's decisions about which communities or animal species are fair game for invasive research have never been based on how useful the results of the research might be or how many human lives "hang in the balance." These decisions have always been based on something much more fundamental: the moral and ethical beliefs that hold sway in that society at the time. This may seem like a semantic point, but it is not. It is a point filled with hope. Because the real question we need to ask is not whether we're willing to sacrifice future medical breakthroughs that chimpanzee research might provide but whether we are willing to continue torturing living, thinking, feeling beings who resemble us in so many profound ways.

In 1993 an international group of philosophers, zoologists, anthropologists, and other academics joined forces in the Great Ape Project (GAP), whose mission is to extend to all great apes the basic legal rights that humans enjoy: the right to life, the protection of individual liberty, and the prohibition on torture. As the founders of GAP, Peter Singer and Paola Cavalieri, write in *The Great Ape Project*, "We now have sufficient information about the capacities of chimpanzees, gorillas and orangutans to make it clear that the moral boundary we draw between us and them is indefensible. Hence the time is ripe for extending full moral equality to members of other species, and the case for doing so is overwhelming."

GAP members are calling on the United Nations to pass the Declaration on Great Apes, modeled on the American Declaration of Independence, which would bring all great apes into a moral "community of equals" with humans. The UN has yet to pass such a declaration. But in 2008 GAP experienced a very important victory in an unlikely place: a committee of the Spanish parliament approved a historic resolution in support of the Great Ape Project, clearing the way for Spain—proud home of the bullfight—to become the first country to grant basic rights to all great apes. Spain can now claim to be one of the most progressive nations on the planet when it comes to animal rights.

Although GAP and GAPA are separate movements, and they measure success in very different ways, they share a certain philosophical underpinning. Each asks a version of the same fundamental question: are we willing to expand our moral circle to include the great apes? In America, at least regarding GAPA, we already have an answer. Polling data from HSUS and NEAVS show that a majority of Americans are in favor of ending painful chimp research, no matter what this would mean for research. This majority appears to be growing every year.

Seventeen years ago, the United States was one of six countries that housed chimpanzees for biomedical research. Today America stands alone on the issue. Countries throughout the world have decided that the slim odds of future medical breakthroughs are far outweighed by the ethical, financial, and scientific downsides to subjecting our closest evolutionary relatives to invasive research. In 2000 New Zealand became the first nation to ban invasive research on great apes, and since then Belgium, Austria, Australia, Sweden, Japan, Holland, and the United Kingdom have all either banned or strictly limited great ape research. Many other countries, including Italy, Norway, and Germany, have avoided using apes in research, although national bans on the practice have yet to be passed. The same is true of my home country, Canada.

In 2004 the Netherlands retired the last of its research chimps, who were the first on Earth to be injected with the HIV virus, and as I write this the European Union is considering a comprehensive ban on using great apes in research. In 2006 the last Japanese pharmaceutical company to use chimpanzees retired its entire colony. Even the Hepatitis Research Foundation, which has conducted extremely intensive biomedical research on chimps for decades at the New York Blood Center's Vilab in Liberia, decided in 2006 to retire their last seventy-four apes to island sanctuaries purchased from the Liberian government. The lab's director, Betsy Brotman, now says technological advances in the field have allowed ethical and welfare issues to finally take precedence. "There are new methods for doing this kind of research," she told the *Sunday Times* in 2007. "We don't need to use chimpanzees."

For more than a century we've shot chimpanzees into space, implanted electrodes into their brains, shattered their skulls with blunt-force trauma, attempted to inseminate them with human sperm, used them as crash-test dummies, exposed them to pharmaceuticals and toxic chemicals, injected them with deadly human viruses, deprived them of their mothers' care, and driven many of them psychotic—all the while protecting our moral position under the legal rubric that a chimpanzee in a biomedical lab is somehow less "endangered" than its wild compatriots in Africa. Now governments everywhere are coming to the conclusion that the costs of that position far outweigh the benefits and that this sort of research needs to stop. As the straight-talking congressman from Maryland, Roscoe Bartlett, told the audience in the briefing room earlier, when it comes to biomedical research on chimpanzees, "the juice just ain't worth the squeezin'."

War Memorials

ON THE Mall, throngs of people mill about at Abraham Lincoln's feet. Many wear identical purple T-shirts stenciled with the slogan HEALTHCARE '09. These people have come to Washington for the same reason Gloria did, for the same reason everyone marches on this city — to bring about change in their lives and in the world. "The roots of politics are older than humanity," writes Frans de Waal, and as I stroll past the Vietnam Veterans Memorial and marvel at the thousands of names carved into the black marble, I realize that everyone has some sort of legacy to uphold. Later, at sunset, I will watch the changing of the guard at the Tomb of the Unknown Soldier in Arlington Cemetery, the most moving tribute of all in the nation's capital.

By law, Gloria cannot accept any more chimpanzees into her sanctuary. She knows that one day, perhaps not too far in the future, the last chimp at Fauna will pass away, and she has begun preparing for that moment. She plans to turn the chimphouse into a museum dedicated to the thousands of apes sacrificed to biomedical research over the last century. She is also designing a commemorative garden — her own personal war memorial — to be planted with flowers from her late mother's gardens and with plaques to honor each of the nineteen chimps who have blessed the farm with their presence. In Gloria's office is a set of urns containing the ashes of Pablo, Annie, Donna Rae, Jeannie, Sophie, and the indomitable Billy Jo. When the garden is ready, that's where she will scatter the remains of her friends.

Gloria has inspired countless people to take action on behalf of chimpanzees in captivity. Most notable are two ex-employees of Fauna, John Mulcahy and Diana Goodrich, who went on to found a refuge of their own, Chimpanzee Sanctuary Northwest, in the Cascade Mountains of Washington State. In June 2008, Sanctuary Northwest became the permanent retirement home for seven chimpanzees.

But sanctuaries, museums, and memorials aside, the Great Ape Protection Act is the real legacy Gloria is chasing. It has taken immeasurable effort by a great many people and organizations over the years to bring GAPA before Congress today — Gloria and Tom are just two small pieces of an intricate lobbying puzzle. But for her, GAPA couldn't be more personal. If the act is passed and signed into law, Gloria might finally find the peace and sense of purpose she has long been searching for.

Chapter 12

THE HAUNTED

I was a coward, and the shame of my cowardice
in that situation haunts me to this day.
— JAMES MAHONEY, *Saving Molly*

The Sky Walk

JEKYLL AND HYDE HAVEN'T missed me one bit. Just back from
Washington, Gloria drops me off outside the Fauna office. As I approach the front door, my swan guards come running around the
corner. One of them—Jekyll, maybe—stretches her wings out as
she runs. The other, probably Hyde, lets loose a series of frazzled
honks and pecks the air with her beak. At first I imagine this to be a
welcoming party, and my heart warms. But as they set up shop between me and the front door and refuse to let me past, I realize that
these two, just like Eeyore, have pledged allegiance to powers I will
never fully understand.

I walk down to the chimphouse, where I find Sue Ellen out on
the Sky Walk. When she sees me coming she sits down, shakes with
excitement, and presses her lips through the caging. I climb up the
stairs and sit on the landing in front of her, tell her I missed her. I
indulge myself by imagining that she missed me too.

Over the next half-hour, the Hoodlums join us on the Sky Walk.
I've been away for only a week, but it feels like months since I last
saw them. I notice tiny changes in each chimpanzee—a new gash
on Regis's forehead, a clump of hair missing from Chance's back,

a toenail that Susie has allowed to overgrow. Dramas old and new have played out in my absence, and I'm sorry I've missed the show.

Soon Regis sits grooming Jethro, who sits grooming Pepper, who sits grooming Sue Ellen, who sits beside Chance, who chows down on a green apple. Tom ambles outside to join us, and the old guy seems positively thrilled to see everyone gathered in one place. He grunts happily as he slumps down in the middle of the crowd, right across from me, and retrieves his own Washington State apple from somewhere up his sleeve. A soft light washes the chimps' faces in a dignified glow. Soon autumn will be in full swing, and I will be preparing to leave my new friends. But for now we sit quietly together, listening to the lowing cattle, the gurgling ducks, reveling together in the peace of a rural evening.

This might sound unforgivably sentimental, but the longer I stay at Fauna the more convinced I am that the chimpanzees have something important to teach me. This is the third and final transformation that occurs in people who work with apes: first we dream about them, then we see our lives in a new light because of them, and then we're left searching for some kind of message from across the chasm. When science finishes narrowing the gap between us and the rest of the apes, this might be one of the few traits we can all agree is uniquely human: we ask why. We search for meaning. We find purpose in our lives by leaving no stone unturned in our search for it.

It Takes All Kinds

THE NEXT morning I arrive early at the chimphouse and find Kim already hard at work. She's putting together the chimps' breakfast bags and delivering morning medications. The building is calm, the apes snoozing. The only sound is Kim, quietly singing to herself in French.

"Should I start spraying down the trolleys?" I ask.

Kim doesn't answer.

"Should I spray these?" I ask again.

No response.

Kim loves the first few hours of the morning. Sleep is still in the air, and Kim is in her element, ticking off items on her mental to-do list.

"Kim?"

Still no response. She walks upstairs with three Dixie cups in hand. A few minutes later, she returns and walks right past me as if I'm invisible.

I've seen something like this before. A few weeks ago, when I was here with Dawna Grow on a Sunday, she was being run ragged, and as she ran to and fro she talked to herself and the chimps. It was as if Dawna, the person, had somehow disappeared.

"Yoko! What can I getcha? Apples? How about apples? Here you go. OK, Jethro. You've had four already. You've had four. Now Regis, here's your yummy pink stuff. Yummy pink stuff with your meds in it. OK, swallow it back, buddy. Swallow it back — aw, gross! Reege! OK, Reege. OK. We're going to try that again. At least she wore pink today, right, Reege? OK, Tommie, take this. Take this. You don't want this? But you *love* endives. You don't want endives. You do want them. You don't want them. You do want them. Oh, Chancey Pants, wait a second, love. Here we go. Show us your finger. Show us your finger. That's a good girl. Look at that! You bashed it up pretty good, didn't you? Let's put this on it. Show us your finger. It's a cream, Chancey. It's a cream. Here. Sniff it. It's a cream. OK? Good girl. It's a cream. Show us your finger. Let's just wipe it on like this. It's a cream. There you go. There you go. There. You. Go. Perfect! Yay, Chancey Pants! There you go! Getting all better! Wait. No. Don't lick it off. No, Chancey. Don't lick it! Don't . . . well . . . as long as it gets inside you somehow."

Those who excel at looking after traumatized animals must also be experts at ignoring the pleas and wailings of their own egos for extended periods. Whenever Gloria or Kim or Dawna sinks deeply into a trance like this, I've learned it's best to just keep busy. So I make the lunch trolleys and wait for Kim to re-emerge. Sure enough, once the breakfast bags and medications are delivered, she's able to return to the here and now.

"If I'm dating someone," says Kim, "they've gotta know right from the start: the chimps are my priority. If Gloria needs me, I drop everything. Most guys want to be the center of attention, but that doesn't work for me. I don't care how good-looking you are."

Kim started working here in 2003 as a volunteer. Two years later, when Gloria offered her this dream job, she immediately quit her job in the city.

"I was really happy there," Kim says, offering Rachel some juice through the bars. "But I'm so much happier here."

"So you'd never leave?"

"What?" Kim gives me a horrified look. "Why would I leave?" Her face flushes. She looks back at Rachel. "I can't even think about that." We listen to Rachel suck on her straw. She is loving the juice. Her amber eyes, usually so glassy, have come alive with the sweetness.

We wait for Rachel to finish every drop. Kim still looks shaken by my question. Then she walks over to Petra's enclosure. "This place has seen a lot of different people," she says as she hands Petra a big bundle of paper towels to play with. "People who don't fit in. Antisocial people. People who are angry. All kinds. Because animals don't judge you like people do. No matter how messed up you are in your head, they'll accept you." Petra reaches the paper towels through the porthole and waves them back and forth as if she's surrendering. Kim crouches down, puckers her lips in mock sadness, mutters something in French. Her performance is spot-on. Petra huffs with pleasure.

One day some years back, Gloria received a strange phone call from a criminal lawyer in Montreal. He'd heard about Fauna and was moved by what Gloria was doing, so he offered his services free of charge if she ever needed them. But that wasn't all. The lawyer said he could send his clients — ex-cons — out to the farm to help now and then. The felons could log community service hours by helping Richard plant trees on the weekends. The men who came to the farm — one of whom was allegedly Irish Mafia — drove luxury cars and were always impeccably dressed. The lawyer sent only four clients to Fauna before Gloria began feeling uncomfortable and canceled the arrangement.

According to Richard, the men were always respectful and very helpful around the farm.

"How do you think we got all those evergreens?" he once asked me with a laugh. "Or the washer-dryer? Or all the TVs in the chimphouse? For a while, we had more Pepsi fridges showing up than we knew what to do with."

Richard's favorite story is about the lawyer dragging one of his clients — a low-level criminal on trial for shooting someone in the foot, whom I'll refer to as Bobby — to a lecture about factory farming at Concordia University. Bobby was so horrified by what he learned there that he immediately vowed to eat only animals that were treated humanely. As Richard said, "There goes the prosciutto." The trouble was, the audience that day was filled with animal rights people, and Bobby was dressed head to toe in expensive leather. After the talk, a few audience members chewed him out: "There's a dead cow in the room!" they yelled. "Who brought the dead cow?" Bobby felt terrible, but there was no way he'd give up wearing leather. "Baby steps," says Richard. "Everyone's gotta start somewhere."

Without exception, the few petty criminals and Mafia soldiers who put in time at Fauna were deeply moved by what the chimpanzees had been through. One or two of the chimps' stories was usually enough to reduce even the toughest Mafioso to tears. Something about the lives of these animals rang true for these hardened men. Perhaps it was their own firsthand understanding of what captivity can do to a person.

Kim's Party Trick

KIM HANDS a bowl of water to Petra, who immediately balls up her paper towel and dips it in the bowl. Then Pettie squeezes the water into her mouth, just the way wild chimps do with balled-up leaves.

While we were away in Washington, Jethro spent a lot of time near the door to Toby's enclosure. According to Kim, Jeffie was asking to be let back in with Toby, and even though they'd recently had that pretty serious dustup, Kim went with her gut. To make sure that the move wouldn't send Toby into hysterics, she pretended to unlock the door separating the two. Toby seemed fine with that, so she unlocked it for real. Jethro ambled inside, and the two chimps have been living peacefully together ever since.

"Jeffie is working on him, right, Pettie?" says Kim, crouching down again in front of Petra. "Jethro's helping Toby figure stuff out." Kim whispers another rapid-fire lullaby in French. Then she is hit softly in the face with a sodden ball of paper towels.

"Hey, you've seen my party trick, right?" Kim asks, wiping her face while giving me the finger. The third digit on her left hand is missing the last knuckle.

Kim was giving Sophie her meds when it happened. Sophie had been unwell ever since her arrival from the Quebec City Zoo with Spock and Maya. The zoo officials had actually considered euthanizing her because she was so sick, but instead they sent her to Fauna. No one knew the extent of her health problems, other than a terrible stomach ulcer.

"Every chimp has one thing they love more than anything," says Kim. "For Pepper it's fresh kale from the garden. For Spock it's a very specific child's toy, the one that makes the balls spin. For Sophie, it's latex gloves."

That day Kim was kneeling in front of the wake-up room, where Sophie was lying on her stomach with her chin on her hands, stubbornly refusing to drink her meds. Kim had been trying for more than an hour to get her to cooperate. That was not unusual, and Kim is incredibly patient. I once watched her persuade Regis, over the course of three whole hours, to drink his smoothie. Kim has no choice. If she doesn't persevere, the chimps won't get what they need.

But no matter what Kim did, Sophie wouldn't budge. So Kim decided to take a break. And as she leaned forward and pushed herself up from the ground, her strict adherence to the Fauna safety protocols wavered for a split second. Her latex-gloved finger slipped beneath the caging, and Sophie grabbed it with her teeth. There was no alarm bark, no screaming. Sophie appeared perfectly calm, as if she were playing. But now she had a latex glove, with Kim's fingers inside, between her teeth.

"I thought I was a goner," Kim says now. "She had my whole hand in there." Kim had to make a decision. She could either sit through the pain and see if Sophie would release her hand, or she could yank very hard to try to free it. The first option was dangerous, because it would put Sophie entirely in control. The second option, though, meant that Kim would almost certainly lose her finger, and perhaps much more, if Sophie became excited or frightened by Kim's sudden movement.

Kim decided quickly. She pulled away as hard and fast as she could, and as she did, Sophie crunched down and removed the top of Kim's middle finger, very neatly, at the first knuckle.

"I didn't look," says Kim. "I just grabbed my wrist and held my arm in the air. And then it started to gush." Blood sprang from her finger like a geyser. By the time she made it over to the stack of clean towels, there were bright red streaks all over the floor, the caging, the laundry machines, and the ceiling. It was a gruesome scene, one Kim's mother wishes she hadn't witnessed. Unfortunately, she was just around the corner in the kitchen when it happened, baking an apple crumble.

Linda called Gloria, who rushed Kim to the emergency room.

Kim went into surgery that night. Her finger bone was protruding, so the doctors had to cut it back in order to close the skin over the top. She was given a series of antibiotics and even an HIV-AIDS cocktail, because Sophie had been in contact with Pepper and Sue Ellen. Kim refers to this precaution as "a total overreaction."

Four days later, she was released from hospital, and the first thing she did was visit the chimps. She remembers walking into the chimphouse and hearing all of them hooting and hollering in greeting. She remembers Regis's reaction in particular. "Reege was adorable. He saw the bandages on my hand, and he just started to shiver. He was so concerned. He would look at my hand and then look to the ground and shake his head. He knew something really bad had happened."

Sophie did, too.

"She refused to look at me at first," says Kim. "But I stayed with her, and in about a half-hour she looked at my hand and she shivered, too." Kim wasn't mad at Sophie. Far from it. The loss of her fingertip had been her own mistake — she had let her guard down for one second and had paid for it.

"I wanted Sophie to see that *I* was sorry," she says. "Sorry for making her feel bad. If she'd wanted to hurt me, she could've done a lot worse. She was just playing. If I hadn't been wearing latex gloves, she wouldn't have chomped my finger."

Kim never considered quitting her job after the incident. She isn't haunted at all by what happened, doesn't wake up sweating in the middle of the night, as many of us would, imagining our hand being chewed off by a chimpanzee. "I lost a finger, and that was really scary," she says now. "But I never dream about my finger. When I dream, I dream about what happened to Toby."

Kim is still moved by the empathy toward her that Regis, Sophie, and the other chimps showed. Her eyes turn glassy as she tells me this story, more than a year after it happened. Knowing what these apes have been through at the hands of humans, she felt deeply touched to receive such compassion from them. She went back to work two weeks after the accident, but not in the chimphouse. Gloria assigned her to office duty for four months until her finger fully healed.

What bothers Kim most about the event was its timing. Three months later, Sophie became the sixth chimpanzee to pass away at Fauna.

"She was really messed up inside," says Kim. "No one knew how bad it really was." The autopsy showed that Sophie's pancreas was either completely shriveled or had been removed years before. So even though Kim had been serving Sophie her diabetes medication that fateful day, without a pancreas to metabolize them, the meds were a waste of time.

The Haunted

WORKING FOR years in a chimpanzee sanctuary carries a high physical toll. The long days, the heavy lifting, and the need to be on the move constantly leads to chronic back problems, shoulder problems, knee problems, bruised muscles, torn ligaments, and countless other aches and pains. Add to this the occasional accident—Gloria once broke three ribs when she slipped down the stairs while pressure washing—and sanctuary workers begin to resemble construction workers in terms of the bodily harm they endure.

But sanctuary employees endure another sort of harm on a daily basis, a less visible yet more insidious kind of trauma that builds up over the years. After living with Gloria, her staff, and the chimpanzees for more than two months, I have no doubt that everyone here—be they human or chimp or pig or llama—shares much more than a few hundred acres of farmland in southwestern Quebec. The trauma here is shared by all, and part of the job description involves allowing yourself to become haunted by it.

Gloria often receives e-mails and letters from people who knew one of the chimps during their research years or, even further back, from the circus or as a cross-fostered child in a human home. These inquiries usually arrive a week or two after a documentary about Fauna has aired in some faraway place. A viewer in Oklahoma or Louisiana or Australia will recognize one of the chimps on the television screen and will be so overcome with nostalgia or grief or guilt that he will write to Gloria as if she had the means to absolve him. The letters are heartbreaking to read and often include a small check. The donations are crucial, as Fauna could never survive without them. But occasionally the tone of a letter is surprisingly defensive. Most of the letter writers are still haunted by what they witnessed, by what they did or didn't do for the chimps, and are desperate to make amends. Others just send a donation as if, for the right price, Gloria might issue them a pardon.

"I've been in touch with a lot of different people over the years," says Gloria. "People who worked with certain chimps. And they often say to me, 'Don't tell anybody that I contacted you. I'm going to give you money, but I don't want you to tell anybody. And I don't want to hear from you again. I'm doing this for Rachel,' or Jeannie, or whomever. 'This is my retribution, how I'm going to pay her back. But I don't want to hear about it and I don't want it in the newsletter. I don't want you to talk about it.'"

Some people, especially those who used to work in a laboratory, are afraid to get in touch with Gloria because they fear reprisals from the biomedical or pharmaceutical companies they worked for. When they send letters or money, they do so anonymously. But these people fear something else as well. "The biggest fear they have is that one day they will have to face the truth about the suffering they caused," says Gloria. "That's why they don't include their names. Most people would prefer to remain in the dark about where their salaries and benefit packages come from."

When the chimps first arrived at Fauna, Gloria vowed that they would never have to see anyone from LEMSIP again. "To me, they were the enemy," she says. "They did all these horrible things.

There was no way I was going to expose the chimps to them again." But one day, by chance, she discovered that she might have to rethink her opinions about some of the lab workers.

Gloria had decided to watch a video of the LEMSIP nursery on the TV in the chimphouse. When she pressed Play, the distinctive sounds of life inside the old laboratory echoed through the building. The chimps reacted immediately. "They heard the banging, the screaming, the men yelling at the animals, and they all came into the privacy rooms to investigate. They started displaying at the television or cowering together up in the corners, hugging each other and trying to console themselves."

The chimps were terrified. And Gloria, feeling guilty for having frightened them, quickly moved to turn the video off. But before she could, a new voice, a female voice, was heard on the tape. It was the voice of Nancy Megna, a former LEMSIP caregiver who now works for NEAVS. Nancy had been one of the Hoodlums' surrogate mothers, and when they heard her voice, the chimps immediately stopped displaying and cowering. They all came to the front of their rooms — continuing to hug each other, but in a completely different way.

"They were happy," says Gloria. "It was as if the scary part of the movie was over, and now they could relax. Nancy was here. Mom was back. That's when I realized I had to let them come."

Over the next few years, realizing that the chimps had actually lost some very important relationships when they were rescued from LEMSIP, Gloria invited some of the lab workers to visit the chimps in their new surroundings. This went against all of her protective instincts and required some heavy-duty rationalization. "Sometimes you have to accept that your children need someone you don't approve of in their life," she says now, referring not to Nancy but to some of the less sympathetic lab techs. "Think of children who are abused by their parents. They still hug their parents, they still love their parents. Think of prisoners who attach themselves emotionally to their prison guards. You need to latch on to something or someone when you're in a terrible situation. It's like Patty Hearst. It's like Stockholm syndrome in another species." As Gloria says this, however, she acknowledges the harsh conclusion: she has to wonder if her own relationships with the chimps are based on a similar sort of dependency.

When Nancy Megna came to Fauna, the Hoodlums were delighted to see her. They spent hours with the woman who had weaned them. James Mahoney also visited a few times, but these reunions were much more conflicted. Some of the older chimps, like Pablo and Billy and Tommie, went wild with anger when they saw their old vet, throwing furniture around their enclosures and displaying ferociously. Sue Ellen, however, could hardly contain her excitement when Mahoney came near, and Jethro, Regis, and Binky were also overcome with happiness. They would run up to the caging when he arrived, reaching out to groom him or play-fighting with each other, showing off to their old alpha male. The teenagers heard Mahoney's familiar Irish lilt as he and Gloria closed the chimphouse each night — "G'night, Binky! G'night, Jethro! G'night Regis!" — just as they had when they were growing up in the lab. But the surreal nature of Mahoney's visits to Fauna may be best summed up by the actions of Petra, who, upon seeing her old warden for the first time since leaving LEMSIP, reached through the caging and slapped him in the face, knocking his glasses to the ground. It was as if she were scolding Mahoney for everything she and her friends had gone through.

Although the lab-worker visits are in part for the chimps' good, Gloria has another motive for them. She wants to know the truth about life inside biomedical laboratories, the truth the researchers and companies don't want the public to hear. And she has found that when lab workers are off the clock and experiencing strong emotions, they often want to share what they witnessed. "When people come here, they tell me stuff," she says. "Horrible stuff. Chimps with no fingers left because they've chewed them all off.

Chimps with concussions from hitting the ground after being darted. Chimps who have such horrible wake-ups from anesthesia that they nearly kill themselves as they thrash around their room. Did you know the only time a chimp was given pain medication was after he'd had a vasectomy? They weren't even allowed a Tylenol, because it would interfere with the science." Gloria collects the lab workers' stories obsessively; they are crucial ammunition for swaying public opinion and getting GAPA passed into law. But she also collects these gruesome tales because she knows that no one else will.

"Over the last twelve years, I've realized you can't force people who worked in the lab to speak out publicly," she says. "You can't. Because they live in purgatory, in their own little hell. Most of them will never be able to deal with what they saw, what they did, what they were a part of—the crimes they committed against the chimps."

One lab technician who visited had to leave the chimphouse after only five minutes. He could barely speak when he saw the animals he used to fear, the animals he used to pump full of darts, enjoying their retirement. Later that night, after a few beers, he finally opened up. He told Gloria about witnessing Pablo take those five darts in his body—he never said so, but Gloria suspects that he was the shooter. Then he shared another memory, the one that had driven him from the chimphouse earlier that day. Once, when he was moving a female chimp between cages, the chimp was rattling the bars so hard that the link between the cages started coming apart. With only seconds to act before the chimp would be free, he panicked and grabbed the only tool at his disposal, a fire extinguisher, and proceeded to bash the chimpanzee's fingers to a pulp.

"A lot of caregivers and lab techs have terrible psychological problems afterward," says Gloria. "They suffer from PTSD as much as the chimps do. They witness violent acts against chimpanzees every single day, and they suffer terribly for it. So when we talk about ending chimp research, it's not just for the chimps' sakes.

We need to end it for the sake of the humans, too." As Judith Herman writes, "Witnesses as well as victims are subject to the dialectic of trauma."

Practice Makes Perfect

AT FAUNA one doesn't have to go far to see the impact that lab work can have on a person. A few days after Kim tells me about Sophie biting her finger, I have a surprisingly candid conversation with a young animal-care worker named Isabelle, whom Gloria had recently hired because of her experience working with captive primates. She recently quit her job in a private biomedical laboratory just outside Montreal, a job that took years of training to qualify for. The lab was home to hundreds of rabbits, dogs, pigs, and monkeys, all the typical research species. But most of the work was testing cancer drugs on rhesus monkeys and crab-eating macaques.

When I ask Isabelle why she quit, she says it was an easy decision. "I quit because they killed six monkeys for practice."

"What do you mean?"

"The technicians needed to practice autopsies. So they killed six of them. I complained to my boss, nothing happened, so I quit."

That wasn't the first time Isabelle registered a complaint. She tells me about a dermal study in which pigs had their backs shaved and then a drug was applied to their bare skin to test toxicity levels. One of the pigs got razor burn because he wasn't shaved properly, and his back became infected. But the researchers refused to stop using the animal for testing. Soon the pig's entire back was one big, rotting scab. Isabelle complained to her boss and even threatened to call federal officials, but nothing changed. "In private labs," she says, "the client holds all the power." By "client," Isabelle means the pharmaceutical company whose drugs are being tested. "Before a lab tech can remove an animal from a test, the client must give permission. This barely ever happens."

As we talk, the oven dings, and Isabelle pulls a tray of roasted pumpkin from the oven. "I was only twenty-two, and I was becoming immune to death," she says. "It just didn't bother me anymore. At first I was worried about the animals. Then I was worried about myself. I am too young to be able to shrug off death. Like yesterday, when the goat died." (One of Gloria's goats recently took ill, and Richard had to euthanize her.) "I didn't even blink. I was carrying her dead body, and I had no problem with it. It was like I was blank inside. Something inside me was gone."

As she spoons hot pumpkin into the blender, Isabelle tells me graphic stories about monkeys spinning in their cages, chewing themselves, sinking into deep depression. "If I'm completely honest," she says, "I'd rather see every single monkey in that lab die tomorrow than have to go through more of those tests." Maybe this is why Isabelle has become immune to death. She doesn't see it as such a horrible alternative to life in a lab.

"I went to a party last week with all my old friends from vet school," she tells me. "We had this huge ethical debate. So many of us are quitting our jobs. We studied for years to make the lives of animals better, but for some reason we all ended up working in the labs."

Isabelle adds soymilk to the blender and purees the squash into a beautiful smoothie. "They'll love this," she says, pouring it into thirteen plastic cups.

Gloria hired Isabelle for her diverse animal husbandry skills. But in the short term, she has been given a very specific task. Gloria's hope is that Isabelle's training will enable her to establish a rapport with Regis and eventually be able to give him the diabetes injections he so desperately needs. Regis still refuses to present his arm, but it is not unreasonable to think that over time, someone with the requisite mixture of experience and patience might break through his fear. So whenever Isabelle is in the chimphouse, she spends most of her time with skinny Reege. She plays with him, talks to him, and tries to get him used to her presence, all in the hope that one day she'll be able to make him better. Today she's making pumpkin smoothies. Tomorrow she might hand Regis his favorite food while holding an empty needle in her other hand. She needs to take the fear out of the object. Although it's a daunting task, Isabelle can take heart in the fact that if the chimps have learned anything so far at Fauna, it is that not all humans are out to use them or hurt them.

A Small Measure

IN THIS idyllic setting, with fresh food, interesting activities, and ample room to socialize, the chimps have been transformed. The lab techs who visit often have trouble recognizing the apes because they've put on so much healthy weight and regrown so much hair. And sometimes, as when a LEMSIP technician named Dave came to visit one day, the visitors experience something even more unexpected.

"I took Dave into the back to see Sue Ellen and Donna Rae," says Gloria. "Pepper was way up on one of the tree structures, but when she saw Dave, she came down in a flash. I never saw anything move so fast in my life." Pepper came running on two feet up to the cage door, her arms in the air, her body pressed to the bars. Then she pushed her face into the bars as hard as she could and smooshed her lips through the caging. "I looked at Dave, he looked at me, I looked at Pep, and I told him, 'She wants to kiss you.' Dave started shaking, and he said, 'No, she doesn't. She hates me.' But Pepper wouldn't leave, and she was quivering, too, in that whole-body quiver."

Eventually, Gloria convinced Dave to approach Pepper. "If he was ever going to pee his pants," says Gloria, "this would have been the time." Dave bent over and slowly touched his lips to Pepper's. The next thing he knew, Pepper was zooming back up to the top of her tree, and he had collapsed in a fit of sobbing.

"I told him he must have done something. He must have been important to her. There must have been something between them.

And he said, 'How? I just worked there.' But then he told me he always loved Pepper. He always thought she was so intelligent, how she made the system work for her. That's the beautiful thing about Pepper. She is so smart, so cooperative. She cooperated to make her life a little bit easier."

The story of Dave's visit is one of Gloria's favorites because Pepper, like Binky, was not supposed to come to Fauna in the first place. Her easygoing nature made her a good candidate for further research protocols, so she was scheduled to move to the Coulston Foundation when LEMSIP closed. It was only when Mahoney temporarily removed Jeannie from the Fauna group that Pepper was added as a last-minute replacement.

"Chimps can tell," says Gloria. "Pepper knew that Dave was a good person. If Dave loved Pepper, she would have loved him back."

Dave was obviously deeply conflicted by what he'd seen and done to chimps at LEMSIP. I don't know what he was hoping or expecting to find when he came for that visit, but I think it's fair to assume he wasn't expecting to receive a kiss from one of the chimpanzees he used to work with. And I can't speculate on what that gesture meant to Pepper; that idea is better left to Gloria or her sister Dawna, both of whom know Pep so well. But it's pretty clear what that kiss meant for Dave: even though he felt he didn't deserve it, Pepper had given him a small measure of forgiveness.

Fall

AUTUMN HAS arrived on the farm, which means it's almost time for me to leave. By four o'clock in the afternoon, the shadows are long on the fields and the cool evening breezes have started up. For the last few days, Linda has been hard at work putting up Christmas decorations in the chimphouse. "I know it's early," she says, "but what the heck, right?" Gold tinsel encircles the pillars, and the caging is strung with blinking lights. By the time Linda is finished, the building looks like an odd fusion of Macy's, Walmart, and Chicago's Lincoln Park Zoo.

Gloria and I share one last, lazy Sunday in the chimphouse. High up near the Sky Walk door, Spock and Maya sit on one side of the caging, opposite Jethro and Regis. The two zoo chimps are grooming the two Hoodlums through the bars, and they all seem to be enjoying themselves. Toby is still living with Jethro occasionally but is steering clear of him today, preferring to stay downstairs in a privacy room next to Rachel. He hasn't fought with Jethro since they battled almost two months ago. Hopefully, Jethro's persistence with him is having an impact.

For the last week or so, Tom has been living in Jeannie's Room. Kim has occasionally let him in with Spock, and the two old-timers seem to have figured out a system that works for them. Whenever the tension in the building rises and Spock starts to panic and throw things, Tom quietly removes himself to the back playroom until the tense mood has eased. And when lunch or dinner arrives, Spock always lets Tom pick from the trolley first. Tom understands that Spock is easily riled, and Spock respects Tom's dominance. These two make life at Fauna look easy.

Gloria and I are arguing over whose cooking the chimps like better. Naturally, I say it's mine, but Gloria refuses to cede the point. She seems to think that removing a twist tie from a bag of raisin bread qualifies her as a chef, whereas I have just boiled an enormous pot full of root vegetables, which I'm about to sprinkle with salt, pepper, paprika, and a dash of thyme.

"Where the hell did you find paprika?" she asks.

"My point exactly."

While the debate goes on, Tom drops down from the second floor and ambles into the wake-up room. He's carrying a big raw potato, and he's found the perfect spot in which to eat it. I walk over and crouch down in front of the old guy, and for the next fifteen minutes, we huff at each other between bites. I am going to miss Tom a lot when I leave. I'll miss all the chimpanzees. I can hardly remember what it's like to wake up in my own bed without Mr. Puppy barking to be let out, without the morning walk along the pond to the chimphouse, without trolleys to restock, smoothies to blend, tensions to weather, relationships to build—without my swan guards to welcome me home at night. When Kim says she has the best job in the world, she is absolutely right.

Having polished off his potato, Tom stands up on all fours, looks at me, nods his head, grabs the hammock behind him, and hurls himself out of the room. I follow, and soon we're making up for lost time, playing the game of chase we missed out on a few weeks ago. We run back and forth, just the way I do with Rachel almost every day now, both of us on all fours, huffing and grunting and pounding on the floor and the cage between us. I can tell Gloria is watching us play. I can also tell she is happy to see it.

It feels remarkable to be accepted by the chimps at Fauna, and it is even more special because I now realize that Gloria takes many of her cues from the apes. She does not make up her mind on how she feels about another human being until she sees how her chimpanzees react to them. The chimps, and especially Tommie, are the judge and jury here. And just as Tom and I run out of steam, he sits down with his back to me and delivers a verdict I have unconsciously craved since I first arrived, a verdict I never expected from old man Tom. With his head turned partway around to see my reaction, he sticks both index fingers through the caging behind his back near the floor. He wiggles them and nods his head a few times. Tom is inviting me to hold on to his fingers.

When Jane Goodall first reached out and touched David Greybeard fifty years ago, the event kicked off an era of scientific discovery that the late evolutionary biologist Stephen Jay Gould considered "one of the great achievements of twentieth-century scholarship." Today the impact of that moment has reached far beyond the realm of science to become one of our most treasured cultural legends. And here is what Goodall writes at the end of her classic book *In the Shadow of Man* about another, equally powerful encounter with David in the jungles of Gombe, when the chimpanzee returned the favor and reached out to touch her hand:

> At that moment there was no need of any scientific knowledge to understand his communication of reassurance. The soft pressure of his fingers spoke to me not through my intellect but through a more primitive emotional channel: the barrier of untold centuries which has grown up during the separate evolution of man and chimpanzee was, for those few seconds, broken down. It was a reward far beyond my greatest hopes.

Everyone lucky enough to commune like this with a chimpanzee feels a similar sense of reward. And it is exactly this feeling that many people hope to find at Fauna. We yearn for a connection with great apes, for the barrier between us to be broken down, if only for a moment. We crave acceptance from animals, and we crave it even more from animals who are our evolutionary cousins, for when we look into their eyes we see ourselves staring back.

So is this the moment for me? Is Tom showing me, by poking his fingers under the caging, that I have earned this contact with him, that even though he's been through hell he trusts me, that he knows my motives are pure? Is this how our story ends? Am I to be rewarded here?

Tom sits perfectly still, waiting for me to touch his fingers and instigate a grooming session. Gloria approaches, aware of the import of the moment. I don't dare touch him without her say-so. Gloria once told me that she always does the opposite of what people expect her to do. Encouraged by this thought, I look up at her.

Gloria smiles a strange half-smile and rolls her eyes, as if she's been both anticipating and dreading this moment ever since I arrived at her sanctuary. Her face flushes. She looks back to Tom, thinks for a while. Tom wiggles his fingers again, jukes his shoulders. Then Gloria opens a kitchen drawer and pulls out a backscratcher.

"He'll understand," she says, and my heart sinks. "He'll understand."

Fantasy Island

THAT NIGHT I call Gloria from my apartment below the Fauna office to see if she's up for one last interview. She agrees but says she'd prefer to do it over the phone. It's late. She sounds exhausted and a little upset. She must be tired of having me around, pushing against her boundaries and asking so many questions, so I begin by telling her about my growing belief that I'm here for a reason that goes beyond the mere writing of a book.

And that's all it takes. As if she'd been expecting me to say this all along, Gloria delivers a monologue like the one she gave on the plane to Washington. This time it's a soliloquy from her office on the other side of the farm. As I listen, with Mr. Puppy fast asleep at my feet, I look out the window and across the paddock to where a lone light still burns in the second-floor window of Gloria and Richard's house.

"Everyone who comes here is looking for something," she says. "Some people realize it, and some people don't. And if the chimps help you find it, well, you're a pretty lucky guy. They have the power to unlock the good things in us. Just look at what Tommie did for Pat. But you know what the philosophers would say? The philosophers would say we're still using them. Even if we think we're here to help, we're still taking from the chimps. This is our relationship with the chimpanzee. Take, take, take, take, take."

Gloria tells me about her wonderful volunteers and about the people who write or donate to Fauna, who've been the greatest inspiration for her. "These people are so unbelievable, so special. They give of themselves constantly, weekly, monthly, yearly, and

I could never do this without them. The chimps need these people in their lives." But then Gloria says that over the years a few volunteers have simply stopped showing up.

"They got their fix," she says. "They got what they were looking for, and then they were gone. I couldn't believe they would leave the chimps. I can understand them leaving me—I don't have enough of an ego to worry about that. But how could you leave *them?* How could you come here for *your* stuff, not *their* stuff? I have no tolerance for that now. People have to stay for the long haul, because chimpanzees are our family. These guys are a tribe of displaced people. The volunteers who stay? Like Kim? Like Derek? There's a long list of them, and they're very important. Important in the world, I mean. Part of that two percent."

I've only met Derek a few times, but I know how deeply connected he is to Fauna. He has volunteered here for years, driving out from the city whenever he can. On his most recent visit, he took off his T-shirt to show me the tattoo he got a few years ago, not long after Jeannie passed away. Behind one of his shoulders, Derek wears a permanent portrait, copied from a black-and-white photograph and rendered in exquisite detail, of Jeannie's face. He told me it gives him comfort to see his friend's face every day.

"Roger Fouts says chimps are the first battleground," Gloria continues. "Because chimps are our primal selves. They tap into our desire to know where we came from, who we are, why we are, all that stuff. That's spirituality as much as biology. My guys have a job to do, and we have to support them in their work. We have to support folks like Tommie. Always, always, always, always support.

"But I have a problem," she says. "It's . . . a big problem." Gloria stops talking. Her breathing turns ragged. "I can hardly watch them in there anymore."

I hear a rustling, as if Gloria has pressed her hand over the mouthpiece. I look out the window toward the farmhouse. The light in her window is still on.

Mr. Puppy quivers through dreamland. Gloria sniffs, sounding a million miles away. Then she continues in a softer voice, so soft I'm not sure she's speaking to me anymore.

"I fight it all the time," she says. "The more I love them, the more I'm with them, the more I know them, the more I can hardly bear to see them in there anymore . . . I can't . . . take the beatings. The breakdowns. The death stuff . . . Carole used to say that if she had to witness one more death in Florida . . . It's just . . . it's so fucking hard. You end up wanting to isolate yourself from it. You stay away. But you're not isolating yourself from it. You're just living in some little fantasy land. Because it's in your heart all the time. It's killing you on the inside. We're eaten up, all of us are, from the inside out."

Gloria stops again. I need to say something here, but I'm speechless. After watching Gloria stoically go about her work for so long, I wasn't expecting this. "You are a rare person," is all I can think to say, but she's not listening.

"That's unbelievable, right?" she says, louder now. "I'm such a fucking coward. 'What do you mean, you can't go in there anymore? You've got to be joking.' I'm a coward. Everyone who does this kind of work needs therapy. All kinds of people have been here to help. Grief people, homeopaths, psychics, pediatricians, hematologists, heart specialists, prison people, chimp socializers. Maybe I need to bring in a therapist." Silence. "Oh, I'm being dramatic today, aren't I?" she says, trying to laugh. "I'm having a bad day with the writer on the phone."

Neither of us says anything. We are steering into difficult territory here, and I should probably let her go. I open my mouth to say so.

"I should have let you touch Tommie today," she says suddenly. "If you could have touched Tommie, you'd understand." Silence. "When you come back . . . You're coming back, right?"

"Of course," I say, struggling. "Of course I'm coming back."

"When you come back, if Tommie presents to you again, I'll be

OK with it. Really. I promise. I want you to have that. I want Tom to have that. I just . . . it's been a long summer. There's been so much to do. There's only so much a person can take."

Now Gloria can hear my own ragged breathing, my own hand pressed to the phone.

"You don't have to apologize," I say eventually.

"Yes, I do," she says.

"No, you really don't."

I feel terrible for having added to Gloria's burdens. She has a job to do, and I've gotten in the way, searching for something I can't even put a name to.

"Can you believe how long they've been here?" Gloria says, brighter now. "Twelve years. They've known me longer than they knew Jim. Binky could live for another thirty-five. We're gonna grow old together, me and the Bub."

Gloria draws a long breath. Mr. Puppy stirs, stretches, falls back asleep. Through the window I see that her office is now dark.

"I want to take them to an island," she says after a time.

"An island?"

"It's another fantasy of mine."

"Fantasy Island," I say.

"Right." She laughs. "Fantasy Island. I live inside a cage, cooking for them and treating their wounds, helping them get better. And they live outside the cage, in their own world, running free. And then one day, eventually, when I'm ready, I'll just . . . I'll just leave the island. I'll leave them behind and they'll be fine. And I'll be fine. And everyone everywhere will be fine."

Chapter 13

THE END OF AN ERA

What we do for ourselves dies with us.
What we do for others and the world
remains and is immortal.

— ALBERT PINE

The First Battleground

FAUNA IS A DIFFICULT place to leave. Even though I've gone down to the chimphouse this morning to say goodbye, and I plan to return when the snows come, as I load my bags into the back of Cyndy's car I feel like I'm ducking out. It seems unfair that I get to go home to my easy life in Toronto, while Gloria, Linda, Kim, and all the chimpanzees have to stay here and put in another long day of work.

As if to make the point clear, when I hop out of the car to open the gate I am greeted by my long-time nemesis, Eeyore. Ears twitching, tail swishing, he brays at me from the other side of the fence, as if scolding me for deserting. Putting aside my irrational fears for once, I walk right up to him, say hello as gently as possible, and place my hand on his muzzle. He leans into my touch, seems to enjoy it; we have a moment, the donkey and I. Then, with a jerk of his head, Eeyore tries to bite me.

Our relationship with the chimpanzee is nearing the end of an era. This has happened before, first when Andrew Battell returned to England from Angola four hundred years ago, bearing news of "two kinds of monsters," and then when Jane Goodall and her mother set off into the Tanzanian rainforest and emerged with the raw materials of a scientific and cultural revolution. Fifty years after that time at Gombe, we have arrived at another moment that may prove just as meaningful. This is the moment when we decide, once and for all, whether chimpanzees deserve to be set free from their bondage to biomedical science. If this were to happen, and the Great Ape Protection Act were to pass, it would be the first time in human history that a global moratorium on invasive research was established for an entire species. Coupled with the recent move by Spain's parliament to support the goals of the Great Ape Project, the passing of GAPA would suggest that we *are* willing to expand our moral sphere beyond the arbitrary boundaries that evolution and culture have thrown up between us. It could be the single greatest expression of human empathy many of us are ever likely to see.

Chimpanzees are the first battleground. If GAPA is successful, it could lead to future victories for other species currently suffering at our hands. Because once a bridge is built across that particular chasm, there will be no removing it, and more traffic will be encouraged to flow. Raymond Corbey, at the end of his *Metaphysics of Apes*, suggests that maybe the great apes are destined to become an entirely different sort of missing link for us, that instead of representing lesser beings in the Great Chain or an evolutionary step toward Western civilization, they might serve "as go-betweens and mediators between humans and other animals, philosophically, scientifically, and morally." This is a wondrous notion.

One of the great gifts that evolution has bestowed upon us is the ability to care for others. Frans de Waal believes we are on the verge of an Age of Empathy, in which we will understand that our culture's obsession with competition and aggression is only half of the human story. "Compassion is not a recent weakness going against the grain of nature," he writes, "but a formidable power that is as much a part of who and what we are as the competitive tendencies it seeks to overcome." Empathic unrest, empathic cognition, empathic dialogue, sympathy, compassion, morality—call it what you will, we are all hard-wired to care for others and to decide for ourselves where that caring begins and ends. The ultimate irony of this story is that this important lesson is now being communicated to us by the lucky few who have spent their careers studying chimpanzees.

Empathy is rooted in emotion, and humans are emotional beings. We hear a song about a heartbroken boy and feel badly for him. We see a photo of a suffering Haitian man and feel sympathy for all of Haiti. We read a book about suffering animals, and we feel empathy for all animals who are suffering. Humans are unique in having the astonishing capacity to extend our sympathies far beyond the here and now, through time and space, to anywhere and anything we choose. It is our culture that decides how large and inclusive our moral circle is, but it is each of us who make up our culture.

Gloria Grow doesn't really think only 2 percent of us are truly conscious or caring. She understands how many things in the world need changing, and she doesn't resent those who choose to champion another cause or fight another fight. All she really wants is for people to make a choice, to become a champion or learn how to fight—to use the gift they've been given.

"As long as you care about something," she says. "Something beyond yourself."

A Vital Force

THE FAUNA sanctuary isn't the product of a midlife crisis. It didn't start with Gloria's visit to Roger and Deborah Fouts in central Washington, or her first visit to LEMSIP, when her heart was stolen by Jeannie. Fauna, and all the stories of resilience and recovery that have been written here over the years, owes its origin to something that occurred more than forty years ago, to a ten-year-old girl play-ing in a tree house in the South Shore town of Croydon.

"I was up the willow tree," Gloria told me. "I was playing by myself, because I didn't have any friends. I heard a loud thump and a screech of tires. I went running around to the front of the house. On the road was a little dog."

Gloria's sisters, Linda and Dawna, were already there, scream-ing and crying. The car was long gone. Blood was everywhere in the street.

"So my mom did what any good mother would do. She went out there, picked up the dog, and brought him inside. She helped us deal with it. She let us be sad and angry. She taught us to respect the dead body. Then she put the dog in a box. We had a funeral for it out back, with a cat, too, and a bird that had just died. We buried the bird in an empty hemorrhoid-cream box—Linda always remem-bers that part. I was the minister. It was a ritualistic thing, a prayer, a circle around the grave. We threw some flowers—my mother had a beautiful garden—then we covered up the hole."

When Gloria was a child, she wanted to become a vet. But her mother wasn't sure her daughter could deal with sick animals. "She didn't think I could handle the blood or the death," says Gloria now. "All because of that day with the dog." But her mother had it all wrong. "I wasn't upset that day because of the blood," Gloria tells me. "And we had animals die on us all the time, so it wasn't that. The most traumatic thing for me was that driver. I couldn't believe someone could hit an animal with his car and just leave it for dead."

In that moment, ten-year-old Gloria experienced something sim-ilar to what her hero, Jane Goodall, experienced at Gombe around the same time, when the young primatologist first witnessed chim-panzees making war. Gloria had caught her first glimpse of the dark side of human nature. And ever since then, she has done everything she can to show that in the face of human cruelty, human empathy is just as vital a force.

I'VE BEEN home only a few weeks when I get the e-mail. It arrives at midnight. The subject line says everything. I pull back from my computer and fumble for my phone. Of course Gloria doesn't pick up. I leave a message and immediately regret it. Now Gloria has a two-minute recording of me blubbering like a child on her phone.

I leave early the next morning for Montreal. The drive takes more than six hours because I have to pull over three times to get hold of myself. When the city's skyline finally appears on my left, most of the buildings are capped with white; Mount Royal is a winter wonderland. Two days ago southwestern Quebec was slammed by the first big snowstorm of the season. As I take the Champlain Bridge to the South Shore, I struggle to fend off the absurd notion that this snowfall was an omen of tragedy.

When I arrive at the farm, the driveway gate is open. Mr. Puppy is standing guard on shaky legs and Mario's truck sits idling by the pond. I drive alongside him, lower my window. Mario has huge bags under his eyes and his face is puffy. He seems to have aged by ten years.

"You can go down," he says.

I park, grab a walkie-talkie from the office, and begin the walk to the chimphouse. Mr. Puppy comes with me partway, but by the time I reach the old LEMSIP cage he's off barking at some demon. In the summer this cage looked like a rusted relic from a medieval dungeon. But now, outlined by a frosting of the whitest snow, the tiny steel box seems as harmless and ephemeral as a cage made of gingerbread.

Last night I dreamt that one of the chimps had escaped and was running through the back pastures. We were all chasing him, but none of us could tell who it was. A gibbon was chasing him, too, which was strange, because there are no gibbons at Fauna. It was still summer. When the chimp finally ran out of breath, he sat down in some tall grasses. Then he took a long drink from a bottle of Pepsi, and I woke up.

Kim meets me inside the door of the chimphouse and collapses into my arms. "It's never going to be the same," she says, sobbing. "I can't believe he's gone." We cry together for a few minutes, neither of us saying anything. Then she takes me into the walk-in fridge, where a black body bag sits atop a yellow stretcher. Kim unzips the bag halfway and pulls back the blanket inside. "I've been coming in every hour or so," she says. "Just to say hello."

Kim leaves for the kitchen. She has twelve grieving chimpanzees to look after. For the first time since I arrived at Fauna months ago, the two of us are completely alone.

Apparently, the fighting between Yoko and Binky continued after I left the farm. During one particularly vicious encounter, Yoko bit Binky on the leg just above the ankle, and ten days later the wound still hadn't healed. To the contrary, it had begun to fester and swell so much that Richard had to perform minor surgery. He drained the wound of a whole bucketful of pus. Soon Binky refused to put any weight on the limb, and he also refused to move to another room. For Gloria, this is always the most worrying sign. When a chimpanzee won't come to the portholes to eat, something is terribly wrong. Binky quickly lost more than fifteen pounds. According to Kim, the once-brawny middleweight had begun to resemble his skinny friend Regis.

Not long after Richard drained the wound, Binky's leg below the knee swelled up enormously, and Richard began to suspect that the leg was in fact broken. That was two days ago. With the Bub sequestered in the wake-up room, the entire staff took turns mothering him after hours, applying antibiotic creams to his ankle, giving him juice spiked with medications through a long straw, hand-feeding him slices of mandarin orange, the only thing Binky was willing to eat. All day long he held his injured leg up, as if he knew this might help the swelling. When he did have to move a short distance, he shuffled around on his butt, holding the injured leg up with one hand. Richard and Gloria didn't have an x-ray machine, let alone one big enough to use on a chimp. They would have to rely on observation to diagnose the Bub. As the wound got worse, this became harder and harder.

Binky's chimpanzee family were deeply concerned. Regis and Jethro refused to leave the privacy rooms, where they could keep a constant eye on their best friend. Back in the lab, in Junior Africa, Reege and Jeffie would become terribly depressed whenever Binky was removed from the unit. So how would they handle the loss, Gloria wondered, if Binky failed to recover? Tom and Rachel, next door in Jeannie's Room, were acting sullen and miserable. Rachel continually tried to get into the Bub's enclosure, grabbing the sliding door and clanging it back and forth all day. She made such a racket that Gloria eventually had to move her to a room across the kitchen. With her concern, Rachel had been keeping Binky awake at night.

By yesterday morning the swelling, coupled with the bandages on Binky's foot, made it look like he was wearing an astronaut's boot. Pus and blood were beginning to seep through the dressings, which had to be changed before Binky started to pick at them. Gloria called Pat Ring. She had seen his Harley in the area recently, so she knew he was in the neighborhood. She asked if he'd mind stopping by in the afternoon to help change Binky's bandages and cheer him up.

Pat said yes, of course. He would never turn down an opportunity to spend some quality time with his friends.

Tom, meanwhile, spent the morning lying on his back in Jeannie's Room, four feet away from Binky but on the other side of the pulley door, keeping watch on the youngster through the cracks. He was very concerned. Perhaps Tom was remembering his own brush with death back at LEMSIP, when Billy Jo had bit him on the foot just days before they were both supposed to come to Fauna. That injury had refused to heal, delaying Tom's arrival by weeks, and even though he survived, it left a terrible mark on the old man's psyche. When Tom finally arrived, it took him months to reestablish his relationships with the others, which had been strained by his prolonged absence. That injury was less severe than the one on Binky's foot now.

So would Binky face a similar fate if his leg started to improve? The Bub would probably have to be segregated from the group for months while his wound fully healed—it was already showing signs of necrosis—and in that time he would likely lose his social status. This injury could be Binky's death knell in a variety of ways, and if anyone at Fauna could recognize this, it would be Tommie. One can't help but wonder what Tom was thinking as he watched Binky, such an important member of his family, young enough to be his biological son, struggling to recover.

It seemed to everyone that the Bub was fading. He was refusing even the oranges now. His leg was swelling by the minute. When Pat showed up around noon, he visited with Binky and hung out with Tom, who perked up at the sight of his old friend. Kim, Linda, and Cyndi kept a vigil at Binky's side as they waited for Gloria to return from the pharmacy, where she had gone to get some more medication for the Bub.

And that's when Tom began gasping for air.

"Pat!" yelled Kim. "What's wrong with Tommie?"

Pat looked over and saw his old friend struggling for breath, apparently choking. When Tom pushed himself up against the bars in distress, Pat panicked. "Open the doors!" he bellowed. Kim ran around and unlocked the door so Pat could go inside with Tom. Now the chimps went berserk. Their screams were deafening. All twelve chimpanzees came down to the privacy rooms to see what was going on. Jethro and Regis made fear faces and hugged each other. Chance was spinning in her room. Rachel pounded on the caging. Spock was throwing his furniture.

Pat approached Tom as calmly as he could. Cyndi ran to the phone to call Mario, then Richard at the clinic. She screamed into the phone, and Richard screamed back. Tom was lying on his side, still unable to get his breath. Pat rolled him onto his back, straddled his body, and started pumping his chest. Nothing. He leaned in and gave Tom mouth-to-mouth. Nothing. Isabelle went inside, too. She intubated Tommie as quickly as she could, inserting a breathing tube into his neck. Nothing. As Kim watched, she suddenly had a horrible thought. She grabbed the nearest phone but found Cyndi on the line.

"Cyndi! Get off the fucking phone! Someone has to call Gloria!"

At that very moment, Gloria was in the pharmacy in Chambly, reaching for her cell phone to call Kim—she'd forgotten the name of one of the drugs she had to buy. As she flipped open her phone, she thought she heard Kim's voice. Sure enough, when she raised the phone to her ear, there was Kim, screaming at Cyndi. "Someone has to call Gloria!"

Gloria's heart bottomed out. She would later tell me that she felt as if an anvil had dropped on her shoulders.

"Kim?" she said. "What's wrong?"

"It's Tommie," sobbed Kim. "It's Tommie. It's Tommie. It's Tommie."

Gloria could hear Pat yelling in the background. She could hear the chimpanzees screaming, too. But she could also hear Richard in his clinic and, even more oddly, she could hear Mario's voice. At the very moment when Tom the chimpanzee was preparing to leave Fauna, Gloria's, Kim's, Cyndi's, Richard's, and Mario's phone lines became crossed. Everyone heard it. No one understands how it happened. As Richard would later say, "That's Bell Telephone for you."

Gloria didn't make it back to the chimphouse in time. Neither did Richard. At approximately 3:15 P.M. on Thursday, December 10, 2009, at the age of forty-four, Tom passed away. Pat says it took about fifteen minutes altogether. Richard believes it happened much faster than that. He suspects Tom had a heart attack, but only an autopsy will tell for sure.

Tom was the most famous chimpanzee in North America no one had heard of. He was the ambassador of Project R&R and the Great Ape Protection Act, the heart and soul of the movement to free all chimpanzees from biomedical research. Tom stood for thousands of forgotten apes, known only by cute names or numerical codes, whose lives have been sacrificed over the last one hundred years in the name of human progress. He did every one of them proud.

It's true that Tom had a troubled life. But thanks to Gloria, Richard, Pat, the Grow sisters, and the chimps of Fauna sanctuary, he had twelve years at the end to recover, to rediscover joy and friendship, to become a chimpanzee again. Now that his life is over, it is impossible to see it as anything but a triumph. Through his remarkable resilience, Tom proved to Gloria that everyone deserves a second chance at life.

Standing beside Tom's body in the walk-in refrigerator, I might easily come to the conclusion that *this* is why I came to Fauna in the first place—*this* is what the chimpanzees had to teach me. I was meant to write Tom's story, and only by attending his autopsy tomorrow—the most important surgery of his surgery-filled life—can I give his story a beginning, a middle, and an end. It is a human impulse to search for these things. The challenge, as the ethicist Margaret Somerville writes, is to continue our search right up to the end, "to make dying the last great act of living."

But I no longer care about such philosophical statements. And dying is no great act. I just miss my friend Tom. I miss spending time with him. I miss knowing that I can go to see him. I miss his being here with his family, with Gloria. I miss his being, full stop.

People say that when you stare at a chimpanzee you experience a rare form of recognition, a spine-tingling acknowledgment of our shared primal self. As I look at Tommie right now, curled up on this stretcher as if he's dreaming of his mother, I recognize nothing. Without his inimitable postures, his grand vocalizations, his subtle body language, his wise gaze — without, in other words, his spirit — Tom looks totally unfamiliar to me, as if the part of him that had known me is gone.

Tomorrow I will stand in the Fauna clinic with a notepad and pen. I will watch as Tom is put through one final indignity, as Gloria holds his hand. And I will record the evidence that emerges from inside his battered body, the proof that Gloria has long suspected lay hidden there. It is a genuine miracle that Tommie lasted as long as he did. This fact fills me with wonder as much as with sadness.

I reach over and cradle Tom's head in my hands. It is so much heavier than I expected. I rub the rough skin of his cheeks, feel the scratch of his hair against my palm, outline the imperfect curve of his ear with my finger. After months of wanting to connect with him, of wanting to lay my hands on him, I have finally, it seems, come to an understanding with Tommie. I wasn't here to touch him or even to tell his life story. I was here to meet the old guy and learn to live with his loss.

AFTERWORD

MUCH HAS HAPPENED since I left Fauna that wintry day. Binky eventually recovered from his injury, although not before going through five surgical procedures on his leg. The wound got worse before it got better, and at one point Gloria was so worried about the Bub that she slept next to him on the chimphouse floor for a night. Finally, after about a month of convalescence, Binky was well enough to spend time with a friend or two. Gloria let Rachel in with him, which made Rachel very happy, and then Jethro went in to cheer up his old buddy.

Soon, and much to her surprise, Gloria noticed Spock asking to join this new group. So she opened yet another door, and since then Spock and Binky have struck up one of the most unexpected friendships at Fauna. The falling-out with Yoko has been very difficult for the Bub, and losing Tom was especially tough for Spock, who had only recently moved in with him. And now Spock has taken Binky under his wing, which has helped soften the blows they both have suffered. "Their friendship," says Gloria, "is one of the sweetest things I've ever seen."

Toby and Jethro haven't had any more serious skirmishes, but Toby is more comfortable living with Rachel, Petra, Chance, and, of course, Maya, than with the males. Only time will tell whether Toby will be fully accepted by the group. Meanwhile, Isabelle's efforts to cure Regis of his fear of needles is going very well. The last

I heard, she and skinny Reege were actually playing together with an empty syringe, a huge step toward his finally getting the medication he needs.

On Capitol Hill, the Great Ape Protection Act has collected 149 cosponsors so far in the House of Representatives but is still in committee, and an identical version of the bill has been introduced to the Senate. This is encouraging, but some vociferous opponents of the bill are beginning to rally their troops. It is now more important than ever to contact your representatives and senators and urge them to pass GAPA.

There is good news from abroad and more trouble at home. The European Union has passed legislation that officially outlaws invasive research on great apes in all member countries. But in a controversial decision in New Mexico, government officials have decided to move nearly two hundred chimpanzees from the Alamogordo Primate Facility (where no research has been conducted on them for more than a decade) to the Southwest National Primate Research Center in San Antonio, one of the most active biomedical research facilities in America. Many of these chimps are middle-aged or elderly, are already infected with multiple strains of HIV and hepatitis C, and for the last ten years have been living in quasi-retirement. Unless American citizens stand up to block these plans, these chimps will end up back in research, suffering countless more traumas for no good reason, and the nation will continue to lag behind the rest of the world on this issue.

Tom's autopsy confirmed that he had suffered a massive heart attack. The official cause of death was cardiomyopathy, "the same thing that kills many lab chimps," says Gloria. But that cold scientific term vastly underestimates the damage that more than thirty years of lab research had done to Tommie. The vet who performed his autopsy had never seen anything like it.

Tom's death left a big hole in the lives of all the chimpanzees and humans who loved him. It will be many years before we can understand the full impact of his loss, both on the chimphouse and on its custodians. But for those left behind, a small measure of solace might be found in the simple lesson that the chimps of Fauna sanctuary have been teaching Gloria for more than a decade now: that no matter what kind of trauma we've been through, we all have the capacity to recover and to help others heal.

HOW YOU CAN HELP THE CHIMPS

1. Give generously to the Fauna sanctuary. Donations will help Gloria and Richard build the Fauna Lifetime Care Fund, which is the best way to ensure that the chimps will always be looked after. For details on how to donate, visit faunasanctuary.org (for American donations) and faunafoundation.org (the main website).

2. Give generously to other chimpanzee sanctuaries in the United States. All of the following are home to remarkable apes with incredible stories:
   Save the Chimps (savethechimps.org)
   Chimp Haven (chimphaven.org)
   Center for Great Apes (centerforgreatapes.org)
   Chimpanzee Sanctuary Northwest (chimpsanctuarynw.org)
   Chimps Inc. (chimps-inc.org)
   Primate Rescue Center (primaterescue.org)
   Chimpanzee and Human Communication Institute
       (cwu.edu/~cwuchci)

3. Write to your congressman or congresswoman and your senators, urging them to support the Great Ape Protection Act. For details and other up-to-date information on GAPA, visit any of these websites—releasechimps.org, pcrm.org/gapa, or humanesociety.org—and take action!

4. Tell your friends and family about the chimps and their stories. The more people who know about them, the more support GAPA will receive.

FURTHER READING

The following books have informed, inspired, and entertained me over the course of writing this one.

Banks, Russell. *The Darling*. New York: HarperCollins, 2004.

Blum, Deborah. *The Monkey Wars*. New York: Oxford University Press, 1994.

———. *Love at Goon Park: Harry Harlow and the Science of Affection*. New York: Basic Books, 2002.

Boyd, William. *Brazzaville Beach*. New York: Harper Perennial, 1995 (reprint).

Cavalieri, Paola, and Peter Singer. *The Great Ape Project: Equality Beyond Humanity*. New York: St. Martin's Press, 1993.

Corbey, Raymond. *The Metaphysics of Apes: Negotiating the Animal-Human Boundary*. New York: Cambridge University Press, 2005.

De Waal, Frans. *Peacemaking Among Primates*. Cambridge, MA: Harvard University Press, 1989.

———. *Chimpanzee Politics: Power and Sex Among Apes*. Twenty-fifth anniversary edition. Baltimore: Johns Hopkins University Press, 1998.

———. *Our Inner Ape: A Leading Primatologist Explains Why We Are Who We Are*. New York: Riverhead Books, 2005.

———. *The Age of Empathy: Nature's Lessons for a Kinder Society*. New York: Random House, 2009.

Field, Tiffany. *Touch*. Cambridge, MA: MIT Press, 2003.

Fouts, Roger, and Stephen T. Mills. *Next of Kin: My Conversations with Chimpanzees*. New York: Quill, 2003.

Goodall, Jane. *In the Shadow of Man*. Boston: Mariner Books, 2000 (reprint).

———. *Through a Window: My Thirty Years with the Chimpanzees of Gombe*. Boston: Mariner Books, 2000 (reprint).

Herman, Judith. *Trauma and Recovery: The Aftermath of Violence — from Domestic Abuse to Political Terror*. New York: Basic Books, 1992.

Lever, James. *Me Cheeta*. London: Fourth Estate, 2008.

Lorenz, Konrad. *On Aggression*. New York: Harvest Books, 1967.

Mahoney, James. *Saving Molly: A Research Veterinarian's Choices*. Chapel Hill, NC: Algonquin Books of Chapel Hill, 1998.

Peterson, Dale, and Jane Goodall. *Visions of Caliban: On Chimpanzees and People*. Boston: Houghton Mifflin, 1993.

Siebert, Charles. *The Wauchula Woods Accord: Toward a New Understanding of Animals*. New York: Scribner, 2009.

Singer, Peter. *Animal Liberation*. New York: Harper Perennial, 2009 (reprint).

Sorenson, John. *Ape*. London: Reaktion Books, 2009.

Yerkes, Robert M. *Almost Human*. New York: Century, 1925.

ACKNOWLEDGMENTS

This book is about the debt we owe to chimpanzees, and through its writing I've built up my own debts to a number of special people. Gloria Grow welcomed me so warmly into her family, showed me what it means to live a compassionate life, and taught me how to listen to a chimpanzee's story. For all this and much more, Gloria, thank you so much. To Kim, Linda, Dawna, Richard, Mario, Cyndi, Isabelle, Tony, Pat, Derek, and Lynda: thank you all for going easy on me, for persevering with me, and for sharing your stories. Smoothie Boy couldn't have done it without you.

Frank Noelker, who provided the chimp portraits, deserves a special mention. Through his incredible photography, Frank gives back a precious measure of the dignity that captive animals are robbed of. To view more of his work, visit www.franknoelker.com.

On the research side, special thanks to Frans de Waal, Lori Gruen, Gay Bradshaw, Alfred Prince, Kerry Bowman, Kathleen Conlee at HSUS, and Juli Kaiss at Zoocheck Canada. This book would have been immeasurably more difficult to write without the comprehensive Project R&R website (releasechimps.org), run by the New England Anti-Vivisection Society. I encourage everyone to visit it.

On the writing side, huge gratitude to my wonderful tag team of editors, Nicole Angeloro and Jim Gifford; to my brilliant copy editor, Peg Anderson; to my squad of superagents, Martha Magor, Anne McDermid, Swanna MacNair, and Hannah Westland; and to all those who toil behind the scenes at Houghton Mifflin Harcourt and HarperCollins Canada. Thanks to the Canada Council for the Arts, the Ontario Arts Council, and the Toronto Arts Council for their support. Also worthy of a pant-hoot or two are Mitch Kowalski at the Toronto Writers' Centre, Richard Poplak, Jonathan Hayes, Giles Blunt, Jason Rothe, Stephen Morris, Chris Patheiger, and Melanie Benwell, all of whom kept me sane or well fed (or both) over the last two years.

To my family—Maureen, Neil, Kathryn, Andrea, Ivy, Momtaz, and Charline—thank you for listening to my endless stories about the chimps and for understanding that my irksome moods had nothing to do with you and everything to do with the work.

And finally, to Samantha, my *lobiwan* and best friend, thank you for being there in Toronto every night when I needed to talk, or weep, or huff with laughter. You jumped headfirst into this journey with me, and as usual, you are the reason we made it.